PRAISE FOR HOW TO MASTER THE MEDIA

"George Merlis knows everything about blasting through the background sound and making your point. He is not just a great coach for acing a media interview. His rules work for all of life. You can use them on TV, at meetings, on job interviews, on dates, or ordering a pizza by phone! He's talking about being the most effective you."
— DIANE SAWYER, ABC NEWS

"The well-prepared interviewer can control the focus and content of an interview with an ill-prepared interviewee. On the other hand, the well-prepared interviewee can always get his or her message across, no matter how skilled the interviewer. George Merlis's fine book details how to meet the media and prevail."
— DAVID HARTMAN, ORIGINAL HOST,
GOOD MORNING AMERICA

"Being media savvy is an essential survival skill in the 21st century. I am constantly amazed at the smart, successful people who stumble and stammer when a camera is pointed in their face. George Merlis's book will help media neophytes become media pros."
— LEONARD MALTIN, FILM CRITIC AND HISTORIAN

"Written concisely, expertly, entertainingly, and - above all else - helpfully, George Merlis' book reveals the secrets of what goes into a good interview and builds up the reader's confidence to plunge into the media fray. The result? Even I'm ready for my close-up, Mr. DeMille."
— STEPHEN M. SILVERMAN, EDITOR,
PEOPLE.COM NEWS DAILY

George Merlis is one of the best TV producers in the business. He wrote this book in self-defense. He's spent his career locked in editing rooms all over the world trying to help people sound intelligent and make their points. And he's tired. Help him out, read the book."
— JOEL SIEGEL, ENTERTAINMENT EDITOR,
GOOD MORNING AMERICA

"Be prepared! George Merlis's book calls upon both interviewers and interview subjects alike to adopt the Boy Scout motto. The interviewer has prepared for your conversation by learning everything about you in advance, so you'd better be prepared to have all the answers in order to successfully handle any media appearance. Merlis's book is the most valuable tool for any media situation."
— ROBIN LEACH, CELEBRITY JOURNALIST

How To

Master
The
Media

Making your message count on the air, in print, or online

by George Merlis

JAAND Books, Los Angeles, CA
www.MasterTheMedia.com

Library of Congress Cataloging-in-Publication Data

Merlis, George, 1940-
   How to Master the Media
       p.   cm.
   includes index.
   ISBN 978-1-4243-3357-8
   1. media training   2. interviews 3. interviewing
on television 4. interviewing in journalism
5. media interviews 6. crisis communications
7. Title.

CONTENTS

CHAPTER 1

MEET AND MASTER THE MEDIA

> **"In the future everyone will be famous for fifteen minutes**
> - *Andy Warhol,*
> *The Andy Warhol Diaries,*
> *July, 1978*

Today, the media's insatiable appetite for material is growing in a geometric progression, and the media universe - the constellations of outlets disseminating news and information - is expanding so fast it's impossible to track. Looking back, Warhol's bold 1978 prediction is today's naïve understatement. Are *you* prepared for *your* fifteen minutes? What about the altogether likely possibility that your fifteen minutes may stretch into fifteen hours, fifteen days, or even fifteen weeks of media attention? It could happen. Today nearly everyone has a camera and is eager to use it. Anyone with a computer can write a blog entry or post a video on YouTube.com. If the material in that posting is sufficiently titillating, embarrassing, funny, or otherwise interesting, mainstream media are likely to pick it up, follow up on it, and disseminate the story even further.

These days, the media cast wide nets and if one of those nets ensnares you, you have two basic choices: to willingly comply with the reporter's agenda - which may or may not mesh with your own - or to master the situation by taking control and working the encounter to your advantage. The difference between compliance and mastery is the set of skills and the body of knowledge presented in this book.

In these pages I've used everything I've learned in my forty year long broadcast and print career to help you master your media encounters. That career has encompassed a lot of interviews.

I have conducted or overseen more than 10,000 print and broadcast interviews in my years as a reporter, editor, and TV producer. They have run the gamut from friendly chats on "Good Morning America" to tough, adversarial confrontations on investigative TV news magazines. I've interviewed a vast number of individuals myself and I've researched, produced, and written major stories - including exposés - for newspapers, magazines, and television networks. Using the knowledge gained in my media career, I have media trained a large and diverse number of spokespersons for more than twenty years. My clients have ranged literally from rocket scientists to rock stars! Whether you're one or the other - or you make your living in another sector of the economy - the easily learned communications skills in this book will help you reach the public through the media.

The skills I teach when I media train people like yourself are based on my observations and practices honed during a full career as reporter, writer, editor, television news producer, and media training consultant. If you are ever interviewed by the media - if you face even a remote prospect of being interviewed - this book will supply you with a storehouse of vital information. These media mastery skills require practice and repetition because some of them - like beginning your answer with your conclusion instead of building up to it - are counterintuitive to many people. The biggest mistake you can make is to treat an interview like a conversation. It is not. No matter how skillful the reporter is in appearing casual and off-the-cuff, he is *working* when he's talking to you. You must look at an interview as work, too. The reporter has a job to do: to ferret out information for his story. You also have a job: to be sure that the information he gets from you is the information you *want* him to get, and only that information.

There are basic skills such as speaking in soundbites, illustrating your key points with word pictures, and keeping your answers short, simple, and comprehensible, that you should acquire whether you are preparing for an appearance on a national investigative broadcast magazine like "60 Minutes," you have been booked for a brief product-plugging appearance on a local radio show, or you are facing an in-depth interview by a well-prepared reporter for a national newspaper like the *Washington Post* or *The New York Times*. Anyone who might one day be called upon by the media to defend a point of view, explain a policy, or to promote a project or product needs to learn how to:

¶ Speak to the media the way the media speaks to us.
¶ Answer a reporter's questions in ways that help both him and you.
¶ Parry a journalist's catalog of dirty tricks.

All this and more are covered in this book. The skills you will learn here include:

¶ Creating your own agenda for an interview.
¶ Working that agenda into the interview.
¶ Protecting yourself in a hostile or uninformed interview.
¶ Reaching beyond the reporter to his viewers, readers, or listeners with your message.

Whether your questions will come from Michael Isakoff of *Newsweek,* Katie Couric of "The CBS Evening News," or from a friendly neighbor who is writing for the local weekly newspaper, that interview is your best opportunity to reach a wide audience with a message. This book, *How to Master the Media,* teaches you to formulate your messages and to work them gracefully and effectively into your interview. Preparation is the key; it helps you do more than merely survive a media encounter, it enables you to triumph. The easily learned set of skills presented in this book can help anyone master the media.

I have designed the book to be a simple step-by-step how-to guide. Whenever possible I've illustrated my points with anecdotes or case histories that serve as object lessons. In addition, this book has an interactive component. Periodically I'm going to ask you to do a little homework, such as filling out some work-sheets in preparation for an interview. These exercises are very important because they will teach you how to get ready for the real thing. After preparing correctly for your interview, you will feel confident about facing a reporter, whether that questioner is a fawning fan or an aggressive inquisitor. Whether or not you use forms like those in the appendix of this book or create your own forms independently, I recommend preparing for all inter-views by creating your agenda on a computer, where it can easily be saved and, if need be, altered for subsequent interviews. And while you're at your computer, you can do the essential research for your agenda, using search engines like Google and relevant publications' web sites. Today, thanks to these online tools, find-ing the facts, figures, references, and statistics for use in your agenda is much easier than it was in the old days of thumbing through an almanac, an encyclopedia, or other reference book.

A word about how I've organized this book: we'll begin by exploring the basic media mastery skills you'll need whether you're interviewed by someone representing a newspaper, a magazine, a company newsletter, or a local or national television news program. These are fundamental communication skills like speaking in complete sentences, keeping your answers concise, and being quoteworthy. You will need to master these skills in order to be a successful interview subject. Then we'll move on to television's unique and specific demands and you will learn the little tricks of the trade that make you a "good guest" or an interesting interview. You'll learn to speak with animation, how to illustrate your points with gestures, and how to engage your interviewer. These television skills are largely matters of style and cosmetics that in no way substitute for substance. They are designed to enhance the meat of what you are saying. Good tele-vision style - making yourself an interesting TV speaker - is no different from good writing style. Good style makes your mes-sage more palatable and comprehensible, whether you are on the page or on the airwaves. As a television viewer you already know this. When you see a bad interview subject, your attention wanders and you absorb little. Watch a good interview subject and your attention remains focused and you take away her principal message points. You will most likely recognize the interview subject next time she is on television and you'll look forward to hearing what she has to say. The good television interview subject informs in an entertaining, engrossing way.

Increasingly, television spokespersons are asked to demonstrate rather than merely talk. More television programs want show-and-tell these days because viewers respond better and remember more if a guest or interview subject can demonstrate as well as talk. So, if you're talking about a new electronic device, you'd better be prepared to demonstrate it. If you're discussing a medical breakthrough, television prefers that you illustrate it by bringing images and narrating over those images. The tricks of this aspect of the spokesperson's trade, which you'll discover in detail later in the book, include knowing how to show objects to a camera, knowing how to move on camera, and knowing how to talk about your subject while demonstrating or illustrating it.

The book also includes specific information on radio interviews, news conferences, and interviews conducted over the phone and via e-mail. In the case of radio, you must rely only on your voice for communication. You'll learn how to energize your voice, how to make your points concisely, and how to insure the audience knows who is speaking. You'll learn that in a news conference, facing fifteen reporters really is not fifteen times more challenging than facing a single reporter, and you'll learn how to dominate one of these group sessions. In fact, it is possible to use the large group to your advantage by focusing your attention on those reporters most likely to treat you and your point of view fairly. You'll learn how the telephone offers us both risks and opportunities; I'll tell you how to avoid the first and take advantage of the second. You'll see how you can capitalize on the fact your interviewer cannot see what you're doing so that a phone interview becomes, in effect, an open-book test where you can have lots of helpful material right in front of you.

ggest you read the entire book and complete all the
exercises well before your first interview. There is a lot of material to absorb in this book and cramming just before your media
"exam" won't work any better than that allnighter you inflicted
upon yourself before finals in college. Moreover, you need sufficient time to process your agenda for each specific interview
and you don't want that process compromised by speedreading.

WHAT IS NEWS?

Because we must address the media world as it is and not
as it should or could be, let me give you two definitions of news;
the dictionary definition and the modern, practical definition.

THE DICTIONARY DEFINITION
News: A report of a recent event;
intelligence; information.

THE PRACTICAL DEFINITION
News: A report that captures and holds
the attention of an audience.

Spurred by today's cutthroat competition for readers,
viewers, and listeners, many American media outlets put a premium on the second definition. Because of that, we increasingly
see many of our reporters, producers, and editors guided by five
"f" words.

THE FIVE "F" WORDS OF MEDIA
Fear
Fury
Fame
Fun
Fascination

Let's examine each one of those "f" words:

¶ **Fear.** The media thrive on scare stories. Threatening hurricanes, earthquakes, tornadoes, volcanic eruptions, possible terrorist attacks, and viral pandemics always command attention. During the summer of 2006 the local Los Angeles broadcast media carried frequent alarmist reports about West Nile virus. To hear them you would have thought there was an epidemic. Quite the contrary was true: local health officials had done a very good job of eradicating virus-carrying mosquitoes. But the steady drum beat of broadcast scare stories attracted and held viewers.

¶ **Fury.** The media are highly biased, but the slant isn't a political bias as some would have you believe. In fact, Ari Fleischer, President George W. Bush's first news secretary, was quoted by the *Washington Post* on January 10, 2005 as saying, "My conclusion is the press is biased - biased in favor of conflict. Conflict comes first...." For the media, especially broadcast outlets, a fear-driven conflict is the best kind of story because producers usually can count on at least one side getting highly emotional. Emotion equals drama and drama commands attention. Thus the emotionally charged pros and cons of that nuclear power plant a utility wants to build a mile away from an elementary school is a great story because it's filled with fear and fury.

¶ **Fame.** The media love to do stories about the famous or those who they can make famous. If cops stop Mrs. Brown from down the street for driving with an unsecured infant on her lap there is no news story. If they bust singer Britney Spears for the same offense, it's a major story. Similarly, the brutal murder of JonBenet Ramsey would have been a routine and quickly forgotten infanticide had there not been abundant child beauty pageant videotape of her, luridly dressed like a sexually precocious nymphet. Those images made it possible for the media to make JonBenet almost as famous in death as Britney Spears is in life.

¶ **Fun.** If it's funny or can be made funny, the media will go for it. Look at the 2006 promotion campaign for the movie "Borat." The film's star, Sacha Baron Cohen, insisted on appearing only in character as a rude, crude, and clueless television reporter from Kazakhstan. An amazing number of real reporters, including some who consider themselves journalists, interviewed Cohen in his Borat character. Why? Because they knew the result would be funny. I'm not talking about the Jon Stewarts and Jay Lenos of this world - they don't pretend to be journalists. But Matt Lauer on the "Today Show" and others across the country - both print and broadcast news people - collaborated with the masquerade because of the fun factor. But be cautious: comedy is a dangerous business, as we'll see later in the book, and generally it should be left to trained and skilled professionals. In the media, the third "f" word, fun, doesn't mean only comedy; fun can also be simply amusing or humorous.

¶ **Fascination.** Any "Gee, I never knew that" moment or device has appeal to the media. For the vast majority of readers of this book who are not famous, the other "f" words are important. But it is likely none is more important than fascination. If you're not famous and you're dealing with something that has neither a fear factor nor any controversial elements, it's incumbent on you to make it fascinating.

HOW THE MEDIA USE INTERVIEWS

Before creating your agenda, you must understand just how important an interview is in the construction of a news story. Interviews, whether used as a source for verbatim quotes or just for editorial background and research guidance, are the basis for most of the news stories we read and see. The print media initially perfected the practice of using the interview as the key building block of a story and the technique was adapted by the broadcast media to meet their unique needs.

THE PRINT MEDIA

Print journalists create stories by interviewing a source or a number of sources and then paraphrasing or directly quoting what the sources said. The journalist/writers then combine these quotes and/or paraphrases with other material, including first-hand observations by the reporter or colleagues, press releases, earlier articles, and research from books, other journals, and the Internet. Using all these elements, they craft a narrative story.

Sometimes the story is from a single point of view as in: "The administration says it is taking steps to ensure that the NOAA, the National Oceanic and Atmospheric Administration has sufficient research funds to examine climate change thoroughly." At other times, the story comes from multiple points of view, as in: "The administration says it is introducing measures to ensure that NOAA, the National Oceanic and Atmospheric Administration, has sufficient research funds to examine climate change thoroughly, however congressional sources say that a substantial number of House members and a few Senators don't believe there is any climate change and will oppose authorizations to study the matter." Either way, the finished story will use quotes and paraphrases from various spokespeople to flesh out the account.

Another type of article, the Q&A, is just that: questions asked by a reporter and the interview subject's answers in direct quotes. It is the print media's equivalent of a live broadcast interview. The only editing that occurs in one of these articles is the condensation of some answers and the elimination of whole questions and answers that, in the reporter's opinion, do not further the flow.

THE BROADCAST MEDIA

Television stories are created by editing together three basic elements: on-camera interviews, on-camera transitions by the reporter, and footage that illustrates elements of the story, which is called B-roll. The B-roll is narrated either by the reporter or by soundbites pulled from the interviews. The narration is called a voiceover; its origin being the phrase "voice over film."

Much of the correspondent on-camera and voiceover material will be created by paraphrasing spokespersons' quotations garnered in interviews. The rest will come from the same sorts of research sources the print reporter used. Radio stories are similarly structured, except that they have no B-roll, but instead include bits of so-called "actuality audio," that is non-speaking sound recorded on the scene of the news story. Actuality audio might include the sound of trees being cut down for a story on shrinking rain forests or the sound of cars' motors and horns for a story on traffic congestion.

The following is an example of how television might report the hypothetical NOAA budget story cited above. Notice how the interviews are key ingredients in the edited news story.

Correspondent on camera in front of the White House: "The administration, saying it is concerned about climate change and global warming, is seeking a supplemental appropriation from Congress to fund research by the National Oceanic and Atmospheric Administration, or NOAA, to delve deeper into the phenomenon, its causes, and its progress."

Video of an orbiting weather satellite, the correspondent voiceover: "The White House feels that two more satellites like this are needed to adequately survey the situation."

White House science advisor, on camera, identified by a "lower-third," a caption giving his name and title: "The president feels that ongoing global climate change will have vast repercussions throughout society and the economy. There are public safety, agricultural, and commercial concerns that we must address. Unless we have adequate information we will be unable to take the needed steps to reduce the warming trend or to accommodate unavoidable results from climate change. Without these two additional satellites we are like surgeons operating in the dark."

B-roll of the Capitol with correspondent voiceover narration: "However, on Capitol Hill, the announcement was greeted with skepticism in some important quarters."

Rep. Rupkins, on-camera soundbite. Lower-third identifies him as chairman of the Ways and Means Committee: "I can tell you that in my district we have not seen any evidence whatsoever of climate change. This so-called global warming story is the biggest fiction story ever sold to the American people and I'm not going to allow this administration boondoggle to get to the floor because those two satellites would be a waste of taxpayer dollars."

Closing summation from correspondent in front of the White House: "So the battle is joined. The administration claims that failure to fund these two satellites will cost the United States dearly in the future, while Rep. Rupkins who represents a small but powerful group of skeptical lawmakers, says he needs proof of global climate change before he will allow a vote on the satellite funding. For now, the purse strings are tied and the administration is searching for a strategy to loosen them."

You can see how the two interviews supplied the spine for the story and how the controversy played a large part in making the report more dramatic. Both spokespersons got in lines that made their soundbites memorable. The science advisor used the simile of the surgeons operating in the dark and the congressman used the metaphor of global warming being the biggest fiction story ever sold to the American public.

LIVE BROADCAST INTERVIEWS

Whether they are broadcast on radio or television, live interviews are segments in which a host interviews a subject for a specific length of time (usually with breaks only for commercials) and, in some cases, invites viewer or listener call-in questions. The interview may be long or short. For example, my *alma mater*, "Good Morning America," and the other morning programs used to schedule interviews to run between five and eight minutes. Today, those morning show interviews rarely run five minutes at their longest. A generation of viewers reared watching MTV and 30-second commercials has learned to absorb information in very brief bursts, and the interview shows are accommodating that shortened attention span. In fact, many viewers won't tolerate longer interviews; they demand that subject and venue change quickly and often. Perhaps we are a nation suffering from attention deficit disorder. Or perhaps we've all learned how to quickly grasp and process a rapid-fire flow of information. Whether that's a curse or a blessing we'll have to leave to social scientists and psychologists. For our purposes it's sufficient to know that the short form live interview is a fact of broadcast life today and spokespersons must learn to communicate concisely.

Of course, there remain broadcasts like "Larry King Live" on CNN and "Charlie Rose" on PBS which will often give over a whole hour or a substantial portion of an entire hour to a single guest or small group of guests. A PBS hour is almost a whole hour - between 56 and 58 minutes - as opposed to a commercial TV hour, like CNN's, which generally runs only 44 minutes with its commercial breaks factored in. (I place "Charlie Rose" in the live category even though it is taped because it is shot "live to tape," with what appears to be only the lightest of editing to accommodate time constraints. If you are lucky enough to rate an invitation to sit at Charlie Rose's round table, you are virtually guaranteed that most, if not all, of what you say in the interview will make it to air. Of course, on the King show, since it is done live, everything you say is broadcast.)

Whatever the length, a live or live-to-tape TV interview gives you the most control, since it goes out to the audience unedited or only lightly edited. The opportunity is there, but so is the challenge. There is no second chance in a live interview, no calling up after the fact and saying, "There's something else you should know...." So it's incumbent on you to get it right the first time, and the skills you learn in these pages will help you to do that.

The key to media mastery is learning how to be interviewed and I want this book to be your bible for media encounters. To that end, let's begin with what I like to call the commandments of interviews. There are five of them; I did not have the temerity to go for ten:

THE FIVE COMMANDMENTS
OF INTERVIEWS
I. Thou shalt be prepared.
II. Thou shalt know to whom
thou art speaking.
III. Thou shalt be quoteworthy.
IV. Thou shalt practice, practice, practice.
V. Thou shalt not lie, evade, nor cop an attitude.

These five commandments should become your mantra when you prepare for any media appearance. I'll discuss them in detail in the next two chapters. Keeping the commandments foremost in your mind and putting them into practice will go a long way toward assuring successful media appearances.

No doubt you have read the assertion that most people fear public speaking appearances more than they fear death. How much more public can an appearance be than a news media interview? And the fact of the matter is we may have to make numerous public appearances, but we only die once. So whether the fear of an interview or speech is greater than, on a par with, or even less than the fear of dying, it certainly is a more frequently encountered dread. It is quite likely that the cause of both fears is the feeling that in these situations we exercise little or no control. That's where this book comes in - at least in public appearance situations. It will help you overcome the fear of interviews and other public speaking events by giving you the tools to take control. When you get through these pages, you'll lose your fear and you'll view media appearances as opportunities, not as threats. The skill set you will learn here will level the media playing field, even tilt it in your favor.

Let's begin our journey to media mastery with the most essential fundamental: preparation. In Chapter 2, you'll learn how to prepare for any interview as I explain the Boy Scout commandments. This chapter will help you create an agenda for an interview. Your agenda is key; without one you are at the mercy of the reporter and he may or may not help you out. With an agenda you can master the media.

THE BOY SCOUT COMMANDMENTS

Over the years I've observed that the most successful interview subjects are men and women who, regardless of what they're speaking about, approach their media encounters with a sense of purpose, a positive - even eager - attitude, and an enthusiasm for their subject. For some outgoing and passionately committed people this attitude comes naturally. For others, this is learned behavior. While I may appear to be describing the ideal television guest, you should bear in mind that the reporter interviewing you for the local newspaper is - like the television viewer - an audience, too. If you can engage a hundred thousand or a million people in a television appearance, the same skills and attitude will enable you to engage that reporter, your audience of one. Successful interview subjects consciously or unconsciously heed a certain interview discipline. To embrace that discipline, you'll need to learn and obey the five commandments of interviews.

If the term *commandments* seems a little strong, that's intentional. You never want to leave your interview performance to chance, so you must play by a strict set of rules. The most effective spokespersons are those who are dedicated to getting out their message in a manner that is simultaneously entertaining, comprehensive, and comprehensible. To become that messenger requires an intense level of dedication as well as strict adherence to the commandments. I call the first two the Boy Scout Commandments because they take their inspiration from scouting's famous motto, "Be Prepared."

To illustrate the importance of preparation, let me tell you about a couple of my earliest experiences as an interview subject: one when I was prepared, the other when I was not. The very first time a newspaper reporter interviewed me was in 1960. The reporter who did the interview was Ed Klein, who became famous later on as the editor of the *New York Times Magazine*, a *Vanity Fair* editor, and as the author of a very controversial book about Hillary Rodham Clinton. All that was in the future; at the time he interviewed me Ed was a reporter for the now-defunct *New York World-Telegram and The Sun*. Ed was assigned to interview me because I had recently been arrested, interrogated, and expelled from the Soviet Union for, in the words of a Moscow police document, "forcing noxious propaganda on unwilling Soviet citizens." (Actually, the Muscovites had been clamoring for copies of a U.S. State Department exchange magazine called *Amerika*.). After interviewing me, Ed wrote a long, complete story filled with direct quotes. It was, as they say in the newspaper trade, "a good yarn" - American college kid caught up in the cold war superpower confrontation, busted on the streets of the Soviet capital, sloppily and ineptly interrogated, and finally tossed out of the country in an exhibition of bureaucratic fumbling worthy of the Keystone Kops. I was very pleased with the piece; it accurately described my adventure and reflected what I said, often using my own words to tell the story.

It was not until years later that I would again be interviewed. Over those years, I went on to earn a degree from the Columbia University Graduate School of Journalism, I became a reporter at the very same *World-Telegram and The Sun* where Ed Klein had worked, and then I became a network television news producer at ABC. In all, about ten years passed between that first interview and my next one. Now over the course of that decade, I conducted hundreds of interviews myself, so you would think I would be prepared when it was once again my turn as an interview subject. Given my journalism career, I was pretty cocky about the interview. Of all people, *I* certainly knew what to do in an interview. This was going to be easy. The reporter who would be interviewing me covered television for the *Daily News*. Moreover, he was an acquaintance of mine and, by coincidence, lived in the same apartment building! I was certainly in comfortable and familiar territory here. The reporter was writing a short piece about some benign situation at ABC News and he just wanted a couple of comments from me about it. The interview was conducted over the phone and I was very much at ease; too at ease, as you'll see. Our conversation was brief, friendly, and casual. And yet the next day, when I read the few paragraphs the reporter had written about the situation, I found them to be oddly unsatisfying. There were no direct quotes; the reporter had paraphrased what I had said.

Apparently, I had failed to express myself in a quote-worthy manner - nothing I'd said warranted a direct quote; I had been neither concise, witty, nor specific enough to earn myself the medal of quotation marks around my own words. That was strange to me because, as a reporter, I was always on the lookout for good quotes for my own stories. Ten years earlier, talking to Ed Klein, I had given him a lot of good quotes. Looking back on that earlier experience, I realized I had been entertaining as well as informative with Ed; I had helped him with that good yarn. The second time around, I contributed nothing beyond basic, factual answers. I made no effort to excite or entertain a reader; I was, sin of all sins, dull! I could - and should - have illustrated my answers with anecdotes and engaging metaphors. Instead, I just answered the questions as if I had been on the witness stand in court - with barely more than "yes" and "no" responses.

The story just sat on the page, drab as a dirty, old, limp mop. I simply had failed to give the reporter enough good material to work with; I'd been unprepared.

COMMANDMENT 1:
THOU SHALT BE PREPARED

What was the difference between those two interviews? In the first I had a good story to tell; an adventure to relate - my arrest and interrogation by the Soviet police, my expulsion from the country, and my hero's welcome in Poland where, despite the Communist government, anything that smacked of anti-Soviet or anti-Russian behavior won applause from the people. Also, I had agenda points to serve: I felt my adventure dramatically illustrated the freedom-smothering effect of life in a totalitarian police state and it showed that the ancient animosities of Eastern Europe continued to smolder even under supposedly like-minded Communist regimes. Additionally, I prepared for that interview, albeit unintentionally. I had told friends and family the story a dozen times or more since my return. With each telling, I refined it, making it a breezier, sometimes dramatic, sometimes humorous tale that included a number of substantive insights. When I was answering Ed Klein's questions, I used the same lines that had been most effective in earlier renditions of the tale. I could not know it at the time, but my refinement of the story by frequently retelling it, prepared me to give a good interview.

In contrast, before my second interview, I gave no forethought to what I might say; I'd been a passive and not at all creative participant with no real story of my own to relate. I had no agenda to press in the second interview; I had no message to get out. I merely serviced the reporter's agenda, which was to learn a few facts about a developing situation at ABC News. And I served that agenda poorly because I wasn't quotable. Had I only known then what I know now, I could have used the opportunity of that interview to not only serve the reporter, but also to promote a new documentary series ABC News was about to launch. But the reporter never asked about that and, since I was slavishly serving only his agenda, I did not even consider working into the conversation a mention of the series. It was a classic missed opportunity.

Yes, an *opportunity*. Every interview is an opportunity; an opportunity to air your agenda. Of course, to do that you must have an agenda. Remembering my missed opportunity in that second interview and in the spirit of "do as I say, not as I did," implant this in your mind: Every time you are interviewed, you should have a prepared story, a point of view, a message, or a series of messages. To go into an interview unprepared, as I did, without an agenda of your own, is to blow a singular opportunity. Unless you are a movie star or hold a high public office, interview opportunities don't arrive every day. In fact, for many of us, interviews are so few and far between, we might consider each one to be a once-in-a-lifetime opportunity. If you know an interview is coming, prepare. In my case, it wasn't as if the columnist had sidled up to me at the local ABC watering hole and casually inquired, "What's new?" No, he had called me up, told me he was working on a story, and asked me if he could get some information from me. I even had to call him back, so there had been some prep time - which I did not use to my advantage.

While I failed to seize that opportunity, I did learn a lesson, and I never made that mistake again.

An Interview Is A Performance

In the first chapter, I wrote that I've media trained spokespersons for many different professions, everything from rocket scientists to rock stars. When I am dealing with the rock stars, I always advise them to think of an interview as a performance. Well, when you're in an interview, get in touch with your inner rock star and perform. What's true for Kelly Clarkson is true for you, too; your interview should be a performance.

I challenge all the entertainers I media train with this thought: "You wouldn't get up on a stage and begin singing without knowing what you're going to sing, would you? You know your music, your lyrics, your instrumentation, and your choreography. You rehearse your material." And the same holds true, I tell them, for an interview. They need to know and rehearse their material and then they need to perform it. Entertainment clients get that right away. For people in business, science, government, and public service, the idea of an interview as a performance may seem a little strange at first. But that changes once I ask them if they have ever prepared for a speech or presentation by writing their remarks and then silently reading them at their desk or computer terminal. If they have, it is inevitable that they have found - once the attention of an audience is on them - that there are phrases the eye skips over and the tongue trips over. Once you accept the notion that communicating effectively requires performing skills, you appreciate the compelling need for knowing your "lyrics," polishing your techniques, and rehearsing your moves.

Of course, I am not suggesting that rocket scientists - or anyone else for that matter - sing and dance for reporters (although that might supply the "fun" element the media love so much). But to make the most of any media opportunity, these clients - and you - need to have an agenda to "perform." In other words, "Thou Shalt Be Prepared."

Positive Message Statements

The first step in fulfilling that preparedness commandment is to formulate an agenda. Your agenda should be composed of what I label Positive Message Statements, what I call "the good PMS." Good PMS? I'll bet that got your attention. And, in fact, that's why I used Positive Message Statements and not some other term like positive message points or positive agenda mes-sages; I wanted initials you would remember, hence Positive Message Statements or PMSs. These are the points you feel you must make during the interview. Although I use the word *positive*, not every message you deliver must wear a big, verbal happy face. Your PMSs could be health warnings, attacks on a political foe's policies, or pieces of crucial, but downbeat, information. For example, not too long ago I saw a public health official interviewed on one of the cable news channels. He was talking about influenza killing more Americans each year than AIDs. This was far from that verbal happy face, but for his pur-poses it was a *Positive Message Statement* because his agenda was to convince more people in the highest risk groups - the elderly and those with compromised immune systems - to get an annual flu vaccination.

Now if you're going to follow that first commandment, Thou Shalt Be Prepared, you cannot leave your PMSs to chance. Instead, after giving serious consideration to what messages you want to get out, you should write them down ahead of time. Make a list and outdo Santa Claus by checking it more than twice. If you're wondering how big a list to make, I advise clients never to go into an interview without at least four or five PMSs. In the Appendix of this book is a worksheet for creating PMSs. I recommend using the printed worksheet as a guide and doing the actual agenda-building on worksheets you create on your computer. That's because the work is easier to save and re-vise in a computer. But regardless of whether you do your agenda on a computer or write it out in pencil on the back of a number ten envelope, before every interview, fill out a new worksheet. If you do this, you'll find that your message state-ments evolve, develop, and grow as you do more interviews. So going through the step of writing out your PMSs anew before each interview is not an exercise in repetition, it is an aid to en-hancing and polishing them. But wait! Before you begin fash-ioning those PMSs, you need to pay heed to the second com-mandment:

COMMANDMENT 2: THOU SHALT KNOW TO WHOM THOU ART SPEAKING

This second Boy Scout or "Be Prepared" Commandment probably has you asking yourself, "Is this guy kidding?" Of course you know to whom you are speaking. You are speaking to a reporter. Maybe it's a reporter for *Business Week.* Perhaps it's the writer/editor/publisher of your local neighborhood weekly. It could be Meredith Viera on "The Today Show." Or maybe it's the deep-voiced reporter for the local all-news radio station. In each case, you're talking to an interviewer, right?

Wrong! You are never talking *to* an interviewer or a reporter; instead you are talking *through* the reporter, to his readers, viewers, or listeners. It's important to plant this fact firmly in your mind before creating your PMSs because the reporter is likely to be better-informed, far more knowledgeable, and even more interested in what you have to say than his audience is. In fact, some reporters, especially on science, political, and technology beats, like to show off their knowledge to their interview subjects, and that display of reportorial sophistication may well lull you into communicating at a level that's out of reach of your real audience: the reporters' readers, viewers, and listeners.

During my seven years at "Good Morning America," ABC's Entertainment Division controlled the show. In the early days, ABC News executives registered loud and frequent complaints about "show biz" people interviewing newsmakers, such as politicians and statesmen. The Entertainment Division yielded to the news executives' complaints, and ordered us to include a news correspondent in any interview with a guest who might make news. Although I came out of news and, in fact, had been plucked from the ranks of ABC News to be a producer at "Good Morning America," I quickly developed my own gripe, directed at those news correspondents forced upon our interviews. My problem with the journalists was that they almost always phrased their questions to newsmaker guests with the assumption that the viewer knew as much as the interviewer. Because these reporters knew the inside stuff and all the arcane background of a story, they based their questions on that knowledge. It was often knowledge most viewers didn't share. It was exclusionary questioning, and too often the answers were equally exclusionary, our guests being only too happy to reply at the level of sophistication of the questioner rather than at the level of sophistication of the viewer. I can't tell you how many times I rolled my eyes in frustration when an ABC News correspondent launched into a complex question about the intricacies of, say, U.N. Resolution 242, without explaining to the viewers what Resolution 242 was. If, as was often the case, our guest replied in equally inaccessible language, it fell to our "civilian" host, David Hartman, to waste valuable air time backing up and filling in the blanks in the viewer's knowledge.

Before he began hosting "Good Morning America," Hartman had been an actor. He never attended journalism school nor did he work as a newsman. But he was an instinctive interviewer and one of his greatest strengths was his gift for asking questions viewers wanted answered; questions phrased in language viewers could comprehend. David never asked questions designed to show off how much he knew.

Some TV critics and more than a few colleagues at ABC News initially belittled David's common man touch, but audiences responded in droves, and within a year of its creation, the upstart "Good Morning America" was solidly beating the long-established "Today Show" in the ratings. That trouncing continued for about a decade until "Today" acquired a production staff and cast that realized viewers wanted information in understandable language, not showoff presenters who were eager to leave viewers in the dust of confusion.

Identifying Your Audience and Your Interviewer's Agenda

How do you go about tailoring the tone and language of your messages to meet the wants and needs of your interviewer's audience? First of all, you need to determine who is in that audience. That's the easiest part of this second preparedness commandment.

All you have to do is read the reporter's publication, listen to her radio station, or watch his television program, and you will be able to determine its target audience. After all, you will want to speak differently to a reader of *Aviation Week* or *Barron's* than you will to the more general audience reading *USA Today* or watching "Good Morning America." Your first job is to analyze who the outlet appeals to and to gauge how it appeals.

In other words, does it appeal to a mass audience by shocking, angering, or frightening them? (Remember the first two of our "f" words: Fear and Fury?) Or does it appeal to the same audience by entertaining them? (Another of our "f" words: Fun.) Does it seek out an audience of sophisticated experts and engage them by offering them detailed and solid information? Or is it a purveyor of general information for a mass audience? You'll need to know so you can gear your communication level up or down to meet the audience's needs.

If at all possible, watch, listen to, or read the work of the individual reporter scheduled to interview you, and take comprehensive notes on your observations. If it's going to be a print interview, read any bylined pieces so you have an idea of whether she comes to the job with a specific attitude or special knowledge. If it's a broadcast, see what tone he adopts with his interview subjects - is he friendly and cooperative or challenging and prosecutorial? You can't change the reporter's manner, but you can prepare yourself so his attitude doesn't surprise you when you face him on camera. Mike Wallace, the attack bulldog of "60 Minutes" was a guest on CBS News's "The Early Show" in January, 2003, and Harry Smith asked him why, knowing his reputation for dogged questioning, people with something to hide submitted to his interviews. It was a good question because anyone who's watched even a modicum of television over the last 30 years knows who Wallace is and what he does in an interview. Wallace answered, "I don't know. Maybe the bad guys don't think they're really in the fraternity until they've been exposed on '60 Minutes.'"

While Mike Wallace is known nationally and his interview tactics are no secret, other interviews may require you to do more homework. You should make every effort to familiarize yourself with your interviewer's work. If he is someone who's free to express opinions - like a columnist - try to gauge his position vis-à-vis your messages. Does the reporter, the publication, or the broadcast have a point of view? What is the outlet looking for, facts or fun? Is it accurate and factual or lurid and sensational? By doing your research, you will know as much as possible and you'll be able to avoid surprises. Over the last several years, reporters have gotten increasing license to inject their attitudes into the news - especially on television. ABC tolerates -

perhaps even encourages - John Stossel's antigovernment, liber-
tarian and contrarian views on "20/20," which he co-anchors.
CNN makes promotional capital of Lou Dobb's crusades against
outsourcing and illegal immigration. On Headline News, anchor
Glenn Beck makes no pretense of impartiality. And, of course,
Fox News is home to a large roster of partisan pundits in its anchor and reporting staff. By doing your research in advance,
you'll know what you're getting into.

Speaking of surprises, I can recall a stunning example
from the early days of "Good Morning America." Back then, we
staged a daily six or seven minute debate that we called "Face
Off." We would select a hot topic and, with David Hartman
moderating, we would have representatives of opposing points of
view argue about it. The goal was to shed some light and maybe
a little entertaining heat on a subject that viewers would find important. One such "Face Off" featured Ron Kovic, the Marine
Vietnam veteran whose combat wounds left him paralyzed. Kovic wrote about the experience in the extraordinary and passionate antiwar book, *Born on the Forth of July*. The subject was
government truthfulness, or lack of truthfulness, during times of
war. Kovic's adversary was Gen. William Westmoreland, the re-
tired former commander of U.S. forces in Vietnam. Normally on
"Good Morning America" we preinterviewed our guests. For
our "Face Offs" these preinterviews were essential lest we find
on the air that the guests agreed with each other. That had happened only once before in the past, and we called that segment a
"Face On." After the "Face On," we determined that we *had* to
preinterview debate guests. However, Gen. Westmoreland would
not make himself available for the preinterview. But since we
knew he and Kovic disagreed, we weren't particularly worried
about staging another "Face On." Had the general submitted to
the preinterview, he might have learned about the passion and
intensity of his opponent. In addition to not submitting to a preinterview, it was clear that the general had not read nor read
much about Kovic's book. Hard as it may be to believe, Westmoreland seemed not to know that this intense, wheelchair-
bound, longhaired, bearded man he faced on the air was a furious
antiwar activist. I sensed the general thought he was sitting
down to a gentlemanly discussion, so he was unprepared for the
articulate and passionate attack Kovic launched. The encounter

left the surprised Westmoreland almost speechless; he seemed stunned by Kovic's verbal assault. It was all very one-sided and one need not have agreed with Gen. Westmoreland to have felt it was a less than satisfying encounter. Just a little preparation would have enabled Gen. Westmoreland to put up his guard and get in his points. But he was unprepared and Kovic pummeled him like a heavyweight pro taking on a lightweight amateur. The best way to avoid an on-air pummeling is to do your homework before sitting down for the broadcast; you need to know as much as possible about both the reporter and about anyone else he will interview for the story or broadcast segment.

How Are Stories Built?

In addition to gauging the attitude of your interviewer, when you are reviewing his publication or broadcast, pay special attention to how it uses quotes . For print media, does the publication write stories by stringing together quotes with little interpretive continuity from the writer? Or is it largely writer opinion and observation illustrated by an occasional, brief quote? In electronic media, do the soundbites run short or long? An analytical viewing will show you that the half-hour network newscasts run very short soundbites while the magazine shows like "20/20" or "Dateline NBC" run much longer soundbites. If you know the style of the publication or broadcast, you can phrase your answers so they get maximum play.

When you do this you help yourself by tailoring your responses to the media making it more likely the media will use them. And you help the reporter by making his job easier, supplying him with quotes and eliminating his need to paraphrase you. If the publication or broadcast uses extensive, technically detailed quotes, providing that detail in your answers helps the reporter write his story accurately. Conversely, if the outlet goes for the "common touch" and you express yourself accordingly, the reporter is more likely to use your direct quotes and not have to work hard simplifying what you said so his readers can understand it. Remember, the more a reporter paraphrases you, the more opportunity there is for your points to lose focus. Reporters want to quote you rather than paraphrase you, but you need to give them the wherewithal to do that.

Crafting Your Messages
for Your Audience

Once you have identified your audience and your interviewer's likely agenda, then you're ready to craft your messages. Think of what you want that audience to know about your program, company, idea, or product and then use the worksheet in the appendix, or one you create yourself, to write out the messages you want readers, viewers, or listeners to take away. When you've finished with your worksheet, take as much time as you need to read your message statements aloud at least twice and think about them with as much detachment as you can muster. They are, after all, your Positive Message Statements. You created them in your self-interest, but you want your audience to be receptive to them. So, the first question to ask yourself is, "Do my messages sound like someone speaking or do they sound too 'literary?'" If the answer is too literary, you're probably writing for the eye not the ear. That is, you're writing something that is more easily absorbed when read than when heard. You want to redraft your agenda points so that they are more conversational. The second question to ask yourself is, "Do they sound like commercials or sermons?" If so, that's probably because you wrote them exclusively from your point of view. Instead, you should adopt the point of view of your ultimate audience. To identify with that audience, think of a radio station whose call-letters are WSIC. Whether your ultimate audience is watching your interview on TV, reading an account of it in a magazine, or listening to you on radio, all audience members have at least this one thing in common: they are all simultaneously listening to WSIC. Whether your audience is the broad-based readership of *USA Today* or the sophisticated scientists who subscribe to the journal *Science*, they are all listening to WSIC. The call-letters stand for:

```
RADIO STATION WSIC
       W: Why
     S: Should
         I
      C: Care?
```

Everyone you are trying to reach with your messages is subconsciously wondering why your PMSs should concern them and how your messages affect them. Remember what I wrote earlier about David Hartman seizing the morning ratings lead by asking the questions viewers wanted answered? Well that works both ways - for the interviewee as well as for the interviewer. You won't always be fortunate enough to have a David Hartman-esque interviewer, one who is seeking information for his viewers. Sometimes your interviewer will be too rushed, too overwhelmed, too indifferent, too expert, or too egotistical to care about the audience. So it's incumbent on you to care. You need to avoid shaping all your messages solely from your point of view. Instead, you need to broaden them so your real audience understands why it should care about them.

Previously, I wrote about the interview with the public health official who talked about influenza killing more Americans each year than AIDs. In a case like that it's pretty self-evident why a listener or reader should care. The information is a matter of life and death. But the challenge is much greater when you are trying to make people care about a message that doesn't concern a life or death issue. How do you make them care if you're the spokesperson for a rock band or an orbiting telescope? What if your interview goal is to promote a new candy bar or a soft drink? You need to step outside your spokesperson's role and ask yourself what it is about your messages would interest you if you were *not* the spokesperson. What about your messages would interest your Aunt Matilda and Uncle Joe? There's always something; your job now is to find it. People respond to a good story, to being entertained, to the opportunity to pursue pleasure, and to advice that enables them to avoid the unpleasant. Not life or death like the flu, but reason enough to absorb and remember your messages. It is your job to make those connections.

Using the copy of the agenda worksheet from the appendix - or the worksheet you created on your computer - rework and fine-tune your PMSs for the WSIC listeners. When you're finished reread them aloud again and then write down specifically how you've answered the WSIC question. Your WSIC response can be just a word or two, like "saves money," "entertaining," "promotes education," "stimulates the imagination."

Ideally, you'll have one of these brief WSIC responses for every one of your message statements.

ADDITIONAL TIPS
FOR SUCCESSFUL PREPARATION

Commandments 1 and 2, Thou Shalt Be Prepared and Thou Shalt Know to Whom Thou Art Speaking, are the most important rules for you to become a successful interview subject.

Knowing before the interview ever begins what you want to say and to whom you'll be saying it is more than half the preparation battle. In fact, having an agenda in advance is the single most important step in girding yourself for an interview, but there are some additional steps that are no less vital in helping you be the best prepared, most elegant and effective interview subject you can be.

MORE PREPARATION TIPS
Be informed.
Eat something.
Arrive early.
Warm up.
Be discreet.
**Don't assume you have
friends in the media.**

¶ **Be informed.** As close to the time of your interview as possible, read a newspaper and listen to a radio newscast. Even better, if you have access to the Internet, visit sites that may contain the latest news about your subject. You want to be as current on your subject as the reporter is likely to be. Remember this: the reporter expects to get information *from* you, not to give information *to* you. Be sure to check out at least one of these sites: Google News, the New York Times - which are searchable - or an Associated Press web site that is constantly updated. In addition to these, there are likely to be a host of web sites that deal with the specific issues you are going to address. You should make it a point to be familiar with their urls so you can visit them immediately before any media encounter.

Let's deal with the first line of websites for checking developments, Google, the New York Times and the AP:

Google news: Go to: http://news.google.com (There is no www.)

The site offers the latest news, but also has a box right next to the Google logo for entering search term keywords. This is the best all-purpose search site for the latest news. The listings are posted in chronological order - the most recent articles are listed first. Enter your search terms and Google's search engine surveys 45,000 news outlets worldwide. The articles are constantly updated. I find it an invaluable tool when media training clients because it gives me insights into the latest news reports about their company or organization, their sector of the economy, or their policies and programs. On a number of occasions I have found grist for the media training mill by checking Google news immediately before beginning a training session. Often I am privy to information the client doesn't know, so I can stump him with questions based on that information.

The New York Times: Go to http://www.nytimes.com.

The box for typing your search keywords is just above the lead story's headline. The pulldown menu next to the box permits you to narrow your search, but also enables accessing articles as far back as 1981.

Associated Press: Bookmark this one; it's long. http://customwire.ap.org/specials/bluepage.html.

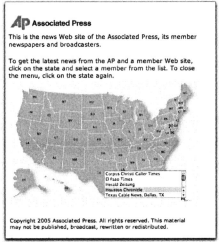

The url takes you to this map of the United States. Click on any state and you'll see a list of AP member newspapers and broadcast stations. Click on any one of these and it will take you to a page hosted by the local outlet but featuring AP news.

If your interview deals with a regional or local matter, be sure to check the web sites of your regional and local publications and broadcasters.

Why do all this homework? Well, you want to be making news, not hearing it. For instance, you surely don't want to learn from the reporter that your company has just declared bankruptcy. In print, your reaction can be embarrassing: "Mr. Kennerly was startled to hear from a reporter that Ynot Industries had declared bankruptcy." On camera, your stunned look will be even more damaging!

¶ **Eat something.** Picture this scene. On "Good Morning America," David Hartman had just introduced his guest, a prominent attorney. David asked her a question and she stammered for an answer. David asked her another question and instead of answering, she leaned back in the chair and her eyes rolled up. "Are you O.K.?" David asked. Unable to answer, her eyes closing, the attorney slowly shook her head. David leaned forward, took her hands and began gently slapping her wrists to get her pulse going. We cut to a commercial. As this dramatic scene was unfolding live on camera, someone phoned 911 and an ambulance arrived before the commercial break had ended. The attorney, who now said she merely felt lightheaded for a moment and blamed the bright, hot television lights, nonetheless agreed to go to the nearest hospital.

Later in the day, she returned to the office to let the show's staff know she was O.K. She told me: "My mother always said breakfast was the most important meal of the day. She never told me *how* important." She had eaten nothing before the show, even though we stocked our Green Room with food. On the air, her blood sugar level dropped sharply, leaving her light-headed and feeling faint. No doubt the stress of the interview environment, which can be an intimidating situation even for experienced interviewees, exacerbated her problem.

Pay attention to what you eat before an interview. Physicians I've consulted on the subject recommend eating complex carbohydrates (like fruit) and avoiding processed sugars, which can make you lethargic. In fact, on the advice of Dr. Tim Johnson, "Good Morning America's" on-camera medical editor, we stocked our Green Room with an ample supply of fresh fruit and a vegetable platter with a low-fat dip in addition to the traditional sticky buns, bagels and sugared pastries. You should avoid alcoholic beverages before an interview; their "calming" qualities are not worth the risk. I've seen more than a few interview subjects show up drunk and slur their way through a conversation with a reporter. In the most extreme case in my career, a famous college football coach was so drunk during a live interview he wet himself and was unaware of it until he got up to leave the set. In addition to booze, avoid carbonated beverages. You don't want to be sitting on camera or in front of a radio microphone stifling belches.

¶ **Arrive early.** On the morning of Ronald Reagan's first inauguration, January 21, 1981, we were broadcasting "Good Morning America" from a temporary studio built atop a high scaffold overlooking the White House. Our first guest for the day, in our 7:00-7:30 half-hour, was Sen. Barry Goldwater. At about 5:30 in the morning, as technicians were still doing last minute checks of gear and David Hartman and the producers were beginning to do a final read-through of the script, one of our staffers burst into the studio and said, "Senator Goldwater's here. He's climbing the stairs." The stairs in this case went three stories straight up without any landings for catching your breath. I knew that the senator had recently undergone hip surgery, so I ran out to intercept him before he climbed all those steps. I wanted to tell him that he was extremely early and might be more comfortable waiting at street level. I was too late; when I got to him he was already halfway up the stairs.

"Oh, it's O.K.," he said. "I always arrive early." "We don't have a Green Room up there," I said. "That's O.K. I'll sit in the corner and read the papers." Under his arm he was carrying several newspapers. Once inside the studio, he took a seat in the back of the small room and read the newspapers he had brought. Then the senator read the newspapers we had on hand and scanned the wire service copy. Finally - when we finished all our briefings - he talked informally with David Hartman and Steve Bell, the show's news anchor.

Sen. Goldwater, a media pro, arrived early for several good reasons. He was insuring he'd be on time, he'd be oriented to the interview's surroundings, he'd be informed (the newspapers and the wire service copy), and he was able to review any prepared messages he might have brought with him. Also, his early arrival gave him the opportunity for an advance chat with his interviewers.

Arriving early is especially important for broadcast interviews. There is nothing worse than rushing into a radio or television studio at the last minute, sitting down and trying to respond to that first question while you are panting like a sprinter, trying to catch your breath. Chances are good you'll be so harried you won't convey your messages effectively.

¶ **Warm up**. As Sen. Goldwater did, chat with the reporter before the interview. Consider it a mental stretching exercise or a warmup before your race. If it's a television interview, introduce yourself to the crew, too. Some TV reporters follow a rigid caste system and will not introduce you to these people, but don't let their rudeness stop you. The camera crew and lighting technicians can make you look good or bad and if you've taken the trouble to say hello to them, they'll treat you better than if you snub them. A skilled practitioner of this tactic was Rosalynn Carter, former President Jimmy Carter's wife. Once, during the 1976 presidential campaign, Mrs. Carter was a guest on "Good Morning America." She took time during the commercial before her appearance to walk up to each cameraman, stagehand, and technician and introduce herself. When she sat down for that interview, there were ten people on the set who would have set things right if even a single hair on Mrs. Carter's head had been out of place. After the interview the future first lady made the rounds again and thanked each person on the set.

¶ **Be discreet.** It is very important when you're chatting up the cast and crew to avoid saying anything you don't want the entire world to know. ("Boy, is our company having a terrible quarter. I don't know if we can avoid bankruptcy. But you won't ask me about that, will you?") Of course you wouldn't do that, right? Well, don't be too sure. I once heard an actress say, "You know, I won't talk about my relationship with X, so don't even bother asking." An early question in the interview was: "You've said you won't talk about your relationship with X. Well, why won't you talk about it?" She wasn't asked about the relationship; the reporter respected her wishes in a literal sense. But the question she actually got sounded a lot more damaging. So instead of talking about what you can't say, use the warmup for what you can say and want to say; your interview agenda.

A good hard and fast rule is this: Whenever you are in proximity to a journalist, you are being interviewed. A print reporter can hear a quote, remember it, and write it down after the fact and use it in her article. A broadcast correspondent can report on the air something you've said to her away from the microphone: "Off-camera Ms. Marmot told me that the Ynot Company is on the brink of bankruptcy...."

You may be asking yourself, "If there is such a big danger of being overly confidential, why bother with the stretch/warmup before the interview? The answer is that the benefits outweigh the risks; with just a little discipline you will be able to use this unique opportunity to plant the seeds of some of your PMSs in the reporter's mind, inviting questions that will elicit those PMSs in formal the interview. So just as you have an agenda for the interview, you should have a Cliff Notes version of that agenda for the warmup as well.

Shortly before President Nixon's resignation in 1974, I produced a story called "The Business of Watergate" for ABC News' weekly magazine show, "The Reasoner Report." The story told how various Watergate figures were cashing in on their notoriety by writing books and giving lectures about the break-in and subsequent cover-up. One of the people I interviewed for the piece was James McCord, one of the Watergate burglars. McCord had written a book called *A Piece of Tape*. While the crew set up the lights and camera in McCord's office in the Washington suburbs, McCord began talking to me about the break-in and gave a couple of details that I'd not heard or read before. So when the camera was rolling, I asked him about them. He repeated them - in the context of their being revealed for the first time in his book. We both went away happy. I had filmed some new pieces of the Watergate puzzle and McCord had a plug for his book. He had used his warmup time with me most effectively.

¶ **Don't assume you have friends in the media.** Does this mean that although you've been friendly with some reporters in the past, you can't ever relax and open up with them? Unfortunately, yes, that's exactly what it means. To illustrate this, take the case of Spiro Agnew.

Agnew was gregarious and outgoing, with a ready smile and a relaxed manner. He'd been the governor of Maryland and in 1968, Richard Nixon selected him to be his vice presidential running mate. Agnew, though a pit bull on the stump, charmed the "boys on the bus," the reporters covering the campaign. In later years he would become the bane of the press corps' existence, the Nixon Administration's point man in its war against the media. Reporters, Agnew would charge in his famously pugnacious 1970 San Diego speech, were "nattering nabobs of negativism." (Here are his exact words: "In the United States today, we have more than our share of the nattering nabobs of negativism.")

But in the early days, Agnew's relations with the reporters covering him were far less confrontational and antagonistic. Agnew was "one of the guys." They may not have agreed with his politics, but "the boys" liked him and perhaps he even thought of them as friends. He certainly thought of Gene Oishi, a Japanese-American reporter who worked for the Baltimore Sun, as a pal; Agnew had known Oishi since his days as governor of Maryland.

One day, Agnew missed Oishi and he asked the other reporters where "the fat Jap" was. Oishi - possibly aware the remark was a joke, possibly because he was not present when the Agnew said it - was unwilling to break the story. Others *were* willing and a few days after Agnew's quip, the *Washington Post* ran the story, forcing Agnew into an embarrassing apology.

Agnew had thought he'd been joking among friends. And, despite Oishi's reluctance to report the candidate's remark, the other reporters did what they saw as their professional duty. The Agnew story is an object lesson in why comedy is best left to comedians.

A more recent object lesson came on November 1, 2006 when, before an audience of college students, Massachusetts Senator John Kerry said, "Education, if you make the most of it, you study hard, you do your homework and you make an effort to be smart, you can do well. And if you don't, you get stuck in Iraq." Coming in the final days of the midterm election campaign, the remark ignited a firestorm, with the White House and sympathetic columnists and commentators claiming Kerry was calling U.S. troops in Iraq uneducated. Kerry defended himself by saying he had botched a joke. Unhappily for him, he botched the joke in front of television cameras, so the words were out there and for a couple of news cycles turned the focus of the election away from the issues and onto the senator's alleged slight of the troops. In a news conference several days later, the senator said what he'd meant to say was "those of who didn't study properly, those who made the decisions, they got us into Iraq." Even in its unbotched form, it was not a particularly funny joke. Spokespeople should be extremely wary about turning comedian in front of the media; just because you can tell a joke to a friend or family member, does not mean you can tell one to a larger audience.

Following Commandments 1 and 2 will prepare and empower you to make your points in any interview. By creating your own agenda you'll gain confidence and avoid the disappointment of missed media opportunities. Knowing what you will and won't say are fundamental to media mastery. Your overall effectiveness as a spokesperson depends on having an agenda of messages that you want the reporter's audience to absorb and making those messages as relevant as possible. You also must express those messages effectively. Now let's move on to the commandments that will help you make your message presentation effective, commandments 3, 4 and 5; what I call the performance commandments.

Chapter 3

THE PERFORMANCE COMMANDMENTS

In our last chapter we dealt with our first two commandments, the preparation commandments - the rules you must obey when *formulating* your Positive Message Statements. The next three commandments deal with *delivering* those messages to the media's audiences. I call these three the performance commandments, because - as I wrote earlier - you should always think of an interview as a performance. Heeding these edicts will make you a better performer. The three performance commandments are:

THE PERFORMANCE COMMANDMENTS

Thou shalt be quoteworthy.

Thou shalt practice, practice, practice.

**Thou shalt not lie, evade,
nor cop an attitude.**

Marshall McLuhan, widely celebrated as the "oracle of the electronic age," coined the phrase, "The medium is the massage," He turned it into the title of a book and that title, almost universally misread as *The Medium is the Message* (with an *e* rather than an *a)* - has licensed an entire generation of spokespersons to think that merely getting their face on television or their name in print is the equivalent of successfully delivering their message. But pay close attention to the exact language McLuhan used: the phrase and the title are a play on words; McLuhan used the word *massage*, not the word *message*. The word play cleverly conflates two meanings: "the medium is the *mass age*" or, the more literal: the medium *massages* our brains just as a masseuse kneads our muscles. With all due respect to the late professor McLuhan, I suggest that for our purposes, we continue the popular misconstruction of his little pun, call it "message" and turn it around. So when you are a spokesperson, your *message* is the message and the *medium* is just that: the mechanism for delivering the message. In other words, the medium is *not* the message. But, with a nod of recognition to McLuhan's pun, the medium does require us to m*a*ssage our m*e*ssage in order to express it most effectively. Each of the different media require that we slightly temper, alter, and tailor our message to accommodate its specific attributes. More on those unique aspects of the different media in succeeding chapters. But for now, let's concentrate on the universal rules for all media; rules which begin with the three performance commandments:

COMMANDMENT 3: THOU SHALT BE QUOTEWORTHY

In the previous chapter I wrote how disappointed I had been when I read the story that emerged from my chat with the *Daily News* reporter who interviewed me at ABC News. He had used no direct quotes, but had paraphrased my remarks and I felt I had been a dull and ineffective spokesperson. I had not taken advantage of the opportunity to get any messages to his readers because I had prepared no messages. I had no agenda; no Positive Message Statements to expound. And whatever expounding I had done in the service of *his* agenda had not been quoteworthy material. In broadcasting terms, I had not spoken in soundbites. After that second interview, I began paying extremely close attention to direct quotes in newspapers and magazine stories. I listened more analytically to television news reports, including those I, myself, produced. I had always been keenly attuned to the attributes of a good soundbite. But now I wanted to codify a formula for quoteworthy messages. I knew a good quote when I read one; I knew a good soundbite when I heard one. But what, exactly, made them good? Until now I had been relying on instinct; I wanted to figure out if I could apply a set of rules to good quotes and soundbites.

What began as a casual investigation into my own shortcomings during a brief phone interview became a thirty-year study. To this day I never read a newspaper, listen to a radio newscast, or watch a TV news program without mentally grading the interview subjects.

Some get an F; they fail miserably. You can tell this group very quickly: usually, not a word of what they said is in direct quotes in a print story. If they are part of a television report, you may see them talking on camera but their words are muted and the correspondent is telling us what they said. This is because they have expressed themselves so badly their actual words are unusable.

Not too long ago, on a local television newscast, I watched just such a "silent interview" in the sports report. A basketball coach was on camera, his lips were moving and no doubt when he was taped, sounds emerged from his mouth. None of those sounds made it to air. Instead, the reporter, speaking voiceover the lip-flapping coach, told us what the coach had said. Apparently he had spoken so ineptly the reporter had to supply a comprehensible version for viewers. The coach's failure was all the more obvious because the reporter used no game or practice video to cover the interview. As a viewer, a producer, and a media coach, I gave the hapless coach a failing grade.

The majority of interview subjects earn a mediocre C. There may be a direct quote from them in print, but most likely it's just a sentence or a sentence fragment. The C interview subject may get eight or nine seconds of a soundbite on television or radio, but often their statements aren't even complete sentences and the correspondent feels compelled to contribute a voiceover introduction to set up the bite or an "outro" to clarify or amplify what the subject was trying to say.

A handful of interviewees earn an A. They are quoted profusely in print. In the electronic media whole sentences - indeed, whole paragraphs - run uninterrupted. A classic A interview subject is former Surgeon General C. Everett Koop. Imposing, deep-voiced, poised and - most importantly - comprehensible, this physician's cameraside manner is probably an outgrowth of the comforting and competent bedside manner he used when he was a practicing physician. News stories concerning Dr. Koop were filled with direct quotes. Television stories featured frequent soundbites. Dr. Koop, by being an A interview subject, in effect, wrote the journalists' stories for them. All A grade interviewees speak in short, comprehensible sentences and there are no ambiguities in their answers. They never equivocate or evade. Also, they use grabbers, word techniques that make a soundbite come alive. A little later, I'll show you how to create grabbers.

Aside from its appeal to our competitive instincts, why strive for an A in an interview? What's wrong with a comfortable C? For that matter, is it a crime to flunk? No, it's not a crime; you won't be left back, sent to detention, ordered to write an essay, or required to take a makeup test. But a failing grade means you have not communicated as effectively as you should; you've missed an opportunity to directly sell your ideas, company, product, or organization to a wide audience. Also, by being a C interview subject you've invited the reporter to paraphrase you and - as I wrote earlier - when a reporter paraphrases, the chances of misinterpretation and distortion increase.

The A interviewee, like Dr. Koop, is in control. He takes advantage of the opportunity interviews afford him to reach large audiences with messages expressed in his own words. To a large extent C, and more so the D and F interviewees, miss out on that opportunity. They are not in control and depend on the reporter to help them convey ideas. The reporter may not accommodate them. Through ineptitude, indifference, or even malice, the reporter may misconstrue, misinterpret, or misstate the message. Many of my media training clients have told me that past interviewers "got it wrong," inaccurately conveying their messages. If you force the journalist to filter your ideas because you don't express them clearly, there is always the risk that the reporter's filter will distort what you want to say. An A inerview subject keeps control by being *quoteworthy*. Giving a reporter good quotes eliminates much of that reportorial filtering.

To be quoteworthy you need to speak in soundbites. A soundbite is the mass media's most valuable commodity - a short, pithy, meaningful statement, a verbal headline.

SOUNDBITES

Critics deplore soundbite journalism as bad journalism. They say that it is vapid, glib, oversimplified. The soundbite, they charge, is the curse of television news and proof of the medium's superficiality. Most of those who make this charge, of course, are print media reporters who often prove their point by citing television's harshest critics in direct quotes; quotes which are suspiciously like soundbites. Just take for example, "Soundbite journalism is infantile, puerile, and futile. It's like a souffle' - all fluff and no substance." A good quote which, if lifted from the printed page and uttered on TV or radio, would be a good soundbite! What is a good soundbite? A brief statement that captures attention, delivers a message, and does it in a way that's sufficiently dramatic or witty to remain in your memory. Good soundbites don't have to come from a politician, an author, a statesman, a movie star, or a philosopher. Anyone can deliver a good, compelling soundbite. Reporting on a tornado that devastated a small Southern town, *The New York Times* quoted a fourth grader as saying, "The good news is we don't have school tomorrow. The bad news is we don't have a school." That's a good, effective soundbite from a ten-year-old. You'll remember that one a lot longer than reading a quote such as, "Our school was blown down in the tornado and now we don't have a school to go to anymore." The fact that the first quote was in a newspaper and not on television or radio is telling. In point of fact, all newspapers and magazines use soundbites - they just call them direct quotes. Soundbites have been around forever, only the name is relatively new. You've come across soundbites in the past. Shakespeare's plays are full of lines that make fine soundbites ("Neither a borrower nor a lender be."). And so is the Bible ("The wages of sin is death."). Soundbites aren't just the currency of literature and religion, either. Virtually every great line we remember from our history courses qualifies as a soundbite. Here are some classic quotes, that illustrate the point:

> *"Give me liberty or give me death."*
> **- Patrick Henry (1775)**

> *"I only regret that I have but one life to lose for my country,"*
> **- Nathan Hale on the gallows before being hanged by the British for spying (1776)**

> *"Here I stand; I can do no otherwise."*
> **- Martin Luther (1521)**

> *"The only thing we have to fear is fear itself."*
> **- President Franklin D. Roosevelt (1933)**

*"It's a recession when your neighbor loses his job;
it's a depression when you lose yours."*
- **Former President Harry Truman (1956)**

You'll notice that most of those soundbites predate television news and three of them predate all electronic media. In fact, Luther's predates the discovery of electricity. Soundbites, or memorable quotes, are the stuff of history, and journalism is history's first draft.

Here's a little homework assignment: next time you're spending a relaxing Sunday with the newspaper or your favorite magazine, compare how much text in a story is within quotation marks with how much is not. When you read the directly quoted material, assess the amount and quality of information in those quotes. Ordinarily, the direct quotes will share two attributes: good solid, comprehensible information and a deft turn of phrase. You can find direct quotes in which only one or another of those attributes will be present, but in those cases, you will notice that it's more likely that a deft turn of language is directly quoted than an inelegantly phrased, information-filled sentence. Typically, reporters will paraphrase the information in the latter, rather than force readers to deconstruct the meandering sentence. That said, the vast majority of words in any given article you'll read in this Sunday assignment will not be direct quotes; the direct quotes will the most significant, the most trenchant statements - if you will, the soundbites.

The New York Times celebrates the best daily soundbite in its Quote of the Day. Over the course of a month I kept careful score of the Quote of the Day and during that period the average length of the quote/soundbite was under 20 words. Most were no more than two sentences and some were as short as a single sentence of as few as 10 words. We'll deal with the ideal construction and length of soundbites a little later on and you'll learn exactly how to express your agenda in compelling soundbites. Many newspapers highlight important quotes by printing them in boldface and enclosing them in a box within the body of a news story. These are called "pull quotes."

Perfecting a Soundbite

Looking back at such masters of soundbites as Shake-speare, John F. Kennedy, Harry Truman, Patrick Henry, Ronald Reagan, Winston Churchill, and so many others - we can see that there is nothing intrinsically wrong with answering a question with a soundbite, especially if the soundbite serves your purpose by vividly illustrating your message. Soundbite journalism gets a bad rap, many consider it "short shrift" journalism - superficial reporting and writing. Also, many soundbites *are* really bad; they amount to little more than vapid slogans, conveying scant substance. This is not necessarily because the interviewee doesn't know his area of expertise. The more likely explanation is he did not have the skill set to make the most out of his media opportunity.

Soundbites for Your
Positive Message Statements

In the last chapter, you created an agenda of Positive Message Statements. That was the first step in producing good soundbites. Your PMSs are the basis for soundbites; the soundbites will bring your PMSs to life, making them compelling to the media. Now let's revisit your messages and create soundbites for them.

First you need to hone your PMSs so they have fine, sparkling, razor-like edges. Next, you'll need to deliver them in an assertive, positive manner without temporizing, compromising, or stumbling. If that sounds daunting, it can be, but only if you don't take the time to prepare. As I wrote earlier, an interview is a performance and the benefits of preparing for that performance are worth the effort. A key part of that preparation is working on your soundbites in advance of every interview; making them sharp enough to cut through the fog and make your messages shine brightly.

The historical soundbites on pages 41 and 42 are uniformly direct, concise, and bold. And short. The longest soundbite I quoted was Harry Truman's witty line about the difference between a recession and a depression. It's a mere 16 words long. Compare his line with a less effective alternate that expresses the same idea:

Truman: "It's a recession when your neighbor loses his job; it's a depression when you lose yours."

Alternate: "It's a recession when your neighbor is out of work; it's a depression when you are."

The difference is that Truman's soundbite is in the active voice, the alternative is in the passive voice: "loses his job" versus "is out of work." The active verb *loses* is so much more powerful than the passive *is out of work.* So use the active voice!

President Franklin D. Roosevelt's "fear" soundbite, "The only thing we have to fear is fear itself," is only ten words long. (It is misquoted frequently in eight words: "We have nothing to fear but fear itself.") The Roosevelt quote is from his first inaugural address, so it was less off-the-cuff than the Truman recession/depression line. It is also likely Roosevelt's memorable quote was the result of fine-tuning by accomplished speechwriters - Roosevelt had successful poets and playwrights on his speechwriting staff. Some of the other vintage soundbites I quoted came from prepared remarks, too, while others were spontaneous. But you need not hire speechwriters and poets to do this work, and you do not have to read your soundbites. In fact, in most face-to-face interviews it would be a mistake to read them. And you do not need Harry Truman's spontaneous wit to come up with them, either. It's a good idea to compose your soundbites in advance and when the occasion presents itself in the form of a question, deploy them from memory.

Harry Truman, in particular, had a gift for concise and telling off-the-cuff remarks, making him a master of the soundbite. He famously said, "If you can't stand the heat, stay out of the kitchen." Another of his favorites was "The buck stops here." He even had a small plaque on his Oval Office desk that read, "The buck stops here." Compare Truman's memorable line to similar sentiments expressed more recently by President George W. Bush: "Presidents, whether things are good or bad, always get the blame." Truman's "buck stops here" is an historic soundbite, the other wound up in a book called *Bushisms*, a compendium of the 43rd president's verbal gaffes. Both quotes have the same basic message, albeit Bush's is more defensive than Truman's. But it is really the memorable language that differentiates them.

In my media training sessions, I've always urged participants not to memorize their entire answers, lest they sound overly rehearsed. But I make an exception for brief soundbites because, unless you've got Harry Truman's unique gift, you'd better plan, write, and rehearse these lines so they'll have maximum effect.

But, please, don't do as our current crop of politicians do and, upon finding a resonating soundbite, repeat it *ad nauseam* for the same audience. Remember Vice President Al Gore's "social security lockbox" in the 2000 presidential campaign? Or President Bush's "stay the course line" about the Iraq war? Both used their terms until they became grist for the mills of comedians. Patrick Henry didn't go around the colonies repeating "Give me liberty or give me death." He said it once in 1775 and it reverberates to this day. (I'll have more to say about "Stay the course" later on when we deal with denying you said something while TV cameras recorded you saying it.)

In general, you can repeat a good soundbite until it runs nationally or until it becomes a cliché. At that point, let the media use the term for you. Lockbox would have been O.K. on a Houston radio station then in a Denver newspaper and later on in a TV newscast in Chicago. But after it was on the network nightly newscasts and on CNN once or twice, Gore probably should have dropped it; chances are good the media would have continued to use it for him.

Do you remember the oft-repeated slogan for eliminating the nation's narcotics problem which Sen. Bob Dole unleashed in his 1996 presidential campaign? Following leaks to the media that candidate Dole was going to unveil a "powerful new slogan to help fight the war on drugs," the senator came out with: "Just don't do it." On the stump he didn't just say it once, he would say it four, five, even six times in rapid succession, turning it into a manic chant. The words might have worked in a one-on-one interview - a masterpiece of brevity in answer to a question. But as a chant, it was not merely seriously wanting; it became comedic. And even after the latenight comics began having fun with it, Sen. Dole wouldn't abandon it; he repeated it during every stump speech in his campaign.

Speak in Complete Sentences

How is it our politicians make so many media mistakes their utterances become the currency of comedy? Media critic Michael Wolff, writing in the December 9, 2002, issue of *New York Magazine*, summed up the situation this way: "All but an exceptional few politicians suck at making, or understanding, media. This is a surprise, because the only thing politicians want to do is get on TV. That's their basic job. But they're talentless. They're zeros."

The paradigm of a long-gone past - making the same speech at every venue - remains in force in political campaigns even today. It is a paradigm established long before there were national media that electronically spread every quote and speech nationwide and then repeated them throughout the 24-hour news cycle. The same holds true for political interviews, too. Frequently, politicians give the same word-for-word answers to questions. While there's nothing wrong with reusing a good answer for new audiences, repeating it for the same audience runs the risk of turning even the best soundbite into a cliché and making the interview subject look overly scripted. For most spokespersons, this isn't a risk because they aren't subjected to the same constant and intensive media attention that politicians must endure.

Today, one thing many politicians *have* mastered is the art of speaking in complete sentences in interviews, and that is a skill you need to learn, too. Delivering your answers in complete sentences enhances your control of the interview because the print reporter interviewing you won't have to add your missing words in brackets and the broadcast reporter won't have to write a tortured lead-in or lead-out to your soundbite. Since filling in your blanks or creating that tortured lead-in or lead-out is extra work, many reporters won't bother doing it; instead they will paraphrase your words - and you want to avoid being paraphrased. In addition, giving the reporter your thoughts in complete sentences means your quotes and soundbites will help you capture the reader's or viewer's full attention.

Most of the time you should incorporate the sense of the question in your answer. Doing this makes it easier for the reporter to use your answer without having to include her question. So, for example, if I asked you, "How's the weather today," you would not answer "It's fine." Instead, you would reply, "The weather today is fine," incorporating the sense of my question in your answer. An added benefit is that when you include the sense of the question in your answer, you buy yourself a little bit of thinking time to decide which of your Positive Message Statements you want to unleash in response. Former Presidents Nixon, Reagan, and Clinton regularly incorporated the sense of a question in their answers. If you listen to the soundbites from their news conferences, you'll notice their statements frequently stood on their own; you understood what they were responding to without having heard the question. I wrote that it is a good idea "most of the time" to incorporate the sense of the question in your answer. The exception to that general rule is the loaded, hostile, negative question like, "Wasn't your failure to alert your investors to the downturn in sales a case of managerial malfeasance?" Obviously, incorporating the sense of that question into your answer - even if the answer is a ringing denial - would be counterproductive. In those instances, omit the sense of the question and just give an answer, remembering to speak in complete sentences.

Earlier, I urged you to be concise and bold with your soundbites. You *can* be too bold. Many years ago I covered a news conference by the leader of the Brooklyn longshoreman's union, the elderly but still combative Anthony "Tough Tony" Anastasio. A strike was looming and, on this particular day, Tough Tony, who looked like a grandfather but talked like the Godfather, told the assembled reporters that if there was not a new contract soon, "The docks is gonna run red wit' blood." His glib and polished second-in-command, Tony Scotto, who was also Tough Tony's son-in-law, quickly interjected: "What Pop means is...."

To those of us covering the news conference, what "Pop" meant was abundantly clear. But I submit that while it was a great soundbite for those of us in the media, it may not have been for Anastasio. It made him appear to be a ruthless thug. As a rule, if you need a "handler" to spin your soundbite, you probably should not have uttered it in the first place.

Additionally, I would caution all spokespersons against "red wit' blood" style soundbites. You really want avoid direct quotes that threaten or condone any illegal activity. If the activity were to come to pass, even without your involvement, your soundbite could be extremely embarrassing, maybe even incriminating. And while it is true that the public's memory is distressingly short, the media's memory is limitless. They archive everything and anything you ever say to the media can be found and reprinted or rebroadcast.

Tough Tony's soundbite probably played well with his restive union membership, but everyone else who heard it was appalled at his naked threat of violence. When making bold statements, you have to assess how they will play not only to the general public but also to specific audiences within the public. In a July, 2003 news conference, President Bush said of the Iraqi insurgency, which was in its early stages: "There are some who feel like that the conditions are such they can attack us there. My answer is bring 'em on." As Bush left the podium after the news conference, his press secretary, Ari Fleischer, privately told the chief executive that he took exception to the "bring 'em on" line because the families of soldiers serving in Iraq might find it offensive and insensitive. The statement struck more than just military families as being insensitive and next day, Fleischer was doing a Tony Scotto to Bush's Tough Tony Anastasio, telling reporters that the president had not meant to invite attacks on American troops: "I think what the president was expressing there is his confidence in the men and women of the military to handle the military mission." Four and a half years later, Scott Pelley of "60 Minutes" asked Bush what mistakes he had made in the Iraq war, and the president answered, "Abu Ghraib was a mistake. Using bad language like, you know, 'bring 'em on' was a mistake." Here was the president ranking an ill-chosen soundbite right up there with the prisoner torture scandal. Do you need any further proof of how important soundbites are?

MORE QUOTEWORTHINESS TIPS

Here are some additional tips to help you obey the quoteworthiness commandment. They are essential for turning your messages into soundbites that will be compelling to the media, make a reporter's job easier, and enhance audience comprehension. Following these tips will make your broadcast soundbites and printed quotes more effective and memorable. I illustrate them with radio station call-letters:

> ### THE SOUNDBITE CALL-LETTERS
> **KPUF: Key Point Up Front.**
> **KISS: Keep it Short and Simple.**
> **KOTJ: Knock off the Jargon.**

¶ **KPUF: Key Point Up Front.** Copy the media's technique and speak the way the media write. Read a news story or listen to a newscast and pay special attention to how writers structure the stories. Typically, there is a headline, then a lead sentence, and then supporting facts. (Broadcast reports often omit the headline, although an introductory line like, "Here's a frightening story from the Centers for Disease Control," is a verbal headline.) The lead sentence is the one that contains the most important information the reporter wishes to convey. For most of us, it is counterintuitive to express ourselves this way. In ordinary conversation, we answer a question with this progression: fact A plus fact B, therefore conclusion C. When we are communicating through the media, we must reverse that: Conclusion C because fact A plus fact B. It may seem illogical to answer questions this way, but there are valid reasons for doing it. In electronic media the listener or viewer doesn't have the advantage that a newspaper or magazine reader has - the ability to go back and revisit a line or a paragraph. I call this the reread factor. So in broadcast interviews it is vital that you get the most important elements up front to set the audience's mental agenda. But I recommend doing this in print interviews, as well, because you'll be speaking to the reporter exactly the way he writes his stories. And speaking this way makes it much more likely you'll wind up in direct quotes and not paraphrases. Also, as a former print reporter, I can attest that my notes were always extremely legible at the start of a response and became more difficult to read as the answer progressed. Get your top ideas out before writer's cramp sets in. (It's worth noting that FDR's "The only thing we have to fear is fear itself" was the fifth sentence in a twenty-minute speech.)

¶ **KISS: Keep it Short and Simple**. Why short? Because if you go on and on and on and on and on and on and on and …. Get the point? If you go on and on in a broadcast inter-view, you're going to lose your listener's interest and she'll forget how you started. In a print interview that listener who's going to lose interest is the reporter, and you certainly don't want that. Why simple? Because if your answer gets too complicated, its WSIC (why should I care?) quotient dwindles. In media training workshops clients always ask me, "How short and how simple?" I'll answer in reverse order:

How simple? My colleague, Kerry Millerick, a producer and very funny on-camera talent, was working on a TV show with a highly respected executive producer. In a script Kerry used the word "acknowledge." "You can't use that word," said the producer. "Why not?" Kerry protested, "Aren't we trying to communicate on the level of a 12-year-old? Every 12-year-old knows what the word acknowledge means." "Twelve?" bel-lowed the producer. "Who told you 12? It's *five*. Five, not 12." With all due respect to the veteran executive producer, he was aiming far too low. So where should you aim? Well, remember the second commandment: Thou shalt know to whom thou art speaking? If your interview is with *USA Today*, "The CBS Early Show," or "Larry King Live," you're reaching a less sophisti-cated audience than if the interview is with the journal *Science* or *Barron's* or *Aviation Week*. For those specialized publications you can hike the sophistication level of your answers to match that of your audience. But for the mass-market media, use an-swers that are comprehensible at the U.S. national average grade level: the education grade level reached by the average citizen. In the United States, that's the tenth grade. In other words, you are talking to a fifteen- or sixteen-year-old. And that's not the teen whiz who built a solar-powered car for his science project; it's the *average* fifteen- or sixteen-year old. But here's a caveat: For emotion-charged stories where fear and fury reign, that highly respected producer who gave Kerry Millerick such grief was nearly right; you have to drop down *four* grade levels. In other words, if you are talking about building a nuclear power plant down the street from a preschool, you'll need to make your points comprehensible to a sixth grader (i.e., an eleven-year-old!) It's necessary to make the points simpler and more basic in these cases because the brain receives and processes emotional argu-ments in a more primitive, survivalist way. Thus, the woman

50

with a master's degree who happens to be the mom of a child in that preschool near the proposed nuclear plant is going to respond to the arguments for and against its construction as if she were a twelve-year-old sixth grader.

How do you determine the grade level of your answers? Microsoft Word has a grade level tool. So, if you craft your soundbites in Word and use the tool, you'll see the grade level. To activate this feature in Word, click on the "tools" menu bar, select options, select the spelling and grammar tab, and select "show readability statistics." Thereafter, running "Spelling and Grammar" from the tools menu yields a report like this:

Readability Statistics	
Counts	
Words	89
Characters	433
Paragraphs	3
Sentences	6
Averages	
Sentences per Paragraph	1.2
Words per Sentence	10.5
Characters per Word	4.5
Readability	
Passive Sentences	0%
Flesch Reading Ease	68.6
Flesch-Kincaid Grade Level	6.2

How short? Follow the 30, 10, 3 rule: The ideal soundbite is *no more than* 30 words. Spoken aloud, it takes *no more than* 10 seconds. And it is no more than three sentences. (The preceding was exactly 27 words long, could easily be spoken in under ten seconds, and was only three sentences.) If you're asking yourself do *all* my answers have to be that short, my response is an emphatic, *no!* The key point, the *soundbite* part of your answer, should follow the rule. That said, make every effort to keep your entire answer no more than thirty seconds. You can say a lot in 30 seconds. As an exercise, try reading aloud from this book for 30 seconds and see how far down a page you get be-fore the clock runs out.

¶ **KOTJ: Knock off the jargon**. According to the *Guinness Book of World Records*, the world's longest acronym is: NIIOMTPLABOPARMBETZHELBETRABSBOMONIMONK-ONOTDTEKHSTROMONT. The Latin letters are an approximation, because they are transliterations from the original Cyrillic. In the old, bureaucratic Soviet Union, those fifty-six letters were shorthand for: "The Laboratory for Shuttering, Reinforcement, Concrete and Ferroconcrete Operations for Composite-Monolithic and Monolithic Constructions of the Department of the Technology of Building-Assembly Operations of the Scientific Research Institute of the Organization for Building Mechanization and Technical Aid of the Academy of Building and Architecture of the USSR." (And you thought the Soviet Union crumbled because it spent itself into insolvency keeping up with the U.S. in the arms race!)

If you spoke that acronym in an interview - although how one could possibly pronounce it is a mystery to me - you would use an appreciable amount of the interview time just explaining it. As dense and incomprehensible as that old Soviet acronym is, the routine jargon you use daily may be just as dense to a reporter and to his audience. The fact is, every business, science, art, craft, and trade has its own jargon. What you and your colleagues instantly understand may leave outsiders in the dust. Sure those acronyms and the catchy lingo make your job easier, but they make the job of an interviewer and his end-user harder. Reporters have to translate your jargon and to avoid that chore, they may just paraphrase you.

Sometimes we encounter dueling jargons - a phrase or acronym that means one thing to you and your colleagues and something completely different to people in another industry or even to people in another company in your own sector. Here's an illustration: I was doing media training at NASA's Jet Propulsion Laboratory, working with the engineers involved in landing the rovers, Spirit and Opportunity, on the surface of Mars. The engineers referred to "EDL." In television production, EDL is an acronym for edit decision list - the time code list generated by an editing system. After the second reference, I stopped one of the engineers and asked, "Why do you need an edit decision list to land on Mars?" He was confused, so I said, "EDL - edit decision list." He laughed and said, "EDL is our acronym for entry, descent, and landing." A good example of dueling jargons.

A good reporter may stop you when you deploy jargon and ask you to define the terms. But that interrupts the flow of thought and steals time better spent casting forth your messages. So make it a rule to avoid jargon. That said, some acronyms have become universally understood and don't need explaining. People may wonder what entity you're talking about if you said "The National Aeronautics and Space Agency," but they will instantly know "NASA." Similarly, FBI and CIA are familiar to all Americans, as is FEMA, in the aftermath of Hurricane Katrina, but other federal government agencies, like HUD, DOD, DOE, and HHS are not. (Translations: HUD is Housing and Urban Development, DOD is Department of Defense, DOE is Department of Energy. HHS is Health and Human Services, but in another example of dueling acronyms, it is also the stock exchange symbol for the company Hartke Hanks, Inc.)

Most jargon mystifies and nearly all acronyms are indecipherable to the public. If you find yourself uttering an acronym, define it after first usage: "HUD - or the Department of Housing and Urban Development - has teams that can regularly visit...."

Now to our three radio stations, KPUF, KISS, and KOTJ, let's add five additional quoteworthiness tips.

FIVE MORE
QUOTEWORTHINESS TIPS
Brand!
"Yes" and "no" are not answers.
Use Grabbers.
Be specific and enumerate.
Avoid weak words like "try" and "hope."

¶ **Brand!** How many times have you tuned in your radio or TV mid-interview and heard an author refer repeatedly to "my book" or "the book?" If he captured your interest, you're going to have a tough time at Barnes & Noble or Walden Books getting even the most helpful clerk to find "The Book" or "My Book." Music artists I train frequently talk about "My CD" or "My Album." When they do that I tell them I'm going to bring out a CD of my own called "My CD" and another called "My Album" because they've been helping me promote them. Similarly, how many times have you heard an interview subject say, "we" instead of giving the name of his company or organization? "We" is not a name. Try, instead, "We at Consolidated Ynot Corporation feel..." Branding is simple: if it's got a name, use it.

Think about the photographs of competitive skiers you see in the sports pages of your daily newspaper. Invariably, the skier holds her skis upright, alongside her head, logo side facing the camera. The skier in the photo is "branding" - planting the name of her ski company sponsor in your head and inferring that if you use her brand you'll ski as well as she does. There can be too much branding. Look at NASCAR race cars. If there were any more company logos posted on those cars they would need no paint. There are, in fact, so many logos that most of us don't pay attention to any of them. NASCAR drivers, too, are logo'd to the max. There is enough reading material on their uniforms to distract you from what they're saying.

The mandate to "brand" is a little less important when you're dealing with the print media - where there's that reread factor and a consumer can hunt earlier in the story to find out what company or organization you're affiliated with. But why make them do the work? If you brand, the reader won't have to hunt. Besides, getting into good habits in one medium pays dividends in all media.

¶ **"Yes" and "no" are not answers.** "Yes" and "no" are the beginning of answers; the door-openers to your real answer. In a trial, an attorney will ask for a yes or no response, but an interview is not a trial. Reporters don't want yeses and nos, unless they are the first word in a longer answer. In an interview, there is no such thing as a yes or no question, even if a reporter poses one that way. How many times have you seen an uncoached, unsophisticated individual who responds "yes" and "no" to most questions? In those instances the reporter often fills in the blanks left by the interviewee - always a less than satisfactory solution. I can recall one such interview on "Good Morning America" when Joan Lunden was interviewing a woman who answered, yes or no - and only yes or no - to whatever

Joan asked. So before moving on to her next question, Joan had to fill in the blanks. The interview went something like this:

> **Joan:** "And so then you went to the hospital and you told them that your baby had a very high fever. And they admitted her?"
> **Guest:** "Yes."
> **Joan:** "Then they told you it was pneumonia?"
> **Guest:** "Yes."
> **Joan:** "But you didn't believe that?"
> **Guest:** "No."
> **Joan:** "You thought your daughter might have an allergy to something she'd eaten?"
> **Guest:** "Yes."

Did Joan have to work extra hard? Yes. Was this a satisfying interview for the viewers? No. Did we ever invite that woman back on the show? No.

¶ **Use Grabbers.** A grabber is a phrase that makes your message come alive. A grabber can be a metaphor, simile, or word picture. It can be a comparison, or it can be a quote or the paraphrase of a quote. A grabber can be an attention-getting fact, like a remarkable statistic. Or it can be an "st" word - that is words that end in the letters "st" ("first," "last," "biggest," "smallest," "brightest," "fastest," etc.). The media love "st" words. A grabber, then, is any verbal turn of phrase that fixes your message in a listener's head by capturing her imagination. It can even be a very brief, illustrative anecdote. Here are some examples of grabbers:

Comparison: "That NASCAR Ford bears about as much relationship to a showroom Crown Victoria as an eagle bears to a ladybug."

Simile: "When the spokesperson got flustered at the news conference all the reporters responded like sharks at a feeding frenzy."

Metaphor: "This proposal is the *Titanic* of economic planning - big, ambitious and doomed to sink" (The three examples above used word pictures, too.)

Quote or paraphrase of a quote: "Preparing for an interview, borrow this thought from John F. Kennedy and ask not what you can do for the reporter's agenda; ask what the reporter can do for your agenda."

Amazing fact or statistic: "In architecture, the Romans got it right. Every stadium and arena in the world uses the very same entrance and exit designs introduced in the Coliseum, back in 80 AD!"

"St" words: "NASA's New Horizons mission to Pluto is the *first* mission to the *last* planet."

Brief anecdote: "I am so convinced the ground water near our plant is safe that I just drank a glass of it and so did my three-year-old daughter."

¶ **Be specific and enumerate.** Citing specifics buttresses your PMSs. The audience can infer the general rule from the specific case, but cannot infer the specific from the general rule. Specifics make a generalization come to life. Also, enumerate. If there are three reasons why your company's plan is beneficial to the community, say, "There are three reasons for this..." and then tick off the three reasons. By citing the number in advance and then listing the points, you not only prepare the listener for them, but you remind yourself to get to all three. It's best to keep the number of points to no more than three or four; that is about the maximum number any reader, viewer, or listener is going to absorb in a single answer.

¶ **Avoid weak words like "try" and "hope."** Try, hope, and hopefully are extremely weak words and usually unnecessary. "We plan to do..." is a lot stronger than, "We hope to do...." Similarly, "We're trying to get out of this situation," is a lot less confidence-building than the far more assertive, "We're going to get out of this situation." As I like to tell clients, "Try never to use the word, hope. Hopefully, you'll try hard enough to succeed."

A Little Homework for You

Now using the grabber worksheet in the appendix, or one you create in your computer, develop grabbers for every one of your PMSs. You'll want to take your time with this exercise; for most of us grabbers don't just spring to mind. The simplest grabbers are comparisons, word pictures, or similes, so try for those first. The best way to craft a grabber is to ask yourself, "What everyday activity or concern can I equate with my message?" Thus, you might come up with, "Having a corporation change its orientation from being a growth stock company to becoming a value stock company is about as hard as making a U-turn in a subway train."

After you've written your grabbers, read them out loud to make sure they sound natural and that you're comfortable saying them. If you find them awkward, you'll want to massage them until they don't sound quite so foreign to you. Keep this worksheet handy on our desk or, if you created it on your computer, on your machine's desktop so they're handy and you can refine them over time. And always remember to jot down new grabbers as they occur to you. It's distressing to think about how many wonderful grabbers are lost forever because their authors felt they could remember them the next time they did an interview and didn't bother to commit them to paper or to a hard drive. It takes a great deal of preparation to appear spontaneous in an interview, but the result is worth the investment in time and effort. Once you're ready with your PMSs and their supporting grabbers, you need to heed the next commandment:

COMMANDMENT 4. THOU SHALT PRACTICE, PRACTICE, PRACTICE

I call this one the Henny Youngman commandment, after the old joke by the late Henny Youngman, whose stock in trade was bad jokes: "Fella comes up to me on the street and says, 'Hey, how do I get to Carnegie Hall?' I says, 'Practice, practice, practice.'" Bad joke; good advice.

Here's an object lesson in practice, practice, practice from another old-time comedian, Milton Berle - the man who virtually invented television comedy. In the early days of "Good Morning America," we booked Berle as a guest on the show. I was thrilled because I had been a fan from a very early age. In fact, I think my parents bought our first television set so I would stay home on Tuesday nights and not slink off to friends' homes to watch Uncle Miltie. During a commercial break, I left the control room and ran down to the dressing room where Berle was waiting so I could thank him for all those years of laughter. The door was open and when I stuck my head in, I saw Uncle Miltie pacing back and forth, an unlit cigar in his hand, muttering. I stepped into the room, introduced myself as the show's executive producer and said, "Mr. Berle, everything O.K.?"

He said, "Yeah, sure, kid." (I was in my forties at the time.) "I was just rehearsing my ad-libs." If a veteran who'd done so much TV that his nickname was "Mr. Television" felt he had to practice, practice, practice before a five-minute interview, all the rest of us should, too.

If you are wondering how to practice for an interview when you don't know what you'll be asked, the answer is that with a little effort you can usually figure out the questions an interviewer will pose. If you did the homework in the last chapter - watched the TV show, read the newspaper or magazine, listened to the radio show - you should have a pretty solid idea of the attitude, level of sophistication, and point of view of your interviewer.

Now it's time to write out his questions so you can practice, practice, practice your answers. But do yourself a favor and don't write questions like, "Gosh, you are a great fellow coming from a great organization. What can you tell me about yourself and about your organization that makes you and it so admirable?" While there are a handful of interviewers who might ask something akin to such a puffball, you'd better count on getting challenging questions. Even the most benign reporter can ask a tough question. In fact, I've created a rule about that:

> **MERLIS' LAW OF INTERVIEWS**
> **Anyone unprepared for tough questions**
> **will be asked tough questions.**

Here's a case history: I was preparing a financial services company for the California test rollout of a new credit card product. They were going to hold a news conference and after I went through the techniques of news conferences with them, after helping them compose their PMSs and illustrate them with grabbers, it came time to put them on camera and take them through a practice interview. But first I asked them what tough questions reporters might ask. The lead spokesperson said, "Oh, we won't get any tough questions. This product is so great."

"O.K.," I said. "Pretend Ralph Nader is coming to the news conference. What will he ask?"

"Well," said the lead spokesperson, "he'd probably ask where he could sign up for our product." That brought laughter from his fellow panelists. I again urged them to think of the tough questions and they kept insisting there were none.

I hardly need tell you what happened the next day when they held the news conference. The first question from the first reporter was worthy of a criminal prosecutor in its tone, severity, and insight. The panel introducing the product just sat at their table with their mouths open. What happened next was the journalistic equivalent of a shark feeding frenzy; the reporters tore them to shreds.

Interestingly, a year after the California introduction of the credit card product, there was a national rollout at a New York news conference and this time the clients drilled extensively, developing persuasive answers to tough questions. They were ready for combat; this time no reportorial onslaught was going to take them by surprise. Curiously enough, nothing happened at the New York news conference. Perhaps lulled by the huge buffet breakfast the client laid out, the New York and national reporters didn't ask a single tough question. But it's better to prepare for the tough questions and *not* get them than to be unprepared and and suffer a barrage of them.

In the next chapter we'll compile a worksheet of tough questions and I'll teach you how to get from a challenging question to your PMSs. You'll need that information before you begin to practice, practice, practice. For now though, let me give you some techniques for practicing.

First of all, practice out loud. I've written that the down side of practicing by silently reading is you won't find the tongue-trippers until you're speaking them to a reporter - when it's too late.

To get used to hearing your message points in response to questions, have someone ask you questions. Ask a colleague, friend, or family member pop questions at you. It's a lot more effective than asking yourself questions. Hearing the questioning words coming from another, external voice, rather than from an internal one, will make them very real to you. Actors always "run lines" with another person - even if it isn't the individual with whom they'll actually play the scene. Running lines helps put those incoming words in a human context. In the same way, hearing questions asked by someone else - even an excessively friendly someone else - is far more useful than imaging the questions coming from a phantom reporter.

There is no substitute for seeing yourself in action on videotape, even if you're prepping for a magazine or newspaper interview, so videotape all practice Q&A sessions. Then watch the tape and grade yourself. Keep your remote control nearby, so you can frequently pause. Review the tape. Have your PMS and grabber worksheets at hand so you can see how many of them you worked into the interview. It is equally important that you identify opportunities where you could have or should have inserted PMSs but failed to do so. Seeing which messaging opportunities you missed in practice interviews will insure you don't miss them when the real interview comes along. Keep practicing until you can work in all your PMSs and grabbers. That's *how* to practice. But before you begin those dry runs, you'll need to learn the fifth commandment, "Thou shalt not lie, evade, speculate nor cop a 'tude." And you should read Chapter 4, "Successful Interview Tools," where you'll learn how the media use interviews, the tricks of the reporter's trade, and the tricks of the interviewee's trade.

COMMANDMENT 5: THOU SHALT NOT LIE, EVADE, SPECULATE, NOR COP AN ATTITUDE

Aside from the moral and ethical imperatives against lying, there are very practical reasons - as evidenced by these two examples, soundbites that will resonate in the pages of history:

"I did not have sexual relations with that woman."
- **Bill Clinton**

A nine-word soundbite with ramifications that rendered a presidency ineffective for months on end.

"Read my lips, no new taxes."
- **George H. W. Bush**

A six word soundbite that may well have cost the first President Bush his second term.

By way of explanation, let's refer to a soundbite that predates sound recording:

"It is true that you may fool all the people some of the time; you can even fool some of the people all of the time; but you cannot fool all of the people all of the time."
- **Abraham Lincoln**

Not all lies and other shadings of fact will be found out; but recent history shows just how damaging lies can be when the bright light of truth shines on them. In a strict, dictionary sense, Clinton was not lying, but rather he was evading - fooling the people - since Webster's definition of "sexual relations" is the act of coitus and, according to the participants, his illicit affair did not involve that specific act. You'll note the president did not say, "I did not have sex with that woman," but said, "I did not have sexual *relations* with that woman." Not a lie, but certainly an evasion.

In the same vein, how costly was it for Martha Stewart, when first accused of insider trading, to put out a story about previously instructing her broker to sell her ImClone stock when it dropped below $60 a share? How much more forgiving would the public have been had she said, "In the excitement of the moment, knowing what I knew, I made a mistake by acting on advance information. It was an unfortunate mistake and to make amends, I am donating the entire profit I made from that sale to the American Cancer Society." When Ms. Stewart finally did do an interview, she spoke with *The New Yorker* magazine - fully two months after the charges first surfaced - and she declined to discuss the details of the case on the record. Jeffrey Toobin, *The*

New Yorker legal correspondent, conducted the interview. In it Ms. Stewart appeared extremely concerned about the public's perception of her but did nothing to court public opinion, lacing her quotes with repeated egotistical comments. In other words, she copped an attitude - a pitfall we'll deal with in a moment. In fact, the Martha Stewart *New Yorker* interview is a virtual textbook example of how *not* to do a print interview. Chapter 8 treats this interview in more detail.

There is another practical reason for telling the truth in interviews and for that one I quote one of my mentors, Elmer W. Lower, former President of ABC News. He used to say, "Always tell the truth. That way you won't have to remember what you said." (Incidentally, that's a good grabber.)

In my earliest days at ABC, before becoming a producer, I was the director of public relations for the news division. A big story was about to break and Elmer told me only that major news was coming, adding, "I'm not going to tell you anything about it so if you get a call from the press, you won't have to lie." The story was that ABC News had hired Harry Reasoner away from CBS News. Not fifteen minutes after Elmer told me he wasn't going to tell me what the big story was, I got a call from a Chicago newspaper columnist who asked me, "What's all this about Harry Reasoner leaving CBS News and joining ABC News as your evening news anchor?"

I could honestly respond, "This is the first I've heard of it. No one's told me anything about Harry Reasoner joining ABC."

What if telling the truth in an interview can land you in jail or subject you to a lawsuit? That would appear on the surface to be a good question, but if either of those scenarios are at all likely, why is your lawyer letting you talk to the media? The news media, after all, unlike Congress, the state legislatures, and the courts, cannot compel you to appear and talk to them. Silence is a more satisfying response than falsehood.

Speaking of falsehoods and misrepresentations, it is essential that you never deny saying something that TV cameras or radio microphones have recorded you saying. In 2006, presidential press secretary Tony Snow claimed that President Bush had used the term "stay the course" only seven times in connection with the Iraq war. That evening the fake news program "The

Daily Show with Jon Stewart," displayed its journalism chops by showing videotape of Mr. Bush saying "stay the course" a total of 28 times. In addition to the "Daily Show" video becoming an instantaneous hit on YouTube, mainstream TV news shows began their own count, finding still more instances of the president using the term. Earlier, in the 2004 presidential campaign, former Vermont Gov, Howard Dean self-destructed his campaign with an on-camera scream to an assembly of his supporters. His campaign manager, Joe Trippi, told some reporters, "He wasn't thinking about the cameras. It was the people right in front of him he was speaking to." A good rule for today's media environment is that when there are reporters or cameras about, you are speaking to *every*body.

THE DANGER OF SPECULATION

We've dealt with lying and evading and the reasons to avoid them are pretty obvious. But what can be the harm in speculating? The harm is that the reporter may not put your comments into speculative perspective. He may quote you without identifying your quote as speculation. And even if he does, the second reporter who picks up the quote may omit the speculative tone. The first time you're quoted, it's speculation. The second reporter writes what you said as fact. By the time the third story appears, your speculation has assumed the authority of holy writ. Here's an object lesson on speculation: a government agency announced a high-tech project that included technology that some people thought was dangerous. To allay fears, one of the engineers on the project said, "Well, this time around we have to use that technology. But by the time we build the next one, alternate technology will be available." That quote appeared in newspapers. Well, the alternate technology wasn't available when they built the second one and opponents of the supposedly dangerous technology sued to block the project, citing - among other things - the engineer's speculative quotation.

Whether it has its roots in speculation or oversight, error has an enormous and enduring shelf life; like the villain in a horror movie, it just won't die. Who can forget the photograph of American and Vietnamese employees clambering up the ladder toward a helicopter atop the roof of the U.S. embassy in Saigon when that city fell to the Viet Cong and North Vietnamese? You know exactly the photo I'm talking about; the ladder bows under the weight of the ten or twelve people on it, a man stands alongside the helicopter, reaching for the person at the top of the ladder. It is an iconic representation of the fall of Saigon. Except it isn't a picture of the U.S. embassy. Dutch photographer Hubert van Es snapped a photo of CIA employees clambering toward a helicopter atop an apartment house near the Saigon embassy. Someone at UPI in Australia distributed it with an erroneous caption and for decades thereafter everyone thought it depicted the evacuation of the U.S. embassy. (You can see the photo by entering "Saigon Embassy, evacuation" in the search box of Google images.)

While the photo caption misidentification is a minor distinction, the endurance of that misinformation illustrates the shelf life of error. So if you speculate in an interview and your speculation is wrong, don't be surprised to find the media clothing your speculative error in the garments of incontrovertible fact.

COPPING AN ATTITUDE

Let's now deal with the last part of the commandment - copping an attitude. The reason for not copping an attitude ought to be self-evident. If you are not an angry young rebel actor, a gangsta rapper, or a professional wrestler (all role players), you do yourself a disservice by copping a hostile, challenging, superior, or arrogant attitude.

Vice President Al Gore's supercilious attitude in the first presidential debate in 2000 cost him dearly in the election. In the lessons unlearned department, Senator John Kerry adopted much the same superior attitude in the first of the 2004 debates, with similar results. Had Gore, in particular, shown some humility, he might have gained enough additional electoral votes to convincingly win the election. Similarly, Martha Stewart's superior *noblesse oblige* attitude contributed to the media frenzy attendant upon her insider trading accusation. More recently, in December, 2005, then-Defense Secretary Donald Rumsfeld won himself few friends in this exchange in a town hall meeting with troops in Kuwait who were awaiting deployment to Iraq:

Soldier: Our soldiers have been fighting in Iraq for coming up on three years. A lot of us are getting ready to move north relatively soon. Our vehicles are not armored. We're digging pieces of rusted scrap metal and compromised ballistic glass that's already been shot up, dropped, busted, picking the best out of this scrap to put on our vehicles to take into combat. We do not have proper armament (sic.) vehicles to carry with us north.

Rumsfeld: "I talked to the general coming out here about the pace at which the vehicles are being armored. They have been brought from all over the world, wherever they're not needed, to a place here where they are needed. I'm told that they are being - the Army is - I think it's something like four hundred a month are being done. And it's essentially a matter of physics. It isn't a matter of money. It isn't a matter on the part of the Army of desire. It's a matter of production and capability of doing it. *As you know, you go to war with the Army you have. They're not the Army you might want or wish to have at a later time.*"

What I find startling is that the defense secretary had already answered the question before he copped his attitude, making it appear that his slighting of the soldier's concern was a gratuitous afterthought. In addition to that first seemingly callous statement, later on Rumsfeld added yet another comment that the troops in the room could easily have construed as dismissive of their concerns about adequate protection: "And if you think about it, you can have all the armor in the world on a tank and a tank can be blown up. And you can have an up-armored Humvee and it can be blown up."

What part of Rumsfeld's answer ran on every newscast in America, was quoted in every newspaper in the world, and was featured on all radio newscasts? The part where he appeared to be patronizing the soldiers he was sending into harm's way: "*As you know, you go to war with the Army you have. They're not the Army you might want or wish to have at a later time.*" If you put a chip on your shoulder, the media will be more than happy to knock it off.

Now that we've gone over the five commandments of interviews and some interpretive analysis, let's move on to practical applications in interview settings. Let's first examine what you can expect to encounter and how you can turn the challenge of an interview into an opportunity to get your message out to a large and interested audience.

Chapter 4

SUCCESSFUL INTERVIEWS TOOLS

In Chapters 2 and 3 you learned how to prepare an agenda for an interview and how to tailor your messages for the media. Now let's look at the most basic media encounter, the interview. You'll want to master a specific set of skills - and understand the tricks of the reporter's trade - before you sit down for an interview. Not all interviews are similar in tone and attitude, so before facing a reporter or taking her interview phone call, you must examine her media outlet and, if possible, her individual work to garner some clues about how she will use your material and how she will treat you in the interview and in the subsequent story. In addition to the tone of the publication or broadcast and the work of the reporter, there are a few additional clues to a reporter's agenda and you'll want to investigate those.

Of course, you're always a leg up on ascertaining her agenda if she's working on a story that you or your organization initiated. When you initiate the story - for instance, by making an announcement of a new product or service or an important discovery - reporters are responding to your agenda, so it is usually easier to keep those interviews on target. But when you are responding to someone else's announcement or to an interviewer's enterprise story - that is, one she initiated herself - the interview agenda is initially in the reporter's hands. Those interviews often require you to do more work to bring the questioning around to your agenda.

The overwhelming majority of interviews are neutral or even friendly - not hostile and adversarial. But be aware that a friendly tone can mask a tough question. Not every inquisitorial reporter comes on with the pit bull determination and toughness of a Mike Wallace on "60 Minutes." In fact, some of the most effective investigative reporters *don't* figuratively grip you by the neck and squeeze; rather, they cordially invite you to hang yourself.

One of the best investigative television correspondents I ever knew was David Schoumacher who worked for both CBS News and ABC News. I worked with David at ABC and found him very effective at getting people to stick their heads in his noose by asking the toughest questions in the friendliest way. He had a warm and charming smile and his tone was never challenging nor prosecutorial. As a result, he was able to get an amazing array of skilled corporate executives and politicians to make incriminating statements in the most matter-of-fact way. Because they were not on the defensive, their protective radar was off and they regularly gave up more information than they ever intended. The lesson here is to listen to the *words* of the question, not the *tone* of the question.

Early in the 20th Century, Ida M. Tarbell, the mother of investigative journalism, worked for years to research her book, *The History of the Standard Oil Company.* It was her masterwork, revealing the illegal practices used by John D. Rockefeller to monopolize the oil industry in the United States. At the time, many men felt women could not grasp complex business concepts and so a lot of executives opened up to the "little lady," never expecting that her steel trap mind was not just grasping but was analyzing and understanding every nuance of what they were saying. They would probably have been far more on guard had they been dealing with a male journalist.

Why rehash this bit of ancient history? To emphasize that the way a reporter looks or acts is not a clue to her goal. Even if it isn't his goal to ask tough questions, I've found that the most benign reporter sometimes comes up with them - despite a total absence of malice. Remember that story I told about the financial services company announcing its new product and getting sandbagged with tough questions because they failed to prepare for them in advance? Well the first question at the news conference, the one that set off the reportorial feeding frenzy came from a local TV *weatherman* whose everyday on-camera persona was lighthearted to the point of being comical. Why the TV station sent a weatherman to cover a financial story, I cannot begin to guess. But the weatherman clearly knew as much, if not more, about the credit card business as he did about the weather, and the question he asked was so tough it left the spokespersons stammering for an answer.

For any interview you do, you want to figure out how your participation fits into the larger picture the reporter is trying to create. So you or your public relations aides should ask some key questions.

FIVE QUESTIONS FOR EVERY REPORTER
1. What is the direction and thrust of your story?
2. Who else are you interviewing?
3. How much of my time will you need?
4. How long will your article (or broadcast story) run?
5. Do you need or want any documentation,
photographs, or videotape?

It's important you get the answers to these questions before the reporter sits down with you for the interview. You can pose them when she calls to arrange the interview or, as a last resort, ask them during the preinterview warmup. Reporters are often asked all these questions and should be willing to answer them. This need not be a long, drawn-out discussion; reporters can answer most of the questions with just a few words. Sometimes she'll tell you she doesn't know an answer. That may be truthful, because the story is a work in progress, or it may be an obfuscation. If you don't get straight answers to three or four of these questions, chances are good the reporter is misleading you about the nature and direction of the interview and you need to be on guard. Later in this chapter we'll review techniques for parrying a tough interview, but first there are some tips for learning beforehand the nature of your forthcoming media encounter. We'll work from the five questions you should ask. Bear in mind, reporters rarely embark on a story before they know the answer to the first one - the story's direction - so if there's an "I don't know" or "I'm not sure" response to this one, chances are the reporter is dissembling and you won't get straight answers to the others, either.

¶ **What's the direction or thrust of the story?** You should ask this in a helpful way; you want to appear cooperative and outgoing. When you get a straightforward answer to this question you can, indeed, be much more helpful to the journalist.

Try asking in a tone like this: "What is your story going to be about? I'd like to know so I can gather and review the appropriate materials and make sure I've got all the facts and figures you're going to need from me." Most reporters want you to be prepared; if you do the research in advance, they don't have to do it after the fact. Often if an interview does go beyond what the reporter indicated in advance, it will be because it naturally flows there. There are, however, a number of reporters and producers - usually working on the investigative publications and broadcasts - who will not give you a straight answer to this question. Ostensibly that's because they want the interview to appear more spontaneous. But actually they want to give you as few clues to their agenda as possible so they can catch you unawares and trap you. That's why it's helpful to review a particular reporter's prior work and learn about her reputation before agreeing to the interview. We'll have more on dealing with this breed of reporter in Chapter 6, "Digging Deep: Investigative Broadcasts."

¶ **Who else are you interviewing?** If he's interviewing four people from your company or organization, you should tailor your answers accordingly. ("Well, you're going to be talking to Sharon, and she is our authority on this issue. My own area of specialization is....") If he tells you he's also going to be interviewing competitors or opponents, you have the opportunity to second-guess what they've told him or will tell him and craft answers responding to your critics while at the same time incorporating your PMSs. Also, knowing whom else he's interviewing gives you the opportunity to suggest additional interview subjects - especially individuals who agree with your point of view. You might say to him, "That's a good list, but you might also want to talk to Dr. Hackley; he's the foremost independent authority in the country on...." Recommending other interview subjects who are independent of your company or organization enhances your credibility with reporters.

¶ **How much of my time will you need?** Knowing the answer to this question enables you to set limits on the length of the interview. If he says, "An hour," you can always say, "I'm afraid I can only spare twenty minutes." Then, if the interview is going well, stay longer. Be aware that some reporters habitually understate how much time they need because they hope that once you're sitting with them, you'll feel awkward about ending the interview. But if you've told the reporter in advance how much time he has, the control rests with you. "Well, Jim, I told you I could devote fifteen minutes to this interview and we've been here for fifteen minutes, so I'm afraid we've got to wrap it up now." Of course, if it's going swimmingly, you can say, "I know I told you I could only spare fifteen minutes for this interview, but I think I can squeeze in another five if you need it." Back when Jimmy Carter was president, I produced a story with Harry Reasoner that included an interview with the national security advisor, Zbigniew Brezinski. Before the camera started to roll, Brezinski asked Reasoner, "How long will this interview run on the air?" Reasoner surprised me by saying, "Six minutes," because I knew the entire story would run no more than six minutes and Brezinski's soundbites certainly would not fill more than a minute of that time. The moment Reasoner asked his first question, Brezinski started the timer on his wristwatch and at the end of six minutes, he removed the microphone and stood up. After Brezinski left the room, Reasoner said to me, "He always does that. He doesn't like to be edited, so he gives you exactly the amount of time you ask for. I said six minutes because I figured that would give us enough time with him to get the thirty seconds you really need."

¶ **How Long Will Your Article (or Broadcast Story) Run?** You can be a lot more expansive and detailed in your answers if the interview is for a *New York Times Sunday Magazine* piece that will run seven thousand words than if it is for a two-minute report on the local TV station's 11 p.m. newscast. You need this information to help you frame your answers appropriately. A truly skilled interview subject like director Stephen Spielberg, for example, gives a short form, quip of an answer to an interviewer who grabs him for a few seconds while walking down the Academy Awards red carpet on his way into the Oscar ceremony. Asked virtually the same question on Bravo Network's leisurely and informative "Inside the Actors Studio" or PBS's "Charlie Rose," Spielberg will give a much longer, contemplative, and thought-provoking response. On the red carpet, he knows that his remarks will be one of dozens used in the Oscar story, so he keeps it short; while the Bravo or PBS shows will focus exclusively or nearly exclusively on his thoughts and feelings, so he can be more expansive.

¶ **Do you need or want any documentation, photographs, videotape?** If you know in advance what support material will be helpful to the reporter, then you won't find yourself opposite her saying, "I have a paper on that. I wish I'd brought it with me." Or, "You know, I've seen a really good photograph that illustrates that point. I don't know where it is, but take my word for it - or take my thousand words for it - it was terrific." Even if in advance of the interview she says she needs nothing, you might want to bring to the interview props and videotape (for television), photographs (for all media save radio) and documentation. Naturally, you'll only be supplying props, videotape, photographs, and documentation that buttress your PMSs. As an example, not long ago I was doing media training for some astronomers who were talking about how different telescopes - infrared, x-ray, and ultraviolet - enhance our view of the universe because they can "see" what optical telescopes cannot. Their message really came home to me when I discovered on a NASA website virtually identical pictures of Saturn taken through optical and ultraviolet devices. The familiar ringed planet in the ultraviolet photo had brilliant auroras at its poles, planetary wonders that were invisible in the optical photograph. I encouraged the astronomers to bring these photos - or others like them - to future interviews to illustrate their point. And you should consider bringing similar visuals if you have compelling images that effectively illustrate or prove your point.

HOW TO MASTER ANY INTERVIEW

Interview mastery *is* media mastery. A simple set of skills will empower you to work your agenda into any interview.

ENABLING YOUR AGENDA,
DISABLING THE REPORTER'S AGENDA

Your goal in an interview is to enable your agenda. As I noted earlier, if the reporter's agenda meshes with yours, then it's relatively easy. If the reporter's agenda diverges from yours, you must first disable his agenda in order to enable yours.

In general, reporters are interested in what's new, unique, and unusual. The cliché is that dog bites man is not news, but man bites dog is news. These days, however, there is a premium on bad and frightening news (the fear "f" word journalism so loves), so dog bites man may once again be news - if the bite is severe enough or if enough dogs are biting enough men so the media can frighten people with a threatening "trend." Conflict and drama also pique the news reporter's interest. And good news such as miracle cures, moneysaving schemes or tips, and safety information are all grist for the journalist's mill. Sometimes, then, your agenda will neatly match the reporter's needs - for instance when you are promoting a book on saving money by reducing energy consumption in your home or giving information about how to safeguard the health of audience members with a new medication or medical procedure. At other times, you may be on the defensive - when critics charge a product, policy or program you advocate is dangerous, costly, or ineffective.

In either case, as with most of life's endeavors, the best defense is an offense. If you have heeded the Boy Scout Commandments in Chapter 2, then you know the PMSs you want to express in your interview, you are familiar with the tone and nature of the publication or broadcast, and you know to whom you are speaking - the end-user, not the journalist. And you know that end-user's level of sophistication. Also you're prepared to answer questions in a short and simple manner, lead with your conclusion, and brand your answers.

Getting your message across to the skeptical WSIC (Why Should I Care) listener is pretty easy when the reporter asks, "Tell me, my friend, have you any Positive Message Statements you'd like my readers [viewers, listeners] to know about?" But in the ten thousand interviews I've overseen or conducted myself, I've never heard that question posed and I certainly never asked it. While reporters won't ask that question, they do come close with the commonplace interview-ending: "That about covers my questions. Is there anything you feel I've left out or that my readers [viewers, listeners] should know?" That question really is the equivalent of the "any Positive Message Statements" question I cited, and you should always take advantage of the opportunity and unlimber a PMSs in response. If you had five points at the outset and managed to work in only three or four of them, go to one of your unused messages. If you've already managed to work in all of them before the "anything else" question, revisit one of them. Revisit either your most important PMS or one you think you may not have articulated very well. You'll likely express it more effectively the second time, and the repetition will put your PMS in mental boldface for the reporter. Repeating a PMS does no harm, especially if you express it in different language the second time.

Reporters ask the "anything else" question at the end of interviews, but there's no guarantee they will ask it. So you should pepper the whole session with your PMSs, and not wait for it.

FOUR STEPS FROM A REPORTER'S QUESTION TO YOUR PMS

Obviously, a direct question that solicits one of your PMSs is the easiest way to work an agenda point into an interview. "So tell me about this new asthma medication your company has developed" is an explicit invitation to enunciate a PMS. Similarly, if the reporter praises you, your company, or your product, that's an open door through which you should push a PMS. For example, if the reporter says, "I'm hearing very good things from asthma patients about this new medication you've brought to market." Your response should not be, "Gee, thanks"; it is, instead, "Yes and that's because...." and continue to a PMS.

If you finish answering a question and the reporter is searching his list of questions for his next query, you can fill the vacuum by saying, "Another thing that asthma sufferers will want to know is...." and go to another PMS. But a word of caution: fill pauses only in a *friendly* interview. A time-honored trick of a hostile interviewer is to pause after you've responded to a tough question, hoping you'll feel the pressure of the silence and go beyond the answer you intended to give. More on that later in this chapter.

If the reporter is not asking puffball questions, not throwing kudos your way, and not searching his notes for his next question, how do you work your messages into the interview?

Well, you cannot do what Henry Kissinger did when he was secretary of state and often began his briefings of State Department reporters by announcing, "Ladies and gentlemen, I hope you have your questions because I have my answers." The State Department press corps was a club of sorts and you can get away with that sort of thing in a club. Because most of us aren't in a club with the reporters who'll be questioning us, so we must build a bridge between the question and our PMSs using the following steps. Keep in mind that all the steps work together; you need to take all four of them.

FOUR STEPS TO YOUR AGENDA
1. Acknowledge the question
with short form answer.
2. Build a bridge.
3. Insert a Positive Message
Statement.
4. Shut up!

Step 1: Short Form Answer. To keep a reporter from asking a question again, you need to pay it some lip service. You don't want to appear blandly evasive. So acknowledge the question first. By acknowledging, I don't mean, "Gee, you should have asked me about Y instead of X and here's my answer to Y." There is no quicker way to turn an interview hostile than by telling a reporter what she should be asking. Incredibly, some people in public life actually do that. Lyndon Johnson was famous for it. "No, no, " he would say, "the question ought to be…." and he'd ask himself a question he wanted to answer. Unless you're president of the United States I suggest you steer clear of that. In fact, it's not a good idea even for the chief executive, since it will breed resentment in the press corps. Let's remember, Lyndon Johnson is hardly the exemplar of presidential success; facing a crushing defeat, he chose not to seek reelection.

The short form answer I'm talking about, rather than being evasive, actually addresses the information sought, but not for long. For example, the question is this: "Why is your company still using the X7 aircraft when everyone feels it's obsolete?" But you are there not to talk about the X7, but rather to extol a new freight service. Well, here's the first part of an answer: **"At Ynot Freight Express, we are convinced the X7, which we've flown for fifteen years, remains viable."** Notice the branding right at the top of the answer. It was "At Ynot Freight Express," and not, "We are convinced." The answer tells you who "we" are.

Step 2: Build a bridge. Bridges need not be very elaborate. They are holding up nothing more weighty than a transition. They don't support your Positive Message Statements, just get you to them. So the simpler and shorter the bridge, the better. "At Ynot Freight Express we are convinced the X7, which we've flown for fifteen years, remains viable. **In fact we're so sure of its reliability....**" As bridges go, this one is pretty long. The bridge you build can be as short as a single word: "but," "however," "and." Or the bridge can be a few words that enable a transition: "on the other hand," "in addition to that," "as a matter of fact."

Step 3: State your PMS "At Ynot Freight Express we are convinced the X7, which we've flown for fifteen years, remains viable. In fact we're so sure of its reliability **that we're using that plane to launch our exciting new freight service which will save our customers a hundred million dollars a year without having a negative impact on our earnings. We call it a 'flying win-win.'"**

Step 4: Shut Up! If you stop talking after delivering your message, the chances are good the reporter will follow up with a question about that message. If you bring the answer full circle, you're giving up control of the agenda. Pretend for a moment you're a reporter and you hear this answer: "At Ynot Freight Express we are convinced the X7, which we've flown for fifteen years, remains viable. In fact we're so sure of its reliability that we're using that plane to launch our exciting new freight service which will save our customers a hundred million dollars a year without having a negative impact on our earnings. So of course we don't consider the X7 obsolete." What's your next question going to be about? The obsolete X7 or the exciting new freight service? The X7, because the answer brought you right back to it. The interview subject didn't shut up. If the answer had ended with the point about the money saving to the customers and the impact on Ynot's bottom line, chances are greater your next question would be about the freight service. "What is this new service?" or "How will this new service save your customers $100 million a year?" or "How can you cut your customers' costs by $100 million a year and not have a negative impact on your earnings?" Any one of those three questions keeps the interview in your PMS territory.

Bridging to a PMS from a question is counterintuitive for many of us. In school our teachers always insisted we answer the question that was asked. Here, we're moving beyond the answer that we would have given in school to make a point we want to stress. In a scholastic setting - even in a social setting - this is bad manners. In an interview, it's part of your job. But here are a couple of caveats about bridging from their question to your answer: be very judicious and don't use bridging to answer to every single question you get. Deploy the technique when it's *reasonable* so you can avoid what I call "segue whiplash." Segue whiplash occurs when the reporter asks you about the X7 aircraft and you bridge to your company's annual Christmas party. You can go from question A to message B, C, D or even E. But you can't get much beyond that. When you do, you're approaching the Henry Kissinger "I have my answers" line or the Lyndon Johnson, "the question ought to be..." attitude.

HELP, I GOT LOST LOOKING FOR MY BRIDGE

Sometimes we start an answer fully intending to bridge to one of our PMSs and discover we forgot to turn onto the bridge. What to do? Here I recommend a technique called "flagging." Raise a flag and tell the reporter what's important. Typical flagging phrases are: "What's really important is..." "I can't emphasize strongly enough..." "What's vital for your readers to understand is..." Not as elegant as "but," "however," "on the other hand," but a flag is a form of bridging. You might also want to flag sophisticated concepts: "This is a complex idea, but it's important...." "I'm going to cite some statistics, and they're really critical...." And, of course, you can use flagging when you find yourself giving an answer that violates our KISS - Keep It Short

and Simple - rule. If you are saying too much that's too sophisticated, flag a condensation of your main message with "The key
point here is…."

THE INTERVIEWER'S TOP SEVEN DIRTY TRICKS

Can you use that bridge-building technique in a tough interview? Sure. In fact, many questions that on the surface appear to be probing or hostile are easier to bridge than questions
that are merely off-point and not asked in a challenging manner.
Below are the top seven reportorial dirty tricks and techniques to
counter every one of them and get you back to your agenda.

Trick 1: Words in Your Mouth. We've all seen this one.
An interview subject gives an answer and the reporter interprets
it for him, putting words in his mouth that he never intended to
utter: "So what you're saying is this decrepit airplane, as near to
retirement as it is, is going to be the backbone of a new service
you're offering your customers?" How do you respond? By taking back control of your words. "No [short form answer - shortest form answer, in fact] what I'm saying is [bridge] we are so
convinced of the reliability of the aircraft that we're building our
exciting new flying win-win service on it; a service that is going
to save our customers $100 million a year." (Notice we've de-
clined the invitation to use the words "decrepit" and "retirement.")

Watch "60 Minutes" or one of the other investigative TV
newsmagazine shows and you'll see this "so what you're saying"
technique used frequently. It is much less common on shows
such as "Today," "The Early Show," or "Good Morning America." A reporter usually follows "What you're saying is" by taking what you've said beyond your original meaning. If the reporter is accurately characterizing what you're saying - which
she may do because your expression of the concept wasn't totally
clear and she wants you to take another crack at it - your response should be, "Precisely. [Short form answer] And, in fact
[bridge] I can add…. [Insert an additional PMS or reinforce your
previous PMS]." I can recall a medical interview where, despite
the reporter's extensive efforts to get a physician to use the word
miracle, the doctor would not characterize a recovery that way.

"So," the reporter said, "what you're saying is this isn't a miracle recovery?" "Exactly," the physician answered, "it is an exceptional recovery, an unusual recovery, and it may offer us clues about how to treat other patients with this condition. That's the way science advances - by analyzing what we know and researching what we don't. It's no accident that the last five letters of 'research' spell 'search.'"

Trick 2: The Big Lie. The very premise of the question is false. Sometimes the reporter does this out of ignorance or shoddy research. And sometimes a reporter throws out a false premise to put her interview subject on the defensive. For example: "We know that the X7 aircraft is so obsolete you are the only freight line in the country to use it." Never accept a false premise; correct it at once. Your correction is all the acknowledgment you need before building your bridge: "No, that's not the case. I know of several other airlines that use the plane. [short form answer]. And, in fact [bridge] we are creating our exciting new flying win-win service around this aircraft...." I saw an interview about a nuclear-fueled vessel in which the interviewer demanded, "Isn't it true that there's enough plutonium in this to kill every man, woman, and child on the planet?" A great scare question if ever there was one. But the "fact" underlying the question was wrong, enabling the interview subject to say, "No, that's not the case at all. The radiation in the vessel is less than normal background radiation in many parts of the world and certainly less than what you experience in a chest x-ray. But, even so, we have encased that material in a fail/safe environment." And he went on to deliver his PMS concerning safety precautions that had been designed into the vessel.

Trick 3: Assault with a Deadly Question. "60 Minutes" correspondent Mike Wallace is singularly adept at this one. The reporter hurls a question at you: hard-charging, accusatory, inflammatory, and filled with hot-button words: "Do you expect that the American people will believe that an ancient aircraft like this is still viable and safe?" Reporters use deadly questions to elicit emotion as much - if not more - than to elicit fact. In response, you must remain unemotional; if you do and the interviewer prods you, he's in danger of looking like a bully. Calmly refute the charge, build a bridge and move on to your PMS: "Why, yes, I expect that the American people to believe in the aircraft [short form answer] and [bridge] so do we at Consolidated Ynot because we're using that aircraft as the basis for our exciting new..... [insert PMS here]." Answer the *words* of the question, not the *tone* of it. Stripped of its dramatic rendering, the question really was, "Is this aircraft still viable and safe?"

Let me give you a case history about the importance of remaining calm in the face of hostile questioning, one in which the target of my investigative report outfoxed me. The story I was producing for the ABC newsmagazine show, "The Reasoner Report," concerned contaminated meat in supermarkets. My correspondent and I confronted a Connecticut State Health Department meat inspector with an accusation that he had taken bribes to look the other way when he found violations in a particular market. We had very specific charges against the man, but they came from a single witness and there was no hard evidence like photographs or documents to back up her assertion. Our only hope to nail the inspector was to get him to admit it or to deny it in a shifty, guilty way - or, better yet, to run away. There's nothing as dramatic in television news as someone running away from the camera with a correspondent in hot pursuit, shouting questions. In the case of the meat inspector, my correspondent threw the bribery charge at him in the form of an accusatory question delivered in the tone and style of a TV prosecuting attorney. At the very least, we expected him to begin sweating and shifting, stumbling and bumbling. But instead, he calmly and simply said, "No. That's not the case. Never happened. I would never do that." Needless to say we didn't use the interview or the charge against him. Had he been media trained, he might have gone on to add, "What I look for when protecting the public health is...."

Trick 4: The Dire Hypothetical. The reporter presents a disastrous scenario and invites you to comment on it: "What would happen if you discovered that the entire fleet of X7s had to be taken out of service immediately to have their engines and controls replaced?" Again, the short form answer is easy. First label the premise of the question: "That's a hypothetical proposition that has no basis in fact or historical record. [short form answer] A much more likely scenario [bridge] is that these planes will continue to serve our customers well as we announce our exciting new...." Your short form answer identified the nature of the question. Then you presented your own, more likely hypothetical scenario, and moved on to your PMS. Sometimes a reporter will invite you to come up with the nightmare hypothetical: "What's the worst thing that can happen?" If he's too indolent to invent his own disaster, don't do it for him. Instead, decline to speculate or present a mild scenario: "The worst thing that can happen is that we may be delayed a few weeks as we do all the engineering tests that guarantee the safety and success of this exciting new...."

Trick 5: The Interruption. Rather than waiting for you to finish a statement, the reporter jumps in, stopping you cold, throwing another question at you. This happens mostly in antagonistic broadcast interviews where the reporter is role-playing. He's the tough, crusading good guy and he's going to get to the bottom of this! The best way to turn this rude technique to your advantage is to highlight the fact that the reporter is deploying it. Answer, "Well, I was about to say ...." And move on to your PMS. Unspoken in your response - but clear to viewers and listeners - is the phrase, "before you so rudely interrupted me." If he persists, you may want to call attention directly to it, "You know, Peter, a number of times you've interrupted me before I finished my thought. What I'd like people to know is...." And insert a PMS right there. Calling attention to his rudeness will usually cure it. Few reporters want to appear to be boors. It is unusual for print reporters to employ this trick; there is nothing in it for them, whereas a broadcast journalist gets to appear tough and uncompromising when he interrupts.

Trick 6: The Filibuster. Some reporters love the sound of their own voices so much - or think they know so much - that they hog *your* interview and just won't shut up. I have found this to be true frequently when the reporter is a specialist who is eager to show off his knowledge. Often his questions are miniature speeches followed by "Would you agree?" or "Don't you agree?" It may be tempting to sit quietly by while the reporter gives you a pass by asking very few questions, but you will miss the opportunity to insert your PMSs if you let him get away with it. What to do? Well, when he throws one of those "Would you agree?" questions at you, say, "Yes." [short form answer] As a matter of fact, [bridge]...." and launch into your PMS. If you disagree, say, "No. [short form answer] In point of fact, [Bridge],..." and deliver a PMS. Now if he persists in these filibusters and doesn't even bother to ask you to agree or disagree with him, it's incumbent on you to find an opening and jump in. Listen carefully and when he makes a point you agree with (or disagree with), express your agreement or disagreement and bridge to a PMS. It's better to interrupt him when he's made a point with which you agree so you won't appear to be *quite* so rude. You can also jump in when he pauses to draw a breath; even the most enthusiastic filibusterer must breathe. While it is usually a good idea to deliver no more than one PMS in a single answer, in this instance make an exception to that rule. In fact, forget the KISS (Keep it Short and Simple) injunction, too. You fight fire with fire and a filibuster with a filibuster. It may be the only way you'll be able to work in any of your PMSs.

Early in my television career I worked with a reporter who had a specialty beat and fancied himself more knowledgeable than most of the people he interviewed. He was, in fact, extremely well-versed and usually was far better able to express the complex ideas of his field than many of the people he interviewed. He really wanted to interview only himself, but the management at ABC News, where we worked, would not have permitted that since audiences would have found it bizarre. Since he couldn't interview himself, he instead made long pronouncements and then asked his interview subjects, "Don't you agree?" After a while some of them were reduced to just nodding assent. It made my life hell when I got back to the editing suite and had to try to cut a soundbite out of the interview. The more media savvy would say, "Yes, I agree...." and then express the same point in their own words, giving me *something* to work with. But many others were struck mute by his egotistical interview style.

Trick 7: The Pregnant Pause. Earlier I told you to take advantage of a pause in a friendly interview. When a reporter searches his prepared questions for the next one to ask, I advised, jump in with a PMS. But don't do it in an unfriendly interview. Hostile reporters use pauses, too, but not to find their next question. They use them as an invitation for you to expand on answers you've already given - invitations to go where you really don't want to go. I first became aware of this practice when I accompanied Harry Reasoner, then anchor of ABC's network newscast, when he appeared as a guest on the "David Frost Show." At the time, British interviewer Frost had talk shows on both sides of the Atlantic and commuted by Concorde from London to New York a couple of times a week. Frost eventually gave up that exhausting schedule and concentrated on his British career, which is why we rarely see him in this country any more. Harry and I had been on a week-long promotional tour for ABC News and the Frost show in New York was our last stop. Having listened to Harry give interviews for a week, I had heard all of his quip-filled, clever answers to the predictable questions. But when Harry delivered one of these to Frost, the Briton nodded, looked at Reasoner, and said nothing. Whereupon Reasoner, feeling the weight of the silence, jumped in and added to his stock answer. Frost did this several times during the interview.

When we left the studio, Harry said to me, "That Frost is a master of the pregnant pause. He got more out of me than any of the other interviewers this week and he did it by keeping his mouth shut." So here's the rule: if your interviewer pauses because he is searching for his next question, jump in. If he pauses because he wants you to go up the gallows steps and stick your head in his noose, don't take advantage of the silence. Usually, it's easy to tell the difference: the question-seeking reporter looks at his notes, sometimes frantically; the pregnant pause reporter looks you in the eye.

In responding to all the dirty trick techniques I've cited, it's really important that you avoid repeating negative phrases or words embedded in the reporter's questions. In a broadcast interview, if you repeat the negatives the audience will hear the loaded words twice: once in the reporter's question and a second time in your answer, as in: "Isn't this nuclear plant just a Chernobyl disaster waiting to happen?" "Why no, it's not a Chernobyl disaster waiting to happen at all...." You don't want to be adding emphasis to the negative words, so don't allow an interviewer to lure you into repeating them. In a print interview, it takes very little for a skilled writer to craft a direct quote using the negative words you've repeated; even if you've repeated them in refutation. Just imagine you're the company spokesman in this line from a hypothetical newspaper story: "'This program is not a Chernobyl disaster waiting to happen,' the company spokesman said." The "Chernobyl disaster waiting to happen" was in the question, but the reporter did not print the question in his story. That's because spokesperson did him the favor of repeating it in his answer. The quote looks pretty bad even though it is a refutation, because it introduces the words "Chernobyl" and "disaster," from a spokesperson who appears to have come up with those dire words himself.

Not long ago, I read a story in the *Los Angeles Times* quoting the spokesperson for an arts center that was having trouble raising money. The center had embarked on a new fundraising scheme and the story quoted the spokesperson saying, "This is not a desperation move." As an experienced reporter, it was obvious to me that the spokesperson's quote came in answer to this question: "Isn't this new fundraising scheme a desperation move?" By repeating the words "desperation move" in his answer, the spokesperson gave the reporter those dramatic words for a direct quote. Sometimes, an interview subject doesn't even need the introduction of negative words in a question. During the Watergate scandal President Nixon told a news conference, "I'm not a crook." Well, no one had asked him if he was a crook. He read that unspoken negative word into a question and used it in his answer. Don't refute what isn't charged, and don't indict yourself by repeating the negative words in a question.

ELEVEN RULES FOR ACING AN INTERVIEW

There are eleven rules you need to follow in order to prepare for and ace a tough or hostile interview. It's a good idea to follow these rules for all interviews, because, as I wrote earlier, even a kindly reporter can turn tough if the situation warrants or if she perceives that it's necessary to adopt that tone to get her story.

Rule 1: Play Reporter. Using Worksheet 4 in the Appendix, write down the toughest questions you can anticipate a reporter throwing at you. If you don't write down and study the questions that keep you up nights, you won't be prepared when a reporter springs them on you. Remember Merlis' Law of Interviews: anyone unprepared for tough questions will be asked tough questions. You might say those who are unprepared are magnets for tough questions.

Rule 2: Answer the Tough Questions. It does you no good to anticipate those tough questions if you don't also prepare your answers. Look at each of those questions and decide which of your PMSs you might be able to work into a response without creating segue whiplash for the reporter. As an exercise, attempt to pair a PMSs with each of the individual tough questions you've come up with. You'll find some tough questions just can't accommodate a PMS. For those questions, come up with short, non-evasive, unambiguous answers. (Emphasis on *short!*) Now just because you have answers to tough questions, don't get cocky and invite them. If they come, use your prepared answers. If they don't come, you're that much further ahead; don't solicit them.

Rule 3: Rehearse Tough Questions. Have someone ask you those tough questions and videotape the session. Tell your inquisitor to be merciless with you. When you screen your tape, grade yourself on how well you did in building bridges from the questions to your messages. Even if you did well the first time, repeat the exercise. You want to get almost comfortable under a barrage of withering questions. The key word here is "almost." You want to be *almost* comfortable, but not *totally* comfortable. You never want to be so relaxed and overconfident in an interview that you forget that you are working - and not simply having a casual chat with a buddy.

Rule 4: Tape the Interview. Your best defense against misquotes in print or having answer A paired with question B in a broadcast story is to record your interview on audio or video tape. Be sure to let the reporter know you are recording it; this will put her on notice that she'd better quote you accurately and in proper context. Immediately after the interview, listen to the recording to make sure you didn't misspeak. If you find you did, call the reporter at once, tell her you gave her an incorrect fact or expressed yourself incorrectly and supply the accurate answer or information. (Be sure to record this conversation, too. It will be your only evidence that you corrected your error). In thirteen states and the Commonwealth of Puerto Rico, laws require that you inform all parties to a conversation or phone call if they are being recorded; the other states and the federal government permit unannounced recording of conversations and phone calls. But it is a good policy from both ethical and practical points of view to announce that you are recording the interview even if your state permits clandestine recording. Ethically, you're laying all your cards on the table. Practically, you're putting the reporter on notice that you're attuned to any potential distortions of your answers. Not too long ago I saw a tape of a client's exhausting thirty-five minute interview with an investigative TV reporter. Having been an investigative producer myself, I saw a number of opportunities where a less than totally ethical reporter might have been able to twist and tilt the client's words to work against him. In this case, the reporter used the interview ethically in his finished piece. I can't say for a certainty that knowing my client was recording the interview contributed to the reporter's ethics, but it could not have hurt.

Rule 5: Bring a Witness. In addition to recording the interview, you should have a witness on hand. It helps to have a knowledgeable colleague from your department or your public relations staff sitting in on the interview. Occasionally, under the pressure of the moment, you might misspeak, give an incorrect fact or figure, or get a name wrong. Your less-pressured colleague can intervene and offer you the correct information. Obviously, this doesn't work in a live broadcast interview, but in other formats it can be helpful. The colleague should not interrupt your answer mid-sentence to correct you. She should wait until you've finished your reply at very least and, in the case of a broadcast interview, she should wait until the camera has stopped recording before speaking up, so that her correction doesn't became a part of the on-air story.

Rule 6: Remain Calm. Sometimes in broadcast interviews the drama of having a flustered or angry interview subject is more important to a reporter than having the facts of a story.

(More on that in Chapters 6 and 7). You can remain in control of the agenda only if you remain unemotional. By unemotional, I don't mean being a flatliner wearing a toe tag on a hospital gurney. I mean avoiding displays of anger or guilty nervousness. Even impatience is perceived as a negative emotion by television viewers. As I've already pointed out, this was something Vice President Al Gore learned in the first 2000 presidential debate with Texas Gov. George W. Bush when he rolled his eyes as Bush responded to questions. Rather than highlight the Texas governor's lack of verbal elegance, Gore's gesture left the impression the vice president was arrogant.

While the challenge to exhibit the correct emotion is especially acute in television interviews, even print reporters can use your facial and verbal excesses if you display them. "His faced flushed with anger and his voice rising, Mr. Goodhue defended Ynot Corporation against...." During the 2004 presidential campaign I read an article in *New York Magazine* about Connecticut Senator and Democratic vice presidential candidate Joe Lieberman that included a quote from his wife, Hadassah. The writer quoted Mrs. Lieberman's words and at the end of the quote did not write, "she said," but rather "she snapped." Those loaded words betrayed Hadassah Lieberman's attitude toward the question. The better prepared you are with PMSs and grabbers, with answers to anticipated tough questions, and with bridges to your PMSs, the easier it will be for you to remain calm and in control and the less "snapping" you'll do.

Rule 7: Don't Go Off the Record. Anything you say to a reporter can be used. She might paraphrase, but the facts can wind up in print or on the air. If you're tempted to go off the record, be aware that reporters, publications, or broadcasters may not protect your identity. You think you've said something off the record, but the reporter thinks it's for attribution and, once he acts on his understanding, it *is* on the record. Even a reporter who promises to keep something you've told him in confidence may succumb to pressure from his superiors to put it on the record. Today, in the aftermath of the trial of vice presidential aide Lewis "Scooter" Libby for lying and obstructing an FBI investigation, a lot of journalists and sources are rethinking the whole concept of off the record. The Libby case, involving the leak of a covert CIA agent's identity, left in its wake several tarnished reputations, destroyed careers, and many newly cautious reporters. In the case of Judith Miller, formerly of *The New York Times*, it also resulted in eight weeks in a jail cell after she refused a judge's order to reveal a news source. (The source turned out to be Libby.) Today, a lot of reporters realize they have been tools of off the record sources who were merely using them, and they may be less willing to accept off the record comments than they were in the past. Additionally, whistleblowers who once would have been willing to share information with reporters anonymously worry that journalists facing time behind bars may well cave and identify sources.

There is a single exception to the rule about not going off the record. I used it effectively when I was executive producer of "Good Morning America," and you can, too - although I caution against using it too often. Simply put, you can use off the record to play a reporter. Back when I ran "Good Morning America," critics and columnists who covered television were always out to skewer David Hartman, the show's genial host. Despite his on-camera guy next door likeability, persistent rumor depicted David as a tough, even unreasonable, taskmaster to the staff. That's just the sort of story the press loves - nice guy on camera, monster behind the scenes. The media relish whipping away the curtain and revealing the Wizard of Oz is just a charlatan. So on numerous occasions, television columnists, many of them old friends of mine, would offer me the opportunity to comment off the record on the supposed dual David Hartmans. If you think about it, it was pretty naïve of them to make such an offer. Whether the story was true or not, what was in it for me if negative stories about the show saw the light of print? Back then we were number one in the morning ratings, convincingly trouncing "Today" week after week, month after month and year after year. If viewers became disaffected because they read unfavorable stories about David and consequently stopped watching, I was going to be one of the first goats sacrificed on the alter of falling ratings. Yet, despite this seemingly self-evident calculus, I got a flood of offers to go off the record and tell the "real" story behind the scenes at the show. Usually I declined those opportunities, but from time to time I would use such an offer to manipulate a reporter. "Off the record," a reporter would urge me, seeking some juicy story about Hartman's off-camera persona. "Off the record," I would say, "David is the hardest-working member of the staff and he demands far more of himself then he demands of any of us." My off the record comment was nothing more than what I always said on the record. In other words, it was simply a way of putting boldface on something I was willing to say on the record anytime and anywhere to any reporter.

Rule 8: Don't Supply Not For Attribution Information. A favorite trick of government and some private sector officials is to give reporters information on a not-for-attribution basis as in: "A high-level official of the Ynot corporation, requesting anonymity, told the Daily Bugle that ...." It's usually pretty easy to trace the source of the quote. So if you're giving a statement "not for attribution" in order to keep out of the whistleblower's spotlight, don't do it; you'll be found out. It doesn't take a very sophisticated reader to figure out who the speaker is in most stories. And in some formats, the speaker is a virtual given. For example, the "high-level State Department official traveling with the secretary of state" who gives all those frank assessments of foreign leaders *is* the secretary of state. Since this charade is no secret to the worlds of politics, diplomacy, and journalism, it is a mystery to me why all parties continue to play it; but the little game persists.

Rule 9: Never Answer, "No Comment." Saying, "no comment" in an interview is like taking the Fifth Amendment in a congressional hearing or in court. True you're within your constitutional rights to avoid self-incrimination, but invoking the Fifth *looks* incriminating. The perception is that the Fifth Amendment invoker has something to hide. Similarly, "No comment," looks evasive, largely because it is evasive. If you can't comment for a valid reason, use that reason as a short form answer and build a bridge to a PMS. Here's how to do it: First, without using the words "no comment," tell the reporter why you can't answer his question. It may be that the query seeks information involving active litigation, and company policy or a judge's admonition prevents you from speaking. It may be that the question is about a matter outside your area of expertise or authority. Or it may be that the answer would reveal proprietary information and put your company at a competitive disadvantage. By announcing why you can't address the question, you've actually given the short form answer that sets you up to build the bridge to your PMS. Without using the loaded phrase, "No comment," here's an example: "I can't answer that because it's a matter that's in active litigation and the judge has imposed a gag order [short form answer] But what I can tell you is...[bridge]" Then insert your message and illustrate it with a grabber. And, finally, shut up! Don't go full circle and finish your answer, "And that's why I can't address your question." If there is no judicial admonition against discussing the case, you can say, "company policy prohibits talking about matters that are in litigation."

Looking back, notice I started the statement with "I can't answer" not "I can't comment." Another alternative is, "I really can't address that because...." And then bridge to what you *can* address.

Rule 10: Don't Guess. Guessing at an answer is dangerous; you could be wrong. But if you don't know an answer, use that lack of knowledge as a short form response: "I don't know. I can find out. [short form answer] But what I do know [bridge] is that .... [Insert PMS]" Don't be bullied into guessing. Following your initial answer a prosecutorial reporter might thunder, "You don't know? You don't know? How can you not know? Isn't it your job to know?" Don't let him shake you up so much that you begin guessing. Stay resolute: "That's right. I don't know, but I'll find out and get that for you. What I do know is...." and move on to a second PMS. If he keeps at it he could well enable every one of your PMSs. It's likely he'll realize this in short order and move on. If the question calls for expertise or information you don't have and can't get, you can answer, "I don't know. It's outside my area of expertise. I'll put you in touch with someone who can help you out. But what I do know is...."

Rule 11: Rephrase the Question. Earlier I wrote that an interviewer will sometimes put words in your mouth. That tactic works both ways. You can put words in his mouth by starting your answer to his question this way: "You're asking me if...." This allows you to restate the question more to your liking. Obviously, this doesn't work with a very simple and direct question like, "How long will it take to clean up the toxic spill in your factory's backyard?" To justify rephrasing, a question has to have some nuance - even some ambiguity - to it. Also, your restatement has to have more than a passing similarity to the original question. For instance, you can't say this: "What you're asking me is how effective our affirmative action policy has been...." if the original question was: "Were you here when the chemical spill polluted the ground water?"

BUT WAIT, THERE'S MORE

Here are some additional tips for effective interviews:

¶ **Be Specific.** As I have mentioned, the media and their audiences love specifics. Anytime you can give a case history or a concrete example of a general concept, you are communicating effectively.

A good rule of thumb is that a reader can infer the general concept from the specific, but cannot infer the specific from the general concept. You can use specifics introducing or concluding general statements. I recommend using them as supporting proof of a PMS and putting them at the end because they invite favorable comment from the reporter or they give him a cue for his next question. It's not enough to say, for instance, "The space program has given society lots of technological and scientific advances." The reader of the newspaper or the viewer of a TV broadcast containing that quote is also listening to that universal radio station WSIC, Why Should I Care. If your quote ends there, he will mentally ask: "Oh yeah, like what?" You need to fill in that blank, to answer that question before he asks it. Give him specifics that back up the generalized statement. For instance, "The space program has given society lots of technological and scientific advances. Walk into the radiology department of any modern hospital and you will see diagnostic tools such as MRIs that were developed as an outgrowth of technology created for the space program." Now he knows why he should care: adaptations of technology created for the space program may one day save his life. The specific brings home the Positive Message Statement.

A specific need not be an itemized list, although that helps. In January, 2003, two U.S. Air Force reserve pilots faced court-martial in connection with a mistaken bombing in Afghanistan that killed four Canadian soldiers. Their first line of defense was that their judgment had been clouded because they had taken Air Force-issued amphetamines, or "go pills," which pilots use to stay alert during long missions. That practice came under scrutiny and the Air Force had a pilot/surgeon explain the use of the pills to the media. He might have said simply, "These pills save lives by keeping pilots alert." But the officer, Colonel Peter Demitry, was ready with what I would call a generalized specific and a few grabbers. Here's some of what he said, speaking of the low-dosage amphetamine tablets issued to pilots. I've put the specifics in **boldface** and the grabbers in *italics*: "It is the *gold standard* for antifatigue. We know that fatigue in aviation kills. We have **the smoking holes, the irreplaceable loss of life.** This is a *life-and-death insurance* policy that saves lives." My only criticism of Col. Demitry's sound bite is its length and the very first word: "it." He should have identified the "it." As good as it was his statement would have been even better, more specific and broadcast-friendly, had he said, "**The smoking holes and loss of irreplaceable lives** prove fatigue kills. Low-dose energizing amphetamines are the *gold standard,* the *life-and-death insurance* policy combating pilot fatigue." (Two sentences, a total of 27 words, and approximately seven seconds to speak.)

¶ **Cool down post interview.** I have concluded interviews and seen the subject leap up out of his seat and begin sprinting from the room, only to be halted by the microphone cable attached to his tie. You, too, may feel like fleeing immediately after your interview, even if it was conducted in your own office. Resist this urge. The post interview cooldown is just as important as the preinterview warmup.

In the cooldown, as in the warmup, you shouldn't say anything to the reporter you don't want the whole world to hear, but you can use the cooldown to plant additional ideas, just as you used the warmup to plant the seeds of questions. For example, don't say, "Gee, I'm so glad you didn't ask me about XYZ; I was really afraid of that one." That injunction may sound like a given to you, but a number of interview subjects have expressed just that sentiment to me over the years using a variety of stunningly naïve phrases like that. My journalistic instinct on hearing this sort of comment is to dive right in, probe deeper, and get them to open up with answers to previously unasked questions. I've even had crews stop packing their camera gear, reset their lights, and begin shooting after an interview subject let slip a similar postinterview expression of relief.

Use the cooldown to suggest additional resources to the reporter - resources that back up your point of view. "You know, if you're interested in learning more about this, I'd suggest speaking to Dr. Hackley. He's done a lot of research in the field." Leave unspoken, "And he agrees with me completely." Or, if you realize that you've failed to get one of your key messages into the interview, bring it up during the cooldown. The reporter may not go for the bait, but you've nothing to lose by dangling it. In a print interview, a reporter can seamlessly integrate that additional message into his story and the reader won't even know it was an afterthought. In a broadcast story, the reporter might use the information by saying on-camera, "Mr. XYZ also told me that Ynot Corporation is contemplating doubling its dividend next quarter." We've all seen this on TV - further information added by the reporter. Chances are the reporter learned these points in the cooldown after the camera stopped and the lights were off.

THE GOOD INTERVIEW, THE GOOD GUEST

In my newspaper years, there were a number of people I would go back to time after time for comments on stories. They were the print equivalent of television's good guests. A good guest or good interview is someone who makes the reporter's job easier by preparing, speaking clearly and comprehensibly, and giving good, pithy, even entertaining, quotes.

Most good guests are thought-provoking. They may accomplish this through deft use of language, introduction of new and fresh information, or insightful viewpoints on information in general circulation. Or they may get our attention by throwing the biggest verbal bricks through the biggest plate glass windows. Think Jesse Jackson on the left and Patrick Buchanan on the right; both convey their points of view through the skillful wielding of entertainingly outrageous soundbites. They delight their core constituencies and infuriate their core opponents. By using hot-button words and provocative phrases, they try to force those in the middle to make a choice - or at least to think about their messages. Whether you are courting controversy or skirting it, you can be a good guest if you are well prepared, use precise language, easily grasped specific examples or case histories, and sprinkle your interviews with trenchant grabbers. When I was executive producer of "Good Morning America," I learned that the prolific author Isaac Asimov lived directly across the street from our studio. Asimov wrote science fact and science fiction books - producing two to three books and dozens of magazine articles a year. So he always had something to talk about. And, as importantly, he was a good talker - articulate, comprehensible, accessible, entertaining. So we hatched a deal with Asimov: any time a guest failed to show up for an appearance on "Good Morning America," we would phone him and he would shave, get dressed, stroll across the street, and fill the absent guest's slot by talking about his latest book or article. It was a wonderful arrangement; he always had something interesting to say and we always had emergency access to a guaranteed good guest. Now maybe your goal isn't to be some publication's or broadcast's equivalent of Isaac Asimov, but you will know you have succeeded if, at the end of an interview, the reporter asks, "That was good. Do you mind if I or my colleagues call on you again in the future?"

DON'T "DO" LUNCH

For me, a meal is a meal and an interview is an interview and you should never mix the two. There are just too many distractions at a mealtime interview. I can almost guarantee that a waiter will intrusively place a dish in front of the reporter just as you're beginning to unleash one of your best grabbers. Also, if the food is good, the reporter may spend valuable time and space praising it in his article. And if the food is bad, he may waste valuable time complaining about it. You've read those stories: first the reporter describes the ambiance, then the diners, then the service and food, and then - almost as an afterthought - she writes about her interview subject and what he had to say. All that verbiage wasted on ambiance, crowd, and food when it could have been about you and your agenda!

Also, all restaurants are full of clatter and chatter, which distract from your primary reason for doing the interview. In the world of broadcasting, you may find yourself trying to talk with your mouth full - which is never attractive. In a print interview, the surroundings may so distract the reporter she misses some of your major points. Finally, if you spill a drink, choke on a forkful of steak, or accidentally drop your butter knife on your lap, the mishap could end up in the article, making you look clumsy, careless, or ill-mannered. Even if the reporter offers to pay for the meal - and *that* will be the day - don't do it. Similarly, an interview over cocktails is an invitation to disaster for obvious and subtle reasons. If the drink you have with a reporter is non-alcoholic or even if an alcoholic drink doesn't affect your performance, she can still write, with perfect accuracy, "Interviewed over drinks, Mr. Fields said....," giving the impression alcohol may have impaired your answers. And if an alcoholic beverage consumed during an interview *does* affect you, it would be exceedingly surprising in this era of tabloid journalism for a reporter not to mention it in her article: "Slurring his words, Mr. Baccus said...."

The tips in this chapter pertain to all interviews in all media. You need to master additional, unique skills to be most effective in broadcast encounters. It won't hurt to employ the broadcast skills in print interviews as well. Communicating with all media using the broadcast skill set will make you a livelier, more interesting, more quoted interviewee. And, you won't have to keep changing styles when going from print to broadcast and back. You can read more on television's unique demands in the next chapter.

CHAPTER 5

CATERING TO THE ONE-EYED BEAST: TELEVISION APPEARANCES

If you are going to appear on television, you must watch television. I don't mean "Heroes" or "The Office," although they're fun to watch. I mean you must watch information programming, news programming, interview programming, and especially programming on which you're likely to appear. Watching a program lets you know what to expect when it's your turn before its cameras. Is the show live and unedited ("Larry King Live," "Nightline," "Meet the Press," "Good Morning America") or taped and edited ("60 Minutes," "Dateline NBC," "20/20")? Is the show serious ("The News Hour," "This Week") or flippant ("The Daily Show," "The Colbert Report")? Are guests interviewed singly or are they pitted against each other? And, if they are pitted against each other, are they expected to have a reasoned conversation ("The News Hour") or engage in an angry shoutfest? (See Chapter 7 on how to handle yourself in a shoutfest.) Does the host have a political or social agenda (John Stossel on ABC, Lou Dobbs on CNN, Glenn Beck and Nancy Grace on Headline News, Bill O'Reilly, Sean Hannity on Fox News) or is he journalistic (Wolf Blitzer on CNN, Margaret Warner on "The News Hour," Tim Russert on NBC)? Does the host listen to answers or just read a list of prepared questions and never follow up? Is he polite (Larry King) or tough to the point of being hostile (Bill O'Reilly)? Is he out for information (CNN's Anderson Cooper) or for a laugh (Stephen Colbert)? Are you seated or standing? Is everyone dressed casually or formally? Are interviews long or short? If it's an edited show, are the soundbites generally lengthy and substantive or brief and vapid?

Watching the show answers all those questions. In addition you'll be able to ascertain the nature of the audience - the people you're really talking to - and what that audience wants to hear about. You'll speak differently to an audience of businesspeople on CNBC than to a general audience like the viewers of CBS News' "The Early Show." You can speak at greater length on some live or live-to-tape interview shows ("Larry King Live," "Charlie Rose") than you can on my alma mater, "Good Morning America." Your audience may be sophisticated and knowledgeable news junkies ("The News Hour") or it may be more frivolous ("The Ellen Degeneres Show," "Live With Regis and Kelly"). The more familiar you are with the show, the talent, and the format, the more at ease you'll be and the better prepared to unleash your PMSs.

THE NATURE OF THE BEAST

Early in my television career I worked for an executive producer who was fond of proclaiming, "Television is a visual medium," and who "watched" the first cut of any report with his eyes closed. He did that so he could get the full essence of the written script and spoken soundbites. Back in those days television news reports were filmed, not videotaped, and the picture and soundtracks were separate. Once, as a gag, I had the editor play a first cut of one of my pieces for Mr. Visual without running the picture. The report ran its full four or five minutes, the screen blank, the sound track at normal level. When the piece ended, the executive producer said, "That was pretty good; let's see it again." Since it was his practice to watch the story the second time through, the editor ran the picture and the soundtrack for that second "viewing."

Notwithstanding my juvenile act of mischievous insubordination, that old boss of mine was right: television *is* much more heavily dependent on images than any other medium. In fact, some stories are almost exclusively picture-driven.

Some years ago, the magazine *Consumer Reports* gave an unsatisfactory rating to an imported SUV because its engineers had gotten their test vehicle to tip over in a high-speed, lane changing maneuver. Well, it was an interesting story to hear on the radio or read in a newspaper, but it was a riveting story to see on television. That was because the magazine supplied networks and stations with tape showing the vehicle speeding into a curve and tipping violently, two wheels lifting off the blacktop. Only a device similar to training wheels that was affixed to the SUV kept it from actually going over on its side. The strong visual impact of this TV story made it impossible for the manufacturer to counter with mere words. Instead, the company had to stage and film its own test of the vehicle.

When you are preparing for a television interview, think about whether there are visuals - tape, stills, animation, even drawings - that will help you make your points. In the SUV case, the best media defense was not a corporate engineer telling TV cameras that the *Consumers Reports* test was biased, but was, instead, videotape of a test commissioned by the manufacturer and conducted by another engineering laboratory.

Television loves visuals, so think visually. Viewers, unlike my old executive producer, will be watching as well as listening, so any images you can produce to buttress what you are saying will help immeasurably.

I had just made this very point in a media training session with some engineers who were about to deploy a device that was nuclear-powered. They feared that antinuclear activists might mount a scare campaign against the device and public reaction would threaten the project. When I told the engineers to think visually, one of them pulled a pencil from his pocket, twisted off the tiny pink eraser, tossed it out on the table in front of him and said, "This is how much plutonium we need for this device." It was a dramatic and graphic demonstration. The most fevered stretch of the imagination could not visualize a nuclear weapon's characteristic and fearsome mushroom cloud fueled by such a trivial amount of material. "Do that in every interview," I suggested. "Especially TV interviews. It should put the controversy in perspective instantly."

Why do presidents enhance their major addresses with charts, graphs, photographs, and even backdrops with key message words printed on them in a repeat pattern? Why do NASA spokespersons at interviews almost always have model spacecraft on the table or desk before them and a handout tape of a mission animation? Why do actors plugging their films on talk shows bring clips or outtakes? Because these simple devices add visual interest to the television coverage, making stories come alive on the small screen. If you think visually, you will ask yourself what images you can offer the television reporter to enhance and illustrate your PMSs. Film, tape, animation, stills, graphs, charts, maps - all can make for a much more interesting television story than just a talking head. I tell my clients, "Television loves toys. Bring a toy and you'll give focus to the interview; you'll own the airtime." By toys I mean props, tape, or other graphic enhancements.

How To Look Good on TV

If I say appearances count on television, I don't want to give the impression, as early practitioners of media training did, that appearances are all that count. Content counts, too. An energetic, attractive spokesperson who says nothing is delivering no message save that she is energetic and attractive.

That said, appearance has unique impact in television interviews. An early - and historically significant - object lesson in how much appearance counts in the medium is the very first televised presidential debate in 1960. Vice President Richard M. Nixon eschewed makeup and so looked ghostly pale on the black-and-white screens of the era. He also sweated profusely - as was his wont throughout his career - and, not knowing where to look, Nixon glanced nervously from side to side. Conversely, Senator John F. Kennedy - guided by instinct or coaching or both - kept his gaze fixed on his questioners, used an orator's hand gestures to help him make his points, and seemed "tanned and fit," probably thanks to Max Factor TV makeup. As a result, people who watched the debate on TV awarded Kennedy a "win."

But the debate was simulcast on radio, and listeners, without the benefit of visual clues, thought the event was more like a draw, with Nixon delivering substantive points in his deep, resonant voice, which contrasted with Kennedy's more reedy tones and his unique Boston accent. The difference was cosmetic; on radio it didn't matter, while on television it was the line between winning and losing. While this may be a sad comment on the state of democracy in the age of television, it is the fact of the matter. If you ignore the cosmetic side of television, thinking that it's not a substantive part of your on-camera presentation, you will likely end up dissatisfied with the way the audience perceives your message.

Despite the importance of the cosmetic side, looking good is not enough on television; it won't overcome a lack of substance. But without paying eye service to the cosmetic demands of the medium, it is hard to convey Positive Message Statements

99

to viewers. Think of television's appearance requirements as the visual equivalent of a clear writing style. In print, dense, garbled sentences don't convey your ideas very well. You strive for clarity in written communication; you don't want the writing to get in the way of your thoughts. On television, your appearance and attitude are your visual "writing" style.

Here, then, are eight simple wardrobe, appearance, and performance rules for television:

> **EIGHT RULES FOR LOOKING GOOD ON TV**
> 1. Dress Right.
> 2. Sit Right.
> 3. Stand Right.
> 4. Move Right.
> 5. Emote Right.
> 6. Look Right.
> 7. Talk Right.
> 8. Leave Right.

¶ **Dress right.** When he was president, Richard Nixon hosted my old ABC News colleague, Gary Herman, and his camera crews for a photo-op "day of leisure" at his Western White House in San Clemente, CA. Normally coat-and-tie formal in all photographs and video, Nixon decided to humanize his image and took his wife, Pat, for an on-camera walk along the beach. Characteristically, the President wore a dark business suit, a tie and lace-up black wingtip shoes. Had he been in a pair of Bermuda shorts and barefoot, the scene would have looked natural and charming, instead of staged and awkward. As ridiculous as the suit-on-the-beach stroll looked, it got worse when a higher than normal wave washed up on shore and the president did a little dance in a futile attempt to avoid getting his wingtips soaked. ABC News did Nixon the favor of not airing that particular bit of footage; showing the President of the United States walking on a beach in business attire was an odd enough visual even without the wave-dodging jig Nixon performed. Today, I am sure a similar bit of embarrassing tape would air repeatedly, first on the network nightly newscasts and then on the latenight comedy shows. For example during the 2004 presidential campaign, candidate John Kerry visited NASA's Kennedy Space Center in Florida. As required when visiting a NASA "clean room," Kerry donned a puffy white "clean suit." The problem was the suit made him look like he was auditioning to be the Easter bunny at a mall department store. The image was run repeatedly - and not just by news outlets. It even popped up in opposition print ads and commercials.

Who has grown up without a parent admonishing at least once: "You're going out dressed like that?" While it ought to be self-evident that a suit on a beach is as out of place as a pair of swim trunks in an office, there are gray areas of dressing for television. So before going on camera, imitate that parent and ask yourself, "You're going out dressed like that?" What should you wear? If business attire is correct for the occasion and for your position, men should wear a dark blue or gray suit without a pattern; women should wear a suit or daytime dress with the same color considerations. Avoid brown suits. President Ronald Reagan was partial to a particular brown suit, which he wore quite frequently. Under certain TV lighting conditions the suit looked reddish, almost the color of rust. Whenever I spotted him wearing it on television I would think, "Reagan's got his rusty suit on today." Wear a solid color shirt or blouse - pale blue is best - and avoid bright colors, striped shirts, ties and scarves. Also, wear lightweight clothing. While television lighting has come a long way since Nixon poured sweat during that initial 1960 debate and modern studios are much cooler, TV lights still are bright, and they generate heat, so you should dress accordingly.

Men should wear over-the-calf socks, so we don't see a slash of exposed flesh between trouser cuff and sock top. Women should avoid overly short skirts; oftentimes you will be seated on a very low chair - with all the hazards that represents. Minimize displays of jewelry - avoid any dangling necklaces that might hit your microphone. Also, if you're wearing a diamond the size of the Rock of Gibraltar on your finger, on your wrist, or around your neck, the chances are pretty good you're not going to connect with the average woman in the audience who could feed her family for a year or more for the price of that stone. The same goes for men's bejeweled pinkie rings and diamond-encrusted wristwatches. When I was supervising producer of ABC-TV's "Home Show," a new co-host joined the cast. She wore a blinding, large engagement ring, so I suggested that she might want to take it off while she was on the air. "Who's going to see it?" she asked, declining my suggestion. The answer to her question was, "Every woman in the audience." When she did her first cooking segment and plopped her hand, adorned with eight or ten carats of flashing diamond, into the pizza dough, it provoked more than a few letters from viewers offended by her ostentatious display of affluence.

If business attire is not appropriate, you should still be dressed neatly, in subdued colors and no stripes. Obviously, if you are the fire boss fighting a blaze in a national forest or a squad leader in a combat zone, neatness does not matter. Avoid shirts and jackets with a logo or a lot of printing on them; you want viewers to be watching you, not trying to read your clothing. The only exception to the logo rule is your own company or organization logo. Then it is merely reinforcing your on-screen identification. In our security-minded world, more businesses and organizations require employees to wear ID tags or badges. You'll want to remove these before an interview; they can create distracting reflections and more than a few viewers will distract themselves by trying to read them while you're talking. Some government agencies prohibit photography or videotaping of employee badges to reduce the risk of someone counterfeiting credentials.

¶ **Sit right.** Your mother was right: sit up straight in your chair. If you've watched interviews with sullen young stars of the music and acting worlds, you know why. Often, they sit on their necks, legs splayed at a wide V and invite your attention to their crotches instead of their faces. Don't copy them; sit the way the Victorians did: perched on the forward two-thirds of the chair, your back not even touching the seat back. It's a good idea to lean in slightly toward the interviewer. When you do, your body language says you are eager to talk with him, and the viewer assumes you are just as eager to communicate with her, too. Leaning back sends the opposite body language signal - you are physically retreating from the interviewer and from the viewer.

Don't fidget! Once again, mom was right. A lot of us channel our nervous energy through our legs. We bounce our knees or drum our foot or - when we are in a chair that swivels - we do a seated version of the old rock and roll dance favorite, the twist. You can guess the kind of message this sends to your viewers. If you plant your feet solidly on the floor, imagining your heels glued to the deck, then it is nearly impossible to drum feet, bounce knees, or swivel your chair. It is a mystery to me why some TV shows furnish interview sets with soft, deep-cushioned sofas or swivel chairs, but they do, so exercise care: don't allow yourself to sink too deeply into the upholstery or swivel dizzyingly in your chair.

¶ **Stand right.** Standing interviews tend to be shorter than seated interviews, in no small part because the interviewer is as uncomfortable standing up as you are. When doing a standing interview, stand up straight; don't slump, but never lock your knees because a lack of blood circulation could cause you to pass out, and lying dazed on the floor is not an effective way to communicate your messages. Stand with your feet about shoulder width apart. This will keep you from rocking from side to side. And, please, keep your hands out of your pockets, it does *not* make you look cool.

SITTING OR STANDING, AVOID THE CUPP

Former Pres. Bill Clinton and former Sen. Bob Dole demonstrate the CUPP, or Cover Up Private Parts position. The CUPP sends a highly-defensive body language message.

I took the CUPP photo on the preceeding page in March 2003, when Clinton and Dole appeared together on the "CBS Early Show." Throughout the five-minute segment, both men sat in the CUPP pose; long enough for me to find my camera, turn it on and take a series of pictures off the TV screen. I found it ironic that a president whose term in office was tainted by a sex scandal and a senator whose first private sector job was as a commercial spokesman for Viagra would adopt that particular defensive posture. (In fairness, Sen. Dole has a valid excuse for the CUPP. His World War II wounds left his right arm paralyzed and he and frequently supports that limb with his left hand.)

¶ **Move right.** Be expressive. Talk with your head, shoulders, and hands. This will give your conversation energy and animation. Why do singers use hand gestures? Why do actors use their hands while delivering dialog? For three excellent reasons:

1. Using your hands helps you make a point. When a singer belts out a lyric about love, she often clutches her hands to her heart and then thrusts them wide. The gestures are helping her tell the story of the song. Similarly, when you say, "This is the biggest thing that's ever happened to our company" and you spread your arms in a modified "Soooo big" gesture, you're reinforcing the point you're making. Additionally, gestures can help you remember. If I were on television right now, telling the viewer why it's important to use hand gestures, I would demonstrate the three points by ticking them off on my fingers. Not only do I reinforce the fact that there are three points, but I also remind *myself* that there are three points I must describe.

2. Gestures attract attention; they make you look active. Let's think back to that 1960 presidential debate. Kennedy dramatized his points with very deliberate, almost karate chop hand gestures. Nixon, for the most part, let his hands rest on the lectern in front of him. Kennedy was interesting to look at - in a positive sense; his gestures helped him create his vibrant, energetic image. What was most interesting about Nixon's appearance was his unfortunate and unrelenting sweat.

3. Gestures help energize your voice. Again, look at singers - they gesture not only to illustrate their songs, they also do it to help them throw their voices to the last row of the highest balcony. For the interview subject, gestures have the added benefit of burning off the nervous energy that he might otherwise express with foot tapping or finger drumming.

A cautionary note: If hand gestures are totally foreign to your nature, skip them. Forcing yourself to gesticulate unnaturally will divert important mental energy away from your Positive Message Statements. If you cannot gesture with ease, you are going to look like some sort of puppet when you force yourself to do it.

¶ **Emote right.** Some years ago, I was producing an interview with the spokesman for an automobile company. What he was saying was serious, the way he was saying it was not. Even though he was giving grim economic news, he had an idiotic grin smeared across his face as if he were doing a commercial for cosmetic dentistry. After a couple of moments, I called for a tape stop asked him why, when he was dealing with a negative story, he looked so happy.

"My media trainer told me I should always smile. It makes me look friendly," he said. And, I thought, it also makes you look indifferent to what you're saying. I suggested that "concerned" was more important than "friendly" in this case and he stopped grinning.

Since I wasn't in the room when he underwent media training, I can't testify about whether or not his recollection of the session was accurate. I hope not; media training like that gives our trade the same kind of reputation the medical profession gets from surgeons who leave retractors inside patients. Regardless of what the auto company spokesman may or may not have been told, it's important that *your* facial expression be appropriate to what you are saying. Go with your gut instincts on facial expressions; you know a big bright smile doesn't mesh with grim news and a mournful look fights an announcement of good news.

¶ **Look right.** In the movie "Get Shorty," John Travolta plays a kindhearted collector for mob loan sharks. His favorite line when intimidating a deadbeat is "Look at me." No threats, no strong-arm stuff, just, "Look at me." When you're doing a

television interview, pretend that your interviewer is that character and has just intoned that instruction. Obey it.

You'll recall that Vice President Nixon had a tough time
deciding where to look when he engaged Sen. Kennedy in that
first debate. Consequently, he looked from side to side and forever earned a reputation for being shifty-eyed. It was such an
enduring image that during the mad merchandising orgy that accompanied the Watergate scandal, a company put out a "Tricky
Dick" watch adorned with a cartoon Nixon whose eyes shifted
back and forth to tick off the seconds.

So where do you look? Right in the interviewer's eyes. But
what if your reporter has an intense, unnerving hypnotic stare or,
more commonly, is not looking at you but down in her lap where
her list of prepared questions is resting? For the former condition, look at a spot on her forehead just above her eyes. For the
lap-looker, direct your gaze at where her eyes would be if she
were looking at you. Staring into someone else's lap is not a
good idea on television.

Normally, I tell clients never to look in the camera unless
they are doing a remote interview - in other words the interviewer is not in the room with them, but across town or across
the country. In that case, treat the lens of the camera as if it were
the interviewer's eye. A lot of people find it disconcerting to engage the wide glass eye of a television lens in conversation. If
that's the case with you, write the interviewer's name on an index
card and ask the cameraman to tape it just below the lens. The
name will engage your eye and there's an added benefit: it reminds you of the reporter's identity and prompts you to use his
name in some answers ("Well, Anderson, we are ready for the
storm....").

There is one other exception to the rule of not engaging
the camera. It needs to be used sparingly, judiciously and only
by certain spokespersons. You may look into the lens of the
camera during a face-to-face interview when you want to share a
moment directly with viewers. Pulling your attention away from
the interviewer and staring down the barrel of the lens can be
extremely jarring so do it with great care and never more than
once during an interview. And, if you're going to do it, then *do*
it. Don't start talking toward the lens and then turn back to your
interrogator before you finish the thought; that destroys the ef-

fect.   Only the most practiced and confident spokespersons should try this direct-to-viewer move.

¶ **Talk right.** As I indicated in Chapter 3, talking to the media is different from talking to your colleagues. You must banish jargon and create a verbal headline for your Positive Message Statement. In other words, lead with your strongest stuff; get that key point up front. You also need to keep it short and simple and to use grabbers to capture a viewer's or reader's attention. For television, you'll also want to inject some energy into your voice; if *you* don't sound interested in what you're talking about, the viewer won't be interested, either. Energy is *not* speed. You don't want to talk so fast that you outpace the listeners' ability to follow your ideas. Additionally, you need to know when to stop talking. You'll want to learn to talk right in four different circumstances: during the warmup, whenever there is a microphone present, when you are doing a mic check, and during the actual interview. Let's review each circumstance:

1. Talk right in the warmup. In the last chapter, I covered the hazards of the warmup gaffe of saying to your interviewer - or anyone who might pass it on to your interviewer - "Gosh, I hope you aren't going to ask me about XYZ."   Saying something like that is a virtual guarantee that "Tell me about XYZ?" will be the first question out of the reporter's mouth when the camera rolls. But this doesn't mean you shouldn't talk at all before your interview. In fact, you should talk about your PMSs in the warmup. Just as "Don't ask me about XYZ" sets the stage for a question about XYZ, so, "You know this new asthma medication has enabled youngsters who previously were housebound to actually go out and join little league teams," sets the stage for this question: "I've heard that this new medication has radically improved the lives of some youngsters. Can you tell me about that?"   The interviewer, armed beforehand with the little league specific, is soliciting that story from you.

Just be sure you remember your own material.   In the Green Room before an interview in connection with a novel I'd written, I joked to the host of a local New York talk show, "When I was a foreign correspondent in Rome and Berlin in the 1960s, I was so poor that I couldn't afford a trench coat; I had to make do with an umbrella." On air, the host, John Bartholomew

Tucker, hoping to elicit the trench coat story asked, "Working in Rome sounds pretty glamorous, but I guess it didn't pay very well?" I had forgotten my own quip and replied, "That's right. I worked for a very tightfisted newspaper." Tucker tried to save the gag. "So, you didn't have a trench coat? What did you have?" he asked. At last I remembered. "An umbrella?" I responded tentatively. He laughed dutifully, even though I'd blown my own joke.

2. Talk right if there's a microphone present. Treat a microphone like a gun. Just as we are taught to treat all guns as if they always are loaded, all microphones should be treated as if they always are on and broadcasting. Never say anything near a microphone that you don't want the whole world to hear. An object lesson cited by every media coach in the country is Uncle Don. It seems Uncle Don had a popular kid's radio show in the 1940s. One Friday he signed off, paused, and then said to his studio crew, "That ought to hold the little bastards for the weekend." The microphone was on, the studio was feeding audio to the air, and the little bastards - as well as many of the little bastards' parents - heard the remark and Uncle Don was fired.

Great story! The only problem is, it didn't happen. The Uncle Don story is completely apocryphal. There was, indeed, an Uncle Don on radio in New York during the 1930s and 1940s, but if he ever referred to his listeners as little bastards, it did not go out over the air. Much as I hate to lose Uncle Don as an object lesson, I still have Ronald Reagan, as you'll see.

3. Talk right in a mic check. Before his weekly radio address one Saturday morning, President Reagan was asked for a mic check. Instead of counting from one to ten - or, as rocket scientists do, from ten to one - the president decided to be funny. "Well," he said, "I've just declared war on Russia and the bombers are on their way." The remark did not go out over the air. But the journalists assembled to cover his weekly address heard it, and they reported it. Why? Probably each reporter feared his competitors would go with the story, so each one defensively wrote it to avoid being scooped. Once the story moved on the newswires, radio stations across the country - which had recorded the joke because they had been rolling tape to capture the president's address - felt free to air it. And they did. Repeatedly. We can argue from now until the cows come home about the sanctity of the private jokes of a public man, but the fact of the matter is President Reagan - who began his working life as a radio announcer - should have known better. As I have already noted, say nothing near a reporter or microphone that you don't want the whole wide world to hear. Remarkably, despite the "war on Russia" embarrassment, Reagan did it *again*! Before another Saturday radio address his microphone check consisted of slamming the rulers of Communist Poland, calling them a "bunch of no-good, dirty bums."

Make better use of your mic checks than President Reagan; a mic check can be very productive. Instead of counting or reciting Lincoln's Gettysburg address when you're asked for a mic check, use the opportunity to state your name, your title, and a topic sentence to help set the agenda. If you do that, no interviewer will ever have an excuse for mispronouncing your name or for not knowing your title. And your topic sentence may well generate a question early in the interview.

Here's a sample mic check: "I'm Captain Picard, commander of the Starship *Enterprise* and I'm here today to tell you why we must defeat the Klingons." Having set that thought in an interviewer's mind, it is likely the first question will be, "Captain Piccard, why do you feel we must defeat the Klingons?" Even if he doesn't ask that, he's certainly not going to mistakenly call you Captain Kirk.

4. Talk right in the interview. Use the interviewer's first name - that's how the viewers know your questioner. It's Diane, not Ms. Sawyer; it's Larry, not Mr. King. This is an *American* rule; check local custom before doing it in interviews with foreign outlets such as Britain's BBC, France's ORTF or Germany's RTL. "Well, Bob...." Is more than just a friendly gesture, it buys you some milliseconds to organize your response without appearing to be stalling. Compare that with the old chestnut "I'm glad you asked me that question" or the never-to-be-employed "That's a good question." Either one of these statements is likely to unleash the aggressive beast in even the most passive house pet of an interviewer. Broadcast reporters and hosts don't want their audiences to think of them as fawning fans - even when they are fawning fans. So telling them in front of those viewers that, in effect, they have given you a "pass go, collect $200" softball may result in a daunting barrage of much tougher questions.

When he was president, Dwight Eisenhower inaugurated the televised presidential news conference. His press secretary, Jim Haggerty, advised the president to buy time for an answer with a phrase like, "Let me say this about that." Good soldier that he was, Ike took the advice to heart - too much to heart. Early verbatim transcripts of his news conferences show virtually every answer President Eisenhower gave began with "Let me say this about that." Eventually the newspapers stopped printing full verbatim transcripts. I suspect most of the material edited out was the "let me say this about that" time-buying phrase.

¶ **Leave right.** Parting may or may not be, in Shakespeare's words "sweet sorrow," but leaving a televised interview the wrong way can give you bitter sorrow. Don't heave a sigh of relief, as if the dentist has just withdrawn his probes from your mouth and freed you from his chair. Chances are better than even the audience will see it, and that gesture will undo much of the good you may have accomplished. Don't leap from your chair and run away. If the camera catches that flight - and Murphy's Law virtually guarantees that it will - the action makes you look like a fugitive. Also, it's likely that there's a microphone attached to some piece of your clothing. If it's a hard-wired microphone you're going to tear your clothing, the microphone cord, or both. You should not bolt from the scene at the end of a print interview, either. A reporter may well characterize your exit in her story as this way: "Obviously relieved, Mr. Goodhue raced from the site even though the interview had been conducted in his own office."

At the end of the interview, don't reach out to shake hands with the reporter. If he extends a hand, take it, but don't initiate the gesture. Most reporters are not expecting to have their hand shaken after an interview and may be so slow on the uptake that their body language undermines your gesture. If the interviewer offers his hand - even if he's guilty of assault with a series of deadly questions - take it and shake hands. Hemingway defined courage as "grace under pressure;" shaking hands with an interrogating bully will be perceived as courageous on your part.

Don't leave with a negative editorial comment. "Boy, you were tough on me." "Thank goodness that's over." "You never asked me about...." First of all, your microphone, still clipped to your clothing, may be transmitting. Second, that's not a good way to add information. The interview may be over but the information gathering isn't. If something has been left out of a television interview and you want to add it, tell your interviewer in a positive way. Rather than: "You forgot to ask me about..." try saying, "I probably should have told you ..." The former implies the interviewer didn't do her job, the latter has you taking responsibility and offering to be helpful with additional information. I have seen recorded interviews conclude and then the interview subject say something like, "You know I probably should have talked about...." Whereupon the reporter said, "Well, let's do a few more minutes so we can discuss that." Even live interviews afford some opportunity. I can recall a guest occasionally coming up with a good point after we had gone to commercial on "Good Morning America." If the point was of sufficient interest, sometimes David Hartman would work it in after the break in a subsequent interview, or on another day, paraphrasing the information or using it as the basis for a question to another guest. It's not the best way to get your point across, but it's better than leaving it unspoken.

TELEVISION INTERVIEWERS:
THE GOOD, THE BAD, BUT RARELY THE UGLY

A few words about television interviewers: More than any other breed of journalist, television reporters serve two agendas - getting information and looking good - although not necessarily in that order. By looking good, I don't mean they want to look like a movie idol or a soap opera star; rather I mean looking good in the viewers' eyes by being perceived favorably. This is understandable since television is a personality-driven business, television performers are ego-driven people, and TV newsrooms are not immune from the personality/ego virus. If you have any doubt about how personality-driven television news is, look at Katie Couric's $15 million a year contract with CBS News. The network hired a personality to *read* the news for a sum that could have fielded 20 to 25 journalists to *cover* the news. The conflict between looking good and gathering information wears many faces in television. Here are a few examples:

¶ The reporter wants to appear tough, seasoned, and uncompromising, but the interview subject/victim is really a pitiable character. The reporter dare not cross the line from inquisitor to bully, so he pulls back on his questioning.

¶ The reporter wants to appear tough and goes only for the jugular despite knowing mitigating facts and circumstances. She tempers anything that will make her appear compromising, even though her really big compromise is with journalism's ethical standards. This tough stance can backfire on the reporter. I can recall one of the CBS News women correspondents who sat in for Diane Sawyer as anchor of the "CBS Morning News" when I was executive producer of that broadcast. She had a reputation for toughness and in an interview with a breast cancer survivor, she got inappropriately rough. In the control room we watched this hard-edged interview in appalled silence. I can only imagine what viewers thought of this woman's misguided hostility. Her attitude, which might have been appropriate with a toxic waste dumper, was misplaced dealing with a woman describing the anguish of a double mastectomy.

¶ The reporter wants to appear to be friendly and charming, so he tempers his questions. During the heyday of the dot-com boom, business reporters fell over themselves doing puffball interviews with executives of startup firms whose sole reason for being was to make money in an initial public offering. In the cold, hard light of the economic realities of today, you would have thought that a lot of the business reporters were paid press agents instead of impartial journalists. I can recall media training one young dot-com entrepreneur and when I sharply challenged his assertion that his company would make money by "monetizing" the "community" of web surfers it was going to create, he said to me, "No one's ever asked me anything like that before." I warned him he'd better prepare for the possibility that future interviews would contain questions like mine. But the truth of the matter was that in the fawning financial journalism climate prevalent at that time, it's likely that the toughest questions he had to answer were mine.

¶ The reporter wants to be "one of the guys." This is especially true in show business and sports interviews, where some reporters want a star's glitter to rub off on them. So instead of asking real questions, the interviewer becomes an "insider" and chats up the subject. Many of the interviews of movie and music stars consist of the reporter gushing all over the artist, praising her work, endorsing her projects, and then popping a mild, "how do you feel about that" sort of question at them.

Why should you care about reporters wanting to look good? Because if you can help the reporter achieve that goal while still serving your agenda, he will cut you a lot more slack than if you're not helping him look good.

The example of a TV or movie star is the easiest to explain. A good movie, TV, or music star makes every television interview appear to be a conversation between best friends, and most of the time by doing that, the star avoids embarrassing - or even substantive - questions. The stars who get beaten up by TV all the time are those who won't take a few moments to play the role of the reporter's buddy. Some interviewers in the show business and sports fields can be both buddy and tough; it is a delicate balancing act, which I think Rona Barrett perfected when she was at "Good Morning America." I can recall Rona asking Gregory Peck about his son's suicide, leaving the normally articulate actor momentarily speechless. I also can recall her asking the late Rock Hudson, who had closeted his homosexuality, about a prank involving someone sending dozens of invitations to the wedding of Hudson and another male actor who was reputedly gay. Hudson, stunned by the question, stopped cold, took out a cigarette, lit it, inhaled deeply, and then quietly and gently said words to the effect, "I didn't think you would ask about that." Then he added, "I thought this was a vicious and hurtful thing and I can shrug it off, but it deeply hurt a very decent human being." It was an extremely memorable moment. Had Hudson considered Rona's depth of knowledge of show business, her insider contacts, and her essential toughness, he might have expected such a probing question.

For those of us who are spokespersons without marquee value, a little flattery can go a long, long way. Even those on-air reporters you would think had developed immunity to flattery are suckers for a complement or a promotional boost. For instance, consider Barbara Walters. On the first night of her brief, disastrous, and largely forgotten tenure as co-anchor with Harry Reasoner of the "ABC Evening News," Walters interviewed Egypt's President Anwar Sadat. Sadat was a master of the media and he took a shot at flattery by commenting on his interviewer's new million-dollar anchor contract, the very first seven-figure talent deal in the history of American television news. The subsequent interview was not terribly probing. Was there a cause and effect? It's hard to say, but it didn't hurt Sadat's cause to compliment his interviewer

It is instructional that the Sadat interview was not broadcast live, but was taped and edited. ABC News elected to leave in Sadat's comment about Walters' salary. *The New York Times* television critic, John O'Connor, pointed to its inclusion as evidence the newscast was more concerned with self-promotion than it was with news; an accurate and telling charge, I think. More recently, I saw an interview with the novelist Nora Ephron during which she castigated the Washington press corps for writing or broadcasting puffball stories about President George W. Bush. To turn the reporters, she said, Bush "complimented them on their tie." Lest you think Ms. Ephron's satirical side was exaggerating, in 2006, during a presidential news conference, Bush complimented a CNN reporter on his "sharp suit" and another reporter on her choice of blouse. The questions that followed the sartorial compliments were not particularly tough.

But wardrobe compliments aside, what do you do with the tough, hard-nosed reporter who wants kick you through five minutes of on-air time? Conventional flattery may not work. As I already noted, you should avoid beginning an answer to a tough reporter's questions with: "Gee, that's a good question" because the cliché is like flapping a red cape in a bull's face. The bull/reporter muses, "If he thinks that's a good question, I'd better toughen up." With this sort of reporter, you need to be more subtle. The reporter wants to appear knowledgeable and smart so play to that desire. Credit the intelligence, wisdom, insight, and research behind the questions. Rather than saying, "That's a good question," begin your answer with, "Your question shows you understand the issue, so no doubt you know...." And move on to one of your PMSs. In effect you are saying, "You know and I know and now we'll share it with the audience so they'll know."

Understand that there are limits to this trick. Flattery is like cayenne pepper. A little goes a long way. Too much will burn you, so flatter, don't fawn.

Going Live:
Challenge or Opportunity?

As I previously indicated, the upside of a live television interview is that it is live, done in real time, and broadcast as it happens so nothing can be edited. The downside of a live television interview is that it is live, done in real time, and broadcast as it happens so nothing can be edited. If you're unprepared, the lack of editing can be a daunting challenge. No one is going to fix anything for you. If your message to the viewer is distorted it will be because you distorted it, not because a producer artfully cut what you said. If you are prepared, you've got total control over everything you say, and since there's no editorial selection process, no one is going to be able to alter what you say.

Another plus/minus - depending on your level of preparation - is that live interviews tend to be much shorter than taped ones. When a correspondent or producer is taping an interview, he may revisit a question repeatedly, seeking the perfect soundbite or seeking to trip you up. That tactic in a live interview is a real turnoff for viewers and can make the reporter look like a bully. There are times, though, when a bullying TV journalist can look good to viewers. That's when she's beating up on a demonstrable cad such as the destroyer of working people's pension plans, a child abuser, or the architect of a cover-up. Mike Wallace has made a long career out of gruff and sardonic interviews with truly bad people. If you are truly bad, avoid live interviews and Mike Wallace. Here are some tips for going live.

> **When You're On Live TV**
> **Arrive Early.**
> **Warm Up.**
> **Be Informed.**
> **Use the Preinterview.**

¶ **Arrive early.** Get to the studio fifteen minutes earlier than your call time. Even if the studio is your office and they've set up a remote link for you to talk from there to the interviewer at another location, get there early. An early arrival lets you take in the geography of the studio before the interview starts, lessening the danger of distraction. If it is a familiar place like your own office, the chances are the crew has rearranged some things, and you want to notice that *before* your interview, not in the middle of an answer. Another reason to arrive early, especially for a live interview: you won't sit down, breathless, have a microphone pinned on, and get your first question while you're hyperventilating.

You'd think a veteran television correspondent would be acutely aware of the importance of arriving early on the set of a live broadcast, but one of the most grievous late arrivals I can recall involved a pro - the late Jules Bergman, ABC News' Science Editor. Some minutes before the launch of Apollo 11, the first moon landing mission, Jules absented himself from the anchor desk to find a restroom. There were portable toilets only yards from our studio, which was atop a doublewide trailer at NASA's Kennedy Space Center. But Jules went off in search of a bathroom with running water and the nearest one was a good quarter-mile away. As the clock ticked down toward air - and toward the historic launch - staffers set out to find Bergman so he could join cohost Frank Reynolds at the anchor desk. I found Bergman strolling back from the distant bathroom, oblivious to the running clock. When I warned him how close we were to airtime, he began running. He arrived at the anchor desk just in time to have his microphone pinned on and his earpiece installed. Then ABC was on the air. Bergman was sweating profusely and gasping so hard he could barely speak. Reynolds had to do all the talking until Bergman composed himself.

¶ **Warm up.** We've already dealt with the importance of the warmup in a previous chapter. But it's worth stressing here because it's more important to plant your PMS seeds before a live interview than any other sort of interview. The reason is simple: at the end of the interview, you won't get that classic "anything else we should know?" question. It just isn't done in live interviews. Moreover, since time in a live interview is finite and precious, you want your interviewer to have good strong clues about what you can talk about before you go on the air.

¶ **Be informed.** As important as it is to bone up on current events before any interview, it's doubly important before a live interview. There is no way to edit out your dumbfounded surprise when the interviewer prefaces a question with, "A little while ago, before we went on the air, your agency's budget was cut in half by the legislature." I have seen several spokespersons terminally embarrassed in live interviews by a reporter who had information that the spokesperson *should* have had.

Not long ago I was media training a number of physicists. On the way to the workshop I heard on NPR that the Nobel committee had just awarded the physics prize. "Aha," I thought. "I'll trip them up with this information." But my workshop participants had also listened to the news, so I was unable to catch them off base. Instead, we worked on using the information about the Nobel Prize to explain the impact and importance of their work and how their research complemented the Nobel prizewinners' earlier work. By knowing the day's relevant news, they were able to give their interviews a timely context.

¶ **Use the preinterview.** Many interview programs, especially the live or live-to-tape shows, have staff members preinterview guests. They do this so that the on-camera interviewer has an advance idea of what a guest is likely to say. You should use the preinterview to stress your PMSs to the producer or booker. Chances are she will work them into the set of questions she supplies your interviewer. On more entertainment-oriented program like "The Late Show" or "The Tonight Show," these preinterviews are the building blocks for an entertaining segment. In these cases the writer may well suggest straight lines for you to deliver to the host or gag lines you can unleash when the host throws straight lines to you. This sort of interview is more about fun than fact, but since a lot of preparation goes into one, and since you have a very strong advance indication of where the questioning will go, you can also figure out how to work your message points into the segment. You should always make yourself available for any preinterview. Some shows have a hard-and-fast rule that guests must submit to preinterviews or they are unbooked.

When I was executive producer of "Good Morning America," we routinely unbooked guests who were uncooperative about submitting to preinterviews. The only guests exempt from preinterviews were persons of extraordinarily high stature, like the president, cabinet members, or heads of state. But, interestingly enough, these high-ranking officials often made available to us staff members who would stand in for their bosses in preinterviews. In my experience, the only category of guests who routinely shunned preinterviews were top corporate executives. They not only did our staff and our viewers a disservice, they also missed a golden opportunity to deliver their company messages because the preinterview is a vital tool for helping create the agenda for the actual interview. Another reason to submit to a preinterview is it will give you some insight into what the interviewer will ask on the air. Once at "Good Morning America" we were preparing for an interview with the nation's top spy, the DCI, Director of Central Intelligence, head of the CIA. He supplied us with an aide who we preinterviewed and then a group of us remained behind in a CIA conference room and discussed the flow of questions we would ask the director. I can't say for a fact that the room was bugged, but the next day when we did the interview, the DCI brought in a looseleaf briefing notebook that his staff had prepared. I was sitting opposite him at the table as he reviewed it and I managed to spy on the top spy, reading the notes upside down as he reviewed them (reading upside down is a skill most newspapermen develop). I read in his briefing book virtually every question we had discussed the day before along with his staff's suggested responses. It might have been a coincidence that his staffers had second-guessed all our questions. I would have been more convinced it was a coincidence if we had discussed them someplace other than a CIA conference room. It's extremely unlikely that you'll have the opportunity to bug the reporter who'll be asking you questions. However, you can often figure out from the preinterview some, if not all, of the questions you'll be asked.

More people get more news from television than from any other medium. Television is especially strong in conveying visual information or information where accompanying visuals help tell the story or illustrate the main points.

As powerful as it is for conveying information that is visual or can be supported by visuals, you should also know that television is the most collaborative of mass media. A newspaper reporter might interview you, research and write the story, and then turn it over to a copy editor for editing and the addition of a headline. But that reporter is largely responsible for the content of the story. In television the information passes through many more hands before it reaches the end-user, and so the opportunity for Murphy's Law to have its way is far greater than in other media. But television exposure is worth the challenge because TV is an attention-commanding medium that plays to far larger audiences than all but a handful of newspapers. Also, effective television communication skills translate well to other media and to daily communication as well. ABC's Diane Sawyer wrote that my rules for interviews "work for all of life. You can use them on TV, at meetings, on job interviews, on dates, or ordering a pizza by phone." I'm not too sure about the pizza ordering application, but in all other respects, I heartily agree.

There is one branch of the television tree that requires special attention and a great deal of care if you're ever asked to appear. This is the investigative program and this branch has been growing lots of leaves lately: the hour-long investigative news shows have proliferated as the broadcast networks seek inexpensive ways of filling airtime. The next chapter delves into how you can survive this these daunting shows.

CHAPTER 6

DIGGING DEEP:
INVESTIGATIVE BROADCASTS

Throughout this book, I have urged you to regard media encounters as opportunities. I've counseled that preparation and attitude will see you though an interview and let you take control, that creating your own agenda and honing your message points will carry the day for you. Now it's time for the "yes, but…" exception to the rule.

The investigative broadcasts like "Dateline NBC," "60 Minutes," "Primetime," "20/20" and similar programs may present an opportunity all right - an opportunity to hang yourself in public. These shows are unlike any other media and they deserve separate consideration. When you're preparing for an interview on one of them, you'll need to deploy a singular strategy; and often it's a *survival* strategy.

When I was the executive producer of the "CBS Morning News," I would sometimes share a lunch table in the CBS Broadcast Center's basement cafeteria with Don Hewitt, the creator and executive producer of "60 Minutes." At CBS News in those days one did not call the on-air result of one's work a "show," but used, instead, the word "broadcast," as in, "That was a fine broadcast this morning."

Presumably, a "show" had the stink of entertainment about it, the unsavory aroma of show business; "broadcast" was a more dignified term befitting our journalistic product. Since I had come to CBS from the scrappy, unpretentious precincts of ABC, I repeatedly made the mistake of calling the program I helmed a "show." What began as a slip of the tongue eventually became an exercise in rebellion; I delighted in the punch to the solar plexus wince the "s" word elicited from CBS News old timers, so I frequently used it.

To my knowledge, the only other person at CBS News in those days who called what he produced a "show" was Don Hewitt. He wasn't being rebellious - he was being accurate. I've heard Hewitt say that "60 Minutes" is a prime time show about the adventures of (at that time) five men who, like the iconic heroes of old western movies, ride into town and right wrongs. Instead of U.S. marshals or Texas Rangers, these five cowboys happened to be newsmen. Hewett's on-screen "magnificent five" back then were Morley Safer, Dan Rather, Ed Bradley, Harry Reasoner, and Mike Wallace.

I'm telling you this so you'll understand that "60 Minutes" and its many imitators are not really fair, impartial renderings of fact. Rather, they are information-based entertainment vehicles, designed to excite an emotional response from viewers. To that end, broadcasting's investigative cowboys load their six-shooters with an interview subjects' words and often shoot him right between the eyes with those words. If you wind up appearing on one of these shows, you've got to be sure you don't give these gunslingers any ammunition they can use against you.

So what should you do when a producer for one of the investigative shows calls and invites you to submit to an interview? Do you blow him off? Do you embrace the opportunity? Do you send someone else into the jaws of hell? Well that depends on whether you are being cast as a good guy or a bad guy.

ARE YOU A GOOD GUY OR A BAD GUY?

It is a rule of theater, movies, and scripted television that you cannot have drama without conflict. You cannot have conflict without at least two contending sides. On one side of the conflict is the hero. On the other side of the conflict is the villain. Good guys vs. bad guys. So it is on the reality-based dramas presented on the investigative TV newsmagazine shows. When the friendly producer from one of these shows phones you to talk about a story, the first question to ask yourself is: "Am I a good guy or a bad guy?" There are no hard-and-fast rules for casting good and bad guys. But in general, certain categories are almost always heroes and other categories villains on these programs. On the next page are lists of persons customarily "cast" as good guys and as bad guys on these programs.

INVESTIGATIVE TV'S WHITE HATS
¶ Environmentalists, unless they commit acts of sabotage, desecration, or physical violence.
¶ Firefighters, unless they are arsonists.
¶ Poor people, unless they are criminals.
¶ One-person law firms whose one lawyer dresses in Wal-Mart suits.
¶ Maverick politicians.

INVESTIGATIVE TV'S BLACK HATS
¶ Polluters.
¶ Lobbyists.
¶ Policemen in small Southern towns.
¶ Rich people, unless they got rich by being actors, singers, comedians, or novelists.
¶ Partners in large law firms who wear $2,500 suits.
¶ Most mainstream politicians, *especially* if they wear $2,500 suits.

Despite those lists, there are no pat answers as to who is a bad guy and who is a good guy. "60 Minutes," in particular, revels in the unpredictable and will frequently lionize someone whom conventional wisdom has branded a bad guy and skewer an individual or company whom conventional wisdom has adorned with the good guy mantle. Just because you've always gotten praise from the rest of the press, there's no reason to assume one of these shows will join the bandwagon. In fact, there's a good chance the show may be trying to flatten the bandwagon's tires.

On the air, "60 Minutes" often give us subtle visual clues about who is a bad guy and who is a good guy. In fact, you can tell one from the other with the sound muted! Everyone - save the show's aging talent - is taped in a close-up. But bad guys are framed in *extreme* close-up and from a slightly lower angle. The show reserves the unflattering "up the nostrils" shot for the villains. Wider framing, shot from eye level or slightly above, is reserved for good guys. The other nonfiction drama shows don't go in for this visual gimmick, although they do like it if the bad guy sweats on camera. Another visual clue is B-roll of the correspondent strolling along, talking to an interview subject. Typically, correspondents stroll only with the good guys because the image tells the audience the correspondent is on his side, figuratively as well as literally.

Obviously, it's too late to prepare your defensive strategy if you learn you're the bad guy after they pin on your microphone and the camera starts shooting up your nostrils. So you must determine in advance whether you're going to be standing shoulder to shoulder with the news lawman or facing him across the O.K. Corral. A little later on in this chapter, I'll give you some tips for determining what role an investigative show has cast for you.

WHAT'S A GOOD GUY TO DO?

This one is simple. If you're confident that you're going to be the good guy in this western, proceed with the investigative show interview the same way you would any other interview. Ready your PMSs and grabbers, anticipate questions you might get, practice your answers, determine to whom you're speaking - the end-using audience of the show - and study the outlet and the individual reporter's style. Do all that and you should be fine; in fact you should emerge not merely unscathed but enshrined. But that's only if you're a good guy.

WHAT'S A BAD GUY TO DO?

If you find Wyatt Earp and his brothers are oiling their Colt .45s and practicing their quickdraws for a journalistic shootout with you, what's your move? Do you saddle up and ride out of town or do you stand up to them? Let me give you two case histories that are valid object lessons in dealing with investigative shows. The main point in each of these object lessons is to always be fully aware of the show's agenda.

Case history I - blocking the story. A foreign-owned automobile company that assembled some of its cars in the United States brought me in to prepare some spokespersons for interviews on a network investigative newsmagazine show. A confidentiality agreement prevents me from revealing the company name and even its home nation, so let's call them Quickcar Motors of Carland.

"What's the story," I asked.

"Oh," said the Quickcar Motors domestic publicity chief, "they're going to do a story about how our local plant uses the same production techniques we use in Carland and how that's revolutionizing assembly line work in the U.S."

I asked him: "Have you ever seen that show do an industrial story? What are they *really* after? What controversies are brewing in your assembly plant?"

After several minutes of insisting that first of all, a network news producer wouldn't lie to him, and, second, the Quickcar production techniques *were* a great story, he admitted that some workers had been expressing grievances about perceived on-the-job racial and gender discrimination. He hastened to tell me the grievances were completely unwarranted.

"Warranted or unwarranted, that's the story the show is after," I said, "Not how Carland production techniques are working in the U.S. The discrimination charge is an investigative story; it has conflict, good guys, bad guys. Building automobiles the Quickcar way has no conflict and no bad guys."

"But there's no merit to the grievances," the publicity man protested.

It didn't matter, I told him. His company had always enjoyed glowing reviews for its products and thus was just the type of big, brightly-lit window investigative reporters enjoy shattering with a well-aimed brick. My client could well have been blindsided with the discrimination accusations had he submitted to the interview without identifying the true purpose of the story. On camera, an unprepared spokesperson might well sputter and stammer defensively, ill-equipped to cite exculpatory statistics. It would have been "guilt by appearance."

Although it meant I lost the opportunity to media train a number of the company's spokespersons, I urged the client to take the calculated risk of not letting the show's cameras into the plant to videotape the assembly line and to decline supplying a spokesperson for an interview. I figured that the story was so heavily dependent on production-line images and an on-camera bad guy, the show could not tell it without Quickcar's cooperation. I was right; the show dropped the story. You, too, may be able to block an unfavorable story by preventing it from being shot, so long as you understand what the real scoop is and what it will take in terms of footage for the broadcast to achieve its goal.

That said, the danger in my approach was that the show might have stationed one of its reporters in front of the plant and taped him saying something like, "They wouldn't let us in," using that fact as an indication of guilt. My calculation was that while the "locked out" stunt would have been pretty good advocacy journalism, it was just too visually lame to make a good network newsmagazine segment. Something like that might have worked on a daily newscast, where the average story is less than two minutes long, but investigative magazine show segments are much longer and almost always require point-counterpoint confrontations. Point-point with no counterpoint is pretty poor drama when stretched over a 10-minute segment.

Case history II - emerging unscathed from the O.K. Corral. Not everyone can shut out the investigative shows. Public agencies, for example, usually can't deny access even to the most predatory journalists; so their spokespersons have to do the best they can to deny inquiring investigative predator/reporters anything to chew on.

A few years ago I prepared a government agency spokesman for an investigative segment on one of the network newsmagazine shows. We knew he was going to be the bad guy. The segment was about a controversial government-sponsored endeavor, and because this one had a high visibility, the show's producer made no pretense about the report's subject when he called to book my client. I helped the spokesperson organize a number of defensive strategies. First, I suggested his public relations representative tell the show's producer that the agency was going to videotape the interview. (Notice, I advocated *telling* the producer the agency was going to tape the interview, not *asking* the producer's permission to tape it.) The TV producer couldn't very well say no, since he was going to have two cameras in the conference room where the interview was to take place. I recommend videotape for archiving this type of show, not audio tape which is adequate for most interviews. Videotape will keep the show exceptionally honest because the omnipresent camera constantly reminds the reporter and producer they'd better deal honestly with your answers and not stick answer C after question A or engage in other editing trickery.

When it comes time to set up for the interview, I always suggest pointing the client's camera not at the spokesperson, but at the reporter. He can't fail to notice it under those circumstances. I'll have more on taping a potentially hostile interview later. Focusing for now on this case, my client's investigative interview was an education in and of itself. In his forty-minute Q&A session, the correspondent used every trick enumerated in "The Interviewer's Top Seven Dirty Tricks" in Chapter 4: he put words in the spokesman's mouth, he asked questions based on false or incorrect information, he assaulted the interviewee with deadly questions, using a tone more appropriate to a criminal court than to an interview. In addition, he asked hypothetical questions, he interrupted answers to throw the spokesman off-message, and he delivered long, hectoring preambles to questions. Finally, there were a significant number of pregnant pauses, invitations for my client to break into jail. He also asked the same questions three, four, and five times, hoping that the spokesman would get so bored with his answers, he would vary them and misspeak.

But my client's spokesperson had already been asked all those questions. Repeatedly. First by me, and then by his public relations department. Many intensive hours of mock hostile interviews enabled him to answer the tough questions and remain in control. In fact, his preparation allowed him to remain so calm and unemotional that he gave the program nothing to use: no embarrassing statements, no nervous stammering, no flashes of anger. The program didn't use one second of the interview they taped with him because my client refused to play his assigned role: the furtive bad guy exposed by the muckraking reporter. So the show found another spokesman from the same agency and interviewed him. Unfortunately for my client, the new spokesman declined media training, so was unprepared for the onslaught and plummeted into a number of avoidable pitfalls.

Through diligent preparation; practice, practice, practice, and a calm demeanor, you can succeed in maintaining your cool and scoring points, no matter how hostile the reporter's intent. It is possible to not merely survive an encounter with "60 Minutes" and its brethren, but to use it to serve your own agenda.

GIRDING FOR BATTLE

Whether you're the good guy or the bad guy, there are seven specific rules of engagement you must follow to make sure you are most effective in an investigative television interview.

PREPARING FOR INVESTIGATIVE TV
1. Determine what role you play.
2. Determine what the other side will say.
3. Write out the interviewer's questions.
4. Craft Your rebuttal/message points.
5. Rehearse the interview.
6. Record the interview.
7. Seize the initiative.

Rule 1. Determine what role you play. In the two case histories I've cited, one client did not know if he was the good or bad guy, and the other was sure he was the bad guy. Ask yourself the following questions to determine if you've been cast as the villain:

¶ **Were you a source when show researched the story?** These investigative shows cost a lot to produce, so they don't just go out and shoot a story. If a TV newsmagazine tries to book you for an interview without having spoken to you at length beforehand, chances are they want to hear what you have to say only when the camera is rolling. In other words, the producers have already made up their minds about the story and your role in it. If you answered "No" to this question, chances are you're the bad guy.

¶ **Does the producer's description of his story sound like the sort of piece that the show normally airs?** If you answered "No," then he's misleading you about the real story the show is producing. Only bad guys are misled.

¶ **In the preinterview, did the producer try to get you to comment off the record or were there echoes of the other**

side's ideas embedded in her questions or attitude? If you answered "Yes," prepare for a hostile interview.

Rule 2. Figure out what the other side will say. Try to learn who your opponents are. Ask the producer or reporter if he will send you a fax or e-mail with a list of everyone else he will interview for the story and those he's spoken to in researching the story. If the producer tells you he doesn't know who else he'll be interviewing, he's not telling the truth. If he does send a list and obvious adversaries are not on it, be suspicious, you're probably being cast as a bad guy. Make your own list of opponents, too, if you decide to go through with the interview this will be useful.

Here's an offensive tip: Whether or not you get a list, write the producer recommending additional people to interview. These should be individuals unaffiliated with your enterprise who agree with your point of view. Your recommendations may be ignored, but if they are not, you've given them leads that will buttress your side.

Using either the producer's list, if you get one, or your own list - or both - prepare a sheet with the points you anticipate your opponents will make. Be specific; your opponents will be specific, and the interviewer will base his questions on those specifics. Put yourself into your opponent's head. Ask yourself what she will have told the producer or reporter off-camera to entice him to do this story. Remember, the more sensational the charge, the more attractive it is to the producer, so don't hold back, even if your opponent's assertions are preposterous! Prepare your list on a computer so you can cut, paste, and insert your rebuttal material.

Rule 3. Write the interviewer's questions. Below each of your opponent's points write a tough, hostile question derived from that point. Don't be diplomatic or shy. Make the questions pointed, direct, and stinging. If you're prepared for the tough questions, you can handle the easy ones. If you're prepared only for the easy questions, the tough ones will throw you.

Rule 4. Craft Your Rebuttal/Message Points. After you've written out all the hostile questions an interviewer might create from your opponent's points, insert a counterargument in the form of an answer for each question. Do this right into your document immediately after the tough question. It is not enough merely to defend yourself in these situations because you don't want to appear to be on the defensive, fighting a rearguard action. Your counterargument answer/points should be strong, positive expressions of your side of the argument.

Rule 5. Rehearse the Interview. Get someone to throw your tough questions at you in a confrontational and challenging manner. If your questioner is a subordinate, assure him you won't hold his demeanor against him. Don't try to question yourself. Even if you have a strong masochistic streak, you're not going to be tough enough.

Have your interrogator get aggressive, even antagonistic; have him ask the same question repeatedly. Have your colleague read the interviewer's dirty tricks in Chapter 4 before he grills you. Videotape the session so you can watch it and analyze your performance. Then do it again. And again. Do it until you are almost comfortable under the withering fire of hostile questioning; until you have learned to ignore the tone of a question and to answer only the substance of the question.

You want to get confident building bridges from tough questions to your rebuttal points. Remember the lesson of Chapter 4: it's often easier to bridge from a tough, hostile question to a PMS than it is to navigate from a friendly, but off-the-point query. Make sure you don't look too programmed; remember it's a *television* interview and the audience can see your face, so you don't want to look and sound like a robot repeating canned answers. You need to be so familiar with your material that you can take advantage of any opportunity to score your rebuttal points, but you want to do it with grace and a degree of dignity. The reporter will ask you the same question repeatedly in different words to get you off-message. You'll want to respond without using the identical, word-for-word answer each time he asks, but you'll still want to use the substance of the same counterargument each time

When you review the tape of your practice interviews, critique yourself mercilessly. Then repeat the exercise. See how many of your rebuttal points you are able to work into the interview; keep an actual count. If you had five points to make, repeat the exercise until you are adept at getting all five points into the practice interview. Let that exercise interview run long; remember these investigative shows may interview you for as long as, well, sixty minutes. They may have at you for that long in hopes you'll hang yourself with a single incriminating ten-second soundbite. It's better to have a colleague beat you up with these questions in the privacy of your own office than to have Steve Kroft do it on "60 Minutes," with the whole world watching. Kroft, interviewed on CBS's "The Early Show" said, "We always know the answers to the questions before we ask them." That's hyperbole; Kroft and his colleagues don't really know what the answers will be before they ask their questions, but they certainly know that they *want* the answers to be. If you don't play along and give them the anticipated answer, the investigative correspondent will probably keep asking that question, hoping you'll eventually respond with the answer he wants. Only practice can keep you from falling into that trap!

Rule 6. Record the Interview. As I suggested earlier, record the actual investigative TV interview on videotape, letting the reporter and producer know you're doing it. It does you less good to have a spycam somewhere in your office than it does to let them see you are archiving the interview. Be aware that it's illegal in some states to clandestinely record another person and it's of dubious morality even where it's legal. Taping an interview keeps the interviewer honest: he won't be tempted to carve up your answers to the point of distorting your position and he certainly won't put answer B to question A. Also, by focusing your camera on the interviewer, you're going a long way toward minimizing the brow furrowing, intense staring theatrics that are the stock in trade of investigative interviewers.

Rule 7. Seize the Initiative. If you think your interview has gone badly and you feel you've suffered a disaster at the hands of an investigative TV reporter, you should consider taking the initiative and getting out in front of the story. These newsmagazine broadcasts can't move as fast as a daily news show or a newspaper, so mobilize your organization's publicity apparatus to get the story out to the public before the investigative story airs. Tell the story from your point of view and tell it with as much fanfare as you can.

THE INVESTIGATIVE INTERVIEW

As for the investigative interview itself, all the rules of interviews - plus the specific rules for television interviews - apply. Read the papers, listen to newscasts, and check online news sources immediately before your interview. You don't want to be caught flat-footed, ignorant of late-breaking developments. If your opponents have web sites, check them out; chances are they have posted their most recent accusations there, charges which may inform the reporter's questions. Here, as a recap, are our key TV interview tips plus one geared specifically to investigative encounters:

¶ **Arrive early.** Even if the interview is in your own office, be there while the crew is setting up; that way you won't be distracted by the equipment and personnel new to the room or by the inevitable rearrangement that occurs every time a TV crew turns an office into a production stage.

¶ **Eat something.** You don't want your blood sugar level falling during an interview. Avoid alcohol, dairy products and caffeine - alcohol does not calm you, it lulls you; milk, cream and other dairy products produce phlegm, which can make your voice very unattractive, and caffeine can make you hyperactive.

¶ **Greet and chat with the producer and correspondent**. Under normal circumstances it is tougher for a reporter to beat up someone she feels she knows, but investigative reporters are generally immune to this sentiment. Still, chatting in advance doesn't do any harm so long as you don't get lulled into a false sense of security by the reporter's or producer's friendly attitude. If you're the bad guy, the assault is coming, no matter how friendly the interviewer is when exchanging preinterview small talk. Use the warmup to suggest the message points you want to work into the interview.

¶ **Expect the worst.** Normally, you would go into an interview expecting that *perhaps* there will be some tough questions. In an investigative TV interview, tough questions are almost guaranteed; even the good guys sometimes get hit with them. If you are the black hat I guarantee you're going to esperience every one of the interviewer's dirty tricks in Chapter 4 and you're going to get them repeatedly. The pregnant pause, the words in your mouth, the misrepresentation of your words, the out-of-left-field hypotheticals, and the accusatory tone - all these will come at you time and again.

Don't let these techniques throw you. The reason the reporter will continue to hammer away with these tricks is simply this: she wants to shake your composure, get you to move off-message, and appear defensive. Stick to your answers, don't change your message points for the sake of change, don't waver from your rebuttal points, don't compromise, and don't let the interviewer pressure you into retreating. Above all, remain calm, composed, unshakable, and positive - and, despite the repeated assaults with deadly questions, stay friendly. The reporter knows that if she gets too hostile with someone who remains reasonable and friendly, she's the one who will lose the audience's sympathy. A final reminder on the pause: in this type of interview, do *not* take advantage of a reporter's pause in the questioning. Normally, when a reporter stops she is busy searching her papers for her next question and it's a good time for you to insert a message. In an investigative or hostile interview, the pause is a trick to get you to expand on an answer you've already given, to go beyond what you really want to say, to break into jail.

POSTINTERVIEW

When your interview with the investigative broadcast ends, don't beat a hasty retreat from the scene. Instead, stick around while the crew packs up, and act as if there are no hard feelings - even if there are. Feel free to suggest additional rebuttal points, other people the interviewer can speak to, and other research material she might consult. Keep your discussion on point and positive. Don't volunteer anything negative ("I'm glad you didn't ask XYZ.") because it could wind up in her completed story with or without attribution to you.

If, after looking at your tape of the interview, you discover that there are valid rebuttal points you failed to make, send them immediately via fax and e-mail to the correspondent, with copies to her producer and executive producer. At the very least, they are ethically bound to consider these points for inclusion into the finished piece and you will be on record as having proffered them.

Also, take the time to analyze the tape and critique how you answered the questions. A thorough review will empower you to avoid any mistakes and to repeat any triumphs in future interviews. If others who share your point of view will be interviewed in the future, give them a heads-up warning about what they're likely to face. Share your experience with them by showing them the tape of your interview. Even if it means they're going to see some of the gaffes you've committed, you will be helping strengthen your side by preparing them for the same sort of onslaught.

BEATEN UP AND BLOODIED, BUT NOT DEFEATED

If the story airs and seriously misrepresents you or your organization, resist the temptation to sit quietly by, licking your wounds. You should complain to everyone and anyone who will listen. Show your tape of the interview to TV critics, journalism professors, even to local affiliates of the network that misrepresented you. Send copies of your tape of the interview and an air check of the broadcast to all these people and to the president of the offending news division and to his network bosses as well. A word of warning: do this only if the misrepresentation is serious, not simply because you've got a bruised ego or because you misspoke on camera. Don't complain if the investigative show got it right.

I can recall a complaint lodged with the president of ABC TV about a segment I produced concerning ARAMCO, the Arabian/American Oil Company. An ARAMCO official claimed we'd misrepresented him when we showed him saying that, although ARAMCO was a publicly traded American corporation, he owed his first loyalty to "his majesty the King of Saudi Arabia." When we filmed the interview, the answer surprised us, so the correspondent, David Schoumacher, asked him the question again. And again. The executive had three chances to give a different answer, perhaps one that mentioned the ARAMCO stockholders, for example. But he rather reverentially repeated the "his majesty the King of Saudi Arabia" answer each time. The interview came at a particularly sour time in Saudi-U.S. relations; the height of the 1973 Arab oil embargo of the United States.

After ARAMCO complained, the president of network came to our editing suite and screened the entire interview. I stood by outside the room, nervously awaiting his judgment and imagining my career going down the drain. When he emerged, the network president said words to this effect: "I can see why he's upset, but he not only said it, he said it three times. He should have thought about how that would look before he opened his mouth, not after we aired it. And he might have taken the Saudi flag off his desk, while he was at it." The ARAMCO executive had miniature U.S. and Saudi flags on his desk and both were visible in the shot. In those times of oil market manipulation the green Saudi flag, with it's Koranic text and prominent sword, was like a thumb in the eye of gasoline-starved Americans. (Note: in 1980, the Saudi government took full control of ARAMCO, but when did our story, the Saudi stake was 25 percent.)

The experience of appearing on an investigative television news program, while not very common, can be extremely intimidating should you find yourself called to the task. Nonetheless, the same tips and techniques needed to navigate effectively in these interviews will help you succeed in interviews at all levels of difficulty. Two similarly daunting interview experiences are the ambush interview and the shoutfest. I'll cover both in the next chapter.

Chapter 7

BUSHWHACKED:
SURVIVING AN AMBUSH INTERVIEW
AND WINNING A SHOUTFEST

Two of the media's biggest interview challenges are the dreaded TV ambush and the broadcast shoutfest. While they are very different experiences, they do share two characteristics: neither is pleasant and neither is particularly conducive to expressing your agenda. Ambush interviewers catch you unprepared; you get no warning and you are without an interview agenda. In a shoutfest, you'll go into the studio with an agenda, but the challenge is having that agenda heard over the competing roar of the other guests. However, you can survive an ambush and you can get your points into even the windiest of shoutfests by putting into practice the following advice.

AMBUSH INTERVIEWS

The ambush interview has been around for a long time. Reporters used ambushes before there was television news; before there was even the medium of television. But ambushes are most effective on TV because they often deliver good, dramatic pictures - crusading journalists accosting furtive interview subjects with little to say and much to hide. That's all an ambush is: an aggressive reporter accosting an unsuspecting - and often unwilling - interview subject in an unexpected location and throwing a succession of questions at him.

Print reporters can ambush you, too, but if you don't answer a print reporter's ambush questions, he is likely to write, "Mr. Richards refused comment." Or "Confronted with questions outside his office, Mr. Richards declined to comment for this article." That's a lot less damaging to Mr. Richards than the television depiction of that same refusal to talk; especially if he demonstrated that refusal by a hasty retreat. What could be better theater than the video image of a portly corporate executive in a gray suit running down a street with a reporter in hot pursuit shouting questions after him? The image is a visual *"nolo con-trendre"* plea to any charge the reporter cares to make.

In his younger years, Geraldo Rivera was the black belt champion of TV ambush interviewers. Today, network news-magazine shows and local station investigative reporters go all-out, seeking confrontational situations where the target subject will take to his heels with the reporter in pursuit. The ambush interview is the modern-day TV equivalent of a western marshal quickdrawing on a bad guy as he steps out of the swinging doors of a saloon.

In this little cowboy drama, the camera is rolling and the microphone pointed like a six-shooter at the subject's throat. There are no niceties, no "Good afternoon, sir, may we ask you a few questions." There is just the challenging first question, usu-ally shouted at top volume, and, if the bushwhackee doesn't an-swer instantly, several more rapid-fire questions, often without time between them for an answer, even if the hapless victim wanted to talk.

What should you do if you suddenly find yourself in this situation? First, don't run away! Instead, stand your ground and talk to the reporter. Before getting into what you *should* say, let me tell you what *not* to say. As an object lesson, let's examine what Dan Rather did when he found himself ambushed. Rather, then at CBS, was confronted on the street outside his office. The perpetrator of the Rather ambush was Steve Wilson, an aggres-sive investigative reporter then working on a syndicated daily newsmagazine show. The supreme irony was that Wilson's am-bush of Rather was a direct outgrowth of a failed ambush Rather had tried to spring.

Sometime earlier, Rather had done a "60 Minutes" story about a storefront physician in Los Angeles who, the program contended, was faking injury reports in an auto insurance fraud. Rather accosted the doctor in the parking lot of the storefront clinic. For some reason, the doctor had a 35-mm still camera hanging from a strap around his neck. Instead of answering ques-tions, the ambush target did what every ambusher hopes for: he turned on his heel and ran away. But every so often, the doctor stopped fleeing, turned around and took still photographs of the pursuing Rather and his crew. It turned out Rather had the wrong man; the prey with the camera was *not* the doctor. Naturally, the sequence wasn't used in the "60 Minutes" story about the alleged scam. But when the real doctor sued the network for libel, all the film shot for the report became evidence in the trial. For unfathomable reasons, CBS's lawyers departed from normal practice and did not object to the introduction into evidence of the unused portion of the film, the "outtakes."

At the time, I was executive producer of "Entertainment Tonight," and our very enterprising reporter covering the story, Scott Osborne, asked the judge whether or not the outtakes - as evidence - weren't public record. The judge agreed and turned over the outtakes to Osborne. We ran a story about the case and featured Rather chasing the wrong man around the parking lot. In the wake of the "Entertainment Tonight" report, Steve Wilson, who worked for another syndicated show, staked out the CBS Broadcast Center on West 57th Street, planning to ambush Rather and ask him about the embarrassing mistake. When Rather emerged from the building on his way to lunch, Wilson and his crew struck, ambushing the ambusher. Wilson popped a tough question at Rather who stopped in his tracks. "Bring that thing up here," the CBS newsman said, indicating the microphone. "You hearing me pretty good?" Rather asked Wilson's audio operator. The man nodded. Rather got really close to the microphone "Well," he resonated, "@%&*#$% you. You got that?" And in case there was any doubt, Rather repeated himself, "@%&*#$% you. Now you got that, right?"

Wilson was speechless and Rather walked away, no doubt confident Wilson had nothing he could broadcast. Like President Reagan with his attempt at humor during a microphone check, Rather should have known better. Not only did Wilson's show air a report on the encounter (with the expletive bleeped but clearly discernible to anyone who had gotten beyond the fourth grade), but they made a copy of the tape available to "Entertainment Tonight" and we ran it, too. Rather immediately apologized, characterizing his remark as "an unchristian thing to do."

Now you're probably asking, "If I don't take flight and if I don't unleash my expletive vocabulary, what am I to do if I'm ambushed by a TV reporter?" I have two hard-and-fast rules for surviving an ambush interview:

Rule 1: Don't run away. If you flee, you will appear to be - and, in fact, you will be - a fugitive from the newsman and the public.

Rule 2: Don't reward an ambusher with an interview. Granting an ambush artist a spontaneous interview is a losing proposition; you need to get out of the ambush situation and buy yourself some time to figure out what the interviewer's story is and what you want to say. To do this, calmly tell the reporter, "I'd like to help you with your story, but since we don't have an appointment and I can't spare the time for you right now, if you call my office, we'll set something up and we can sit down and do a comprehensive interview."

Other perfectly plausible reasons for postponing an ambush include:

¶ "I'm not really current on the subject and I don't want to speculate or give misleading information. Let me find out more about it and get back to you and we can set something up so your viewers get the full story."

¶ "Company policy prohibits talking to the media about a case that's in litigation, and since this matter is a subject of litigation, I'm afraid all I can say is that the courts will decide the matter on its legal merits." (Use this only when the ambush pertains to a case in litigation.)

¶ "The judge hearing this case has imposed a gag order on any potential witness. Since there's a possibility I could be a witness, if I speak to you I would be violating that order and face contempt of court charges. So until the gag order is lifted, I'm afraid I can't discuss this at all." (Use this only when there is such a judicial order.)

Notice in the first two instances, you've stated a desire to help the reporter and have invited him to call you for an appointment. His response will likely be to shout more questions or even make threats such as, "Well, we're going to have to go without your side of the story." Remain calm and steadfast, *don't* be intimidated by this tactic. Give him nothing more than, "I'm sorry you feel the need to go ahead with your story without complete information, but I've explained that I'm willing to talk to you at a later time." He will probably keep sticking the microphone in your face in hopes of vexing you into an outburst or a flight, but resist the urge to shout or flee. It's unlikely he'll ever use on the air your calm invitation to a sit-down interview because it would raise the question in the viewer's mind of why he didn't take you up on that invitation.

Understand that an ambush TV interview is a theatrical, not a journalistic, tactic, and in the event you find yourself in this situation, you should play the role of the sober, reasoned, cooperative but, alas, unavailable statesman. More often than not, doing that takes all the drama from this particular aspect of the reporter's story and it's highly unlikely he'll consider that performance worth any airtime. For example, had Dan Rather said to Steve Wilson: "I'm sorry, Steve, but I'm late for an interview of my own and I have to leave now, but I'll be happy to talk with you at a later time and date. Just call my office and make an appointment," no one would have run a clip of him saying that. In fact, Rather had an even better calm and rational way out of the ambush. Wilson's story *did* involve an active legal case, and CBS corporate policy prohibited discussing current or pending litigation. But instead of using that completely legitimate excuse for not speaking to Wilson; Rather embarrassed himself, giving Wilson and "Entertainment Tonight" a great story.

If you saw the Michael Moore documentary, "Bowling for Columbine," you can take as another object lesson Moore's ambush of Dick Clark. In the film, Moore approaches Clark who is sitting in the back seat of an open minivan. The minivan's motor is running, Clark is talking to the driver, and it is obvious that he is in a rush to get somewhere. (This ambush took place long before Clark's 2004 stroke, when he was going full bore on all cylinders and was one of the busiest producers and stars in the television industry.)

Without explaining what the interview is about, Moore begins peppering Clark with questions. Clark, surprised by the cameras has no idea of the subject matter. There is no way Clark could have been aware that Moore was trying to assign a portion of blame to Clark for a school shooting. As broad a stretch as this may seem, here is the backstory: The very young son of a welfare-to-work mother in Michigan found a gun in his uncle's home, took it to school, and accidentally killed a classmate. Moore's contention is that if the welfare-to-work mom had been home, the incident would not have happened. And, since the welfare-to-work mother waited tables in a restaurant owned by

Dick Clark, Clark had some responsibility for the gun tragedy. Unaware of the subject, Clark answers the first couple of questions from Moore, although it is clear from his tone and attitude that this is a major inconvenience, that he is in the dark about the subject matter, and that he is in a desperate rush to get somewhere.

Quickly, Clark realizes that this is a hostile ambush for which he is unprepared and he snaps to the driver of the van, "Let's get going," and vigorously slides the door shut. As a journalist, I found Moore's stretched logic and his tactics shocking, but many others I spoke with said they thought Moore had done a good job of "getting" Clark. In point of fact, Clark "got" himself. The tie between Clark and the shooting was so tenuous that it bordered on the ludicrous for Moore to try making the connection. However, by reacting emotionally, Clark gave Moore all the drama the filmmaker needed.

I think it is entirely likely Moore would not have used the encounter at all had Clark said, "I'm sorry, Michael. But as you can see we're on our way to a meeting and we're running late. I'd be happy to talk to you sometime, but you have to understand that I'm really very busy right now. Why don't you call my office and set something up. Again, sorry, but we've got to go; we can't keep these people waiting." Then Clark could have gently slid the door closed and had his driver pull away, leaving Moore with film of Clark being polite and nothing more

In that scenario, when Moore called the office, Clark's staff could have learned the purpose of the interview and Clark could have made an informed decision about whether or not he wanted to participate. Had he not participated, the worst Moore could have done was stand outside Clark's California office building or Clark's Michigan restaurant and announce to the camera, "Dick Clark refused to talk to me."

Now you may be wondering what chance you have in an ambush situation if a veteran, accomplished interview subject like Dick Clark can be tricked into delivering that bit of defensive theater? Well, you probably have a *better* chance than Clark did. Until that point, most interviews with Dick Clark were about his large number of successful entertainment projects, so he often gave interviewers his time because it almost always accrued to his benefit to do so. It's likely Clark was habitually less on his guard against a hostile interview - especially one on such an arcane subject - than you or I would be.

The bottom line is, if a camera appears out of nowhere and it's accompanied by an aggressive reporter shouting questions, it's an ambush and you gain nothing by stopping and accommodating the reporter. You cannot win one of these encounters because you won't be prepared, so you need to excuse yourself gracefully and avoid the interview by inviting the reporter to meet with you in a more formal setting.

HOW TO WIN A SHOUTFEST

Compared to an ambush, a televised shoutfest is a picnic, an opportunity for you to shoehorn in some of your messages despite some daunting challenges. There is a long-running trend in television news interview programs that is distressing for those who tune in to glean information: the proclivity to feature bitterly partisan and emotionally hectoring "experts" and "analysts" engaging in furious shoutfests. These loud-volume pundits think they win over the viewer by drowning out their opponents. Audiences must be responding to this heat-instead-of-light approach because the ranks of these unpleasant exercises in sound and fury are multiplying while the serious journalistic efforts like PBS's "The News Hour" and "Charlie Rose" are the exceptions rather than the rule. In general, the shoutfests deal with political and social matters. If you are the spokesperson for a political, social, or even an economic issue that might spark controversy, you may be invited on such a program. If, on the other hand, you are the spokesperson for a new product or service or for a scientific breakthrough, it's unlikely you'll be asked to appear in one of these raucous encounters.

The first rule if you're scheduled to appear on a shoutfest is to watch the show so you can identify the style and agenda of the host. Most hosts of these shows have an ideological bias, and it's best to know if that bias favors your angels or your devils. Watching will also give you insights into how far he'll let the talkover go before intervening.

Preparation, as always, is key to mastery, however in a shoutfest you need to abandon reasoned argument and become a sloganeer. Prepare your slogans by reducing your PMSs to their barest essentials, to the equivalent of verbal headlines. When you're on the air, simply shout them unabashedly into the fray whenever you can. In this effort you'll find an ally in human biology, because often your best opportunity to shoehorn in a point is when an opponent takes a breath. Fortunately, even the most long-winded proponent must draw in as well as expel air.

In a shoutfest, toss out all rules of etiquette. You don't need to be responding to a question and there need be no context to your PMSs; you need only the space to ram them in. Most of what viewers are hearing is babble anyway, so if you can launch a PMS in the clear, the audience is going to assume it had a context. It's even possible that your PMS may lead the moderator to follow up with a direct question or, at least, steer the discussion into consideration of what you want to talk about. Conversely, it's important for you not to get drawn too deeply into your opponent's tirade, lest you wind up just shouting responses no one is going to hear anyway. You really don't want to address his points or, at least, you don't want to answer them in any detail, because if you do, you're serving his agenda and the audience hears his points twice, making them that much more accessible.

What I recommend makes no conversational sense at all, but watch the shows - what about them does make sense? They feature three, four, or five people trying to out-yell each other, often all of them speaking at the same time - if speaking isn't too generous a word for it. Complex issues are reduced to angry slogans. So if you can deliver the few seconds of light amid the many minutes of heat, you've gone a long way toward winning. One added thought: don't be shy. If you've ever watched a show with three or more panel members - such as Bill Maher's "Real Time" on HBO - you've probably noticed in almost every edition, one of the panelists plays the role of shrinking violet, getting only a tiny fraction of the airtime grabbed aggressively by the others. On these programs, if you are shy, retiring, reticent - even polite - you're going to be that shortchanged panelist. It may go against your personal grain, but you've got to jump in with both feet and swing away. Let the other panelists fend for themselves; your concern is your agenda and expressing it, nothing more.

PLAYING FOR LAUGHS

Bill Maher's "Real Time" show brings up another new phenomenon: the comedic news or news interview program. The most prominent and successful of these ventures run back-to-back four nights a week on Comedy Central: "The Daily Show with Jon Stewart," and its spinoff, "The Colbert Report," starring Stephen Colbert. Each show features a single interview per episode and these interviews are an opportunity to reach a young and interested audience - one highly valued by advertisers. Of the two, "The Daily Show" is the far more desirable venue because Stewart, while always looking for a comedic opportunity, will allow a guest to make agenda points. Colbert, on the other hand, is playing a role throughout his show, a living cartoon version of Fox News' Bill O'Reilly. The comedian, acting his fake outraged, reactionary personality, is altogether too willing to sacrifice ideas on the alter of his fictional persona. Stewart will treat many of his interview subjects with affectionate respect; Colbert, wrapped in his playacting role, will "dis" anyone and everyone for a laugh. A handful of guests can work with Colbert's act and share in the fun. Many more, however, are discomforted by the obvious role-playing and fail to get much information across.

As a rule, ambushes, shoutfests, and fake news shows are not ideal venues for expressing your Positive Message Statements. In the first, you probably will be accosted without any PMSs at hand. You may be able to dredge up a few from memory, but it's just not worth the effort to try; you're better off excusing yourself from the encounter and inviting the reporter to speak with you after you've taken the time to prepare for the onslaught. In the second, you find yourself in a competition that is more theatrical than journalistic. Shoutfests place greater value on the entertainment aspects of passionate yelling and mindless invective than they do on the intellectual content of your statements. In the last - the fake news show - the premium placed on comedy may endanger your agenda. Far more civil - and far more conducive to calm, rational, and even *thorough* expression of ideas - are print and online interviews. I'll deal with those in the next chapter.

Chapter 8

TAKING NOTES:
PRINT AND ONLINE INTERVIEWS

When it comes to information-gathering techniques, the oldest and the newest of the media share more similarities than differences. Stories in newspapers, magazines, and in online news outlets are often the work of a single reporter, as opposed to the work of a team (as in TV), and print and online outlets are generally able to devote more space than broadcasters to most stories. Print and online media are better venues for analytical journalism and for stories requiring detailed, intricate, and complex data. Since print has been around longer, let's begin with that venerable medium.

PRINT INTERVIEWS

Print was the first mass medium and to this day is generally the most thorough of all the various forms of media. Movable type, perfected by Jonhannes Gutenberg in the 15th century, enabled printers to report and disseminate news within just a few days or even hours after they learned of it. Since printing eliminated the arduous labor of hand-copying all documents, written material became less expensive and literacy exploded - reading was no longer the exclusive province of the clergy, the nobility, and the very wealthy. As literacy spread, newspapers were born and in just a few short centuries their circulation expanded geometrically, reaching impressive levels in America during the early 20th century. In those times, competition for readers and for advertising dollars was, for the most part, among the print outlets, not between them and other media. In cities such as New York, there were more than a dozen daily English-language newspapers and dailies printed in Chinese, Greek, German, Italian, Russian, Polish, and Yiddish. Adding the weekly community and ethnic newspapers brought the total of newsy journals in that city alone to more than 100! Even back in 1961, when I was graduated from Columbia University's School of Journalism, there remained four citywide mass-circulation morning daily newspapers and three afternoon dailies. Today there are three citywide dailies where there were seven. That total, however is two more daily newspapers than most American cities have.

While the commodity of the broadcast media is time, the equivalent commodity in print journalism is space. On a big news day, a paper can add space by simply adding pages. It can get bigger or smaller as dictated by the space needs of either the day's news or advertising or both. An hour of broadcast time is fixed by the speed of the earth's rotation and so it is an absolute: sixty minutes. An hour cannot be expanded to sixty-two minutes to accommodate a big story. And, in fact, a commercial broadcast hour is really closer to forty-four minutes, once you subtract the time for ads and promos. If you're thinking that's skimpy, consider that the ratio of editorial content to advertising is four-to-one in broadcasting but more like one-to-one in print. In fact, some newspapers print more advertising than news, especially in their Sunday editions, while no news program runs more minutes of commercials than minutes of news content. Another difference: publications have the reread factor - if you don't understand a sentence, or can't identify a spokesperson, you can slow down and analyze the sentence or search earlier in the story for the spokesperson's affiliation. But broadcast journalism doesn't have that luxury: you get it first time it's read to you or you miss it. In fact, when you are the reader, you can study a complex story slowly or zip through a simple one quickly. In TV and radio, the pace of the story is completely out of your hands. A corollary to the reread factor in print journalism is the disregard factor. You can toss out those advertising supplements on Sunday, skip the display ads, and just concentrate on the news stories. There are ways to skip the advertising in a linear medium like television: you can use the commercial breaks to go to the refrigerator or to the bathroom, or you can buy and use a digital video recording device like TiVo, which can fast-forward through commercials. But for most TV viewers and for all radio listeners, where there is no TiVo device available, random access to information is not an option. Also, print media usually offer a table of contents or a news index, so you can turn directly to the information you want. In broadcasting, you can skip through content only using a TiVo-like device, but even with one of those gadgets there is no index or table of contents to aid your search for information that appeals to you.

Despite the greater news-to-advertising ratio in broadcasting, on a routine basis the print media allot far more space to news than broadcasting allots time. When I worked on newspapers, all the space devoted to material other than advertising and regular features like stock tables and comic strips was called, rather inelegantly, the news hole. In the middle of the 20th century, when there were so many newspapers looking for material to fill their news holes, legions of print reporters worked the streets and phones to develop stories. The ranks of publications, especially dailies, has thinned, and uncompromising economic dictates from profit-driven corporate owners have resulted in combine sweeps through the editorial offices of the surviving newsrooms, reducing those legions of print reporters to mere squads. My local newspaper, *The Los Angeles Times*, hard on the heels of winning a batch of Pulitzer prizes, announced yet another round of editorial staff cuts mandated by its Chicago-based parent company. This, unfortunately, is not unusual. In 2007, the *Philadelphia Inquirer* pink-slipped 68 of its 412 editorial employees and Time, Inc. cut loose 172 of its editors, reporters, and writers. These substantial cuts were part of a national trend which, in 2006 alone, saw *17,809* media jobs eliminated. That is the disturbing total offered by the outplacement consulting firm Challenger, Grey & Christmas. Even though editorial ranks may be thinning and the number of newspapers continues to spiral downward, print remains the medium where your message is likely to get its most thorough examination. So it's important to consider how you best communicate to readers through the remaining inky wretches who practice the ancient craft of print journalism.

THE GRAMMATICAL IMPERATIVE

Back in the 1960s when I was a reporter for the now-defunct *New York World-Telegram and The Sun*, the city's mayor was Robert F. Wagner, an affable career politician who served three four-year terms. Mayor Wagner routinely butchered English syntax when he spoke. In fact, he often tortured grammar until it screamed for mercy. And mercy is what grammar got from the print reporters covering the mayor because just as routinely as Wagner tore sentences apart, we reporters put them back together for him. Back then, reporters were in the habit of doing the mayor - and other interview subjects - the favor of "fixing their quotes." We did not change the meaning of what they said - we just improved their grammar and syntax, making it seem they were speaking better English. It was repair work we performed with barely a second thought.

Today reporters and editors no longer repair an interview subject's butchered phrases. The party responsible for this is the same beast that slew all those New York newspapers: television. As my print colleagues and I saw fewer of our number and more TV crews at news conferences, we also saw the light of truth - or the light of the dead-on accurate quote. I couldn't very well fix Mayor Wagner's quote in the *World-Telegram* if my reader was going to put down the paper, turn on the television, and see the butchered original for himself.

The wording of your quotes in print interviews is exclusively in your hands, so make every effort to speak clearly, grammatically, and in complete sentences. The most fixing a reporter might do is to add words you've omitted, enclosing them in brackets. But today's print reporters won't do you the favor we used to do Mayor Wagner of quoting you as saying what you would have said had you said it correctly.

It's more important to speak grammatically and in complete sentences for print media than it is for broadcast. Broadcasters are not as likely to toss out a grammatically fouled-up soundbite as are print reporters. There are two reasons for this. First, broadcasting needs soundbites, even if they are imperfect. If a broadcast reporter paraphrases everything an interview subject says, the story will look and sound boring; it will be a reportorial monologue. So broadcast journalists will cut you more slack and use an almost grammatical soundbite just for the sake of getting another voice in the story. Second, broadcasting is just not as discriminating about proper English. Nearly half a century ago, John Hohenberg, one of my professors at Columbia's School of Journalism, used to rail, "Broadcast copy is bad copy." If you listen carefully to what's said and read on radio and television today, you'll agree. A good deal of what broadcast reporters say is grammatically incorrect. This is true not only when they are speaking off-the-cuff, but also when they are working from a prompter or script. They write the stuff ungrammatically! Yes, broadcasting's casual, even indifferent, attitude toward grammar infects its written material in addition to the ad-libbed bits. If you had the opportunity to read most radio and television news scripts, you would find they are rife with incomplete sentences and sloppy syntax. "More than" routinely becomes "over" in broadcast scripts, as in, "He worked for the city for over thirty years." On television, things are "real good," as opposed to the correct "really good." The difference between "lie" and "lay" seems beyond the ken of most broadcasters. Also, very few *literally* know the difference between "literally" and "figuratively." Why are radio and television news scripts so cavalier about language? Because, broadcasters claim, they are writing for the ear and not the eye. So in the grammatical skid row of broadcasting, your ragged, sloppy soundbite doesn't particularly stand out. On the other hand, readers of newspapers and magazines see your syntactically-challenged quote surrounded by prose written and edited in conformity to the rules of grammar. Because of this, a print reporter is less likely than a broadcaster to use a really badly constructed direct quote, preferring instead to paraphrase you. Do yourself and the print reporter the favor of giving him quotes he can use, not quotes he'll have to paraphrase. Also, it doesn't *hurt* to be grammatical on radio and TV.

It's a good idea, too, to include the sense of the question in your answer. Remember, in Chapter 3 I noted that if I ask you, "How's the weather," instead of replying, "It's rainy and windy," you should say, "The weather is rainy and windy." While "It's rainy and windy" is a complete sentence, it isn't as quoteworthy as the sentence that incorporated the sense of the question. Extending that thought, if you asked me, "Why do you feel interview subjects should incorporate the sense of a question in their answer?" I could respond, "It's important because it gives them control of their quotes, buys them a little thinking time, and makes the reporter's job easier, enabling her to use the quote without having to set it up." But that answer forces the reporter to set up my quote: "Asked why it is important for an interview subject to include the sense of a question in his answer, Merlis said,..." Instead of writing that, it's likely the reporter would just paraphrase my answer. A better response from me would begin, "In my book, *How to Master the Media*, I suggest incorporating the sense of a question in an answer because...." With that approach I included the sense of the question, and managed to do a little branding.

SUBJECTIVITY AND OBJECTIVITY

Print is at once the most subjective and objective medium. Let's deal with objectivity first. As a general rule print media devote many more column inches to stories than broadcast devotes time to the same story. The exception, of course, is saturation coverage - the sort of broadcasting we saw on 9/11, after the space shuttle Columbia burned on reentry, and in the extensive coverage of hurricane Katrina. Broadcasters call this sort of reporting "wall-to-wall" coverage, and these marathons are the exception. As a rule, if you were to read aloud a newspaper account of most stories, it would far eclipse the account of the same event in a typical newscast. For example, I read aloud an article in a recent *Los Angeles Times* about shelters in St. Louis that were overwhelmed by a flood of newly homeless persons. The exercise took me seven minutes. That's nearly a third of the twenty-two minutes of editorial content in a half-hour newscast. Similarly, if you set in type even a substantial television news story and printed it in newspaper column form, its brevity would be startling - no TV news story would run more than three or four column inches. This difference enables a greater amount of both objectivity and subjectivity in the print media.

The relative abundance of space that a newspaper or magazine can devote to a story enables objectivity; there is space in a print story for all sides to be expressed and for those expressions to run long enough to be thorough explanations. If you are a spokesperson for one of those sides, the effectiveness of your advocacy is up to you. If you give good quotes, they'll be used, and if you don't, you'll be paraphrased. If you can make your Positive Message Statements relevant and telling, they'll be in the story. If you can be specific, there's room to include the specifics you cite. In the homeless shelter story, for instance, the reporter detailed four case histories, including one of a single mother who moved into a homeless shelter because, although she had a full-time job, her rent ate up more than half her income. Ironically, her job was as a social services counselor, helping needy families find resources. That specific made the story dramatic and vivid. It is my guess that had a local commercial television station done that same story, it would have run 90 seconds to two minutes and, knowing the medium as well as I do, I'm confident the report would have told *only* that ironic story of the homeless social worker and not reported on the wider - and more important - trend that it illustrated.

In a story with several contending points of view, print is apt to give more space to the debate. If equal treatment of your idea and an opposing idea fill six column inches of newspaper space, the equivalent amount of broadcast time simply wouldn't be available in a daily newscast. Additionally, because television is so dependent on images and both radio and television are so dependent on soundbites, they are less likely to run subjective opinion or analytical pieces. Usually, the pictures and soundbites are wanting in these stories, so they don't make very compelling viewing or listening; subjective and analytical journalism is pretty much the province of the print media. A recent major exception: the anchors on some of the all-news channels have been given license to exhibit subjectivity and anchor opinions are increasingly being expressed - often with vehemence.

In the fall of 2002, Senate Majority Leader Trent Lott made a feeble joke during the celebration of Senator Strom Thurmond's 100th birthday. Noting Thurman's Dixiecrat run for the presidency in 1948, Lott said that had Thurman, an outspoken segregationist, won "we wouldn't have had all these problems over all these years." Seeing how the media covered this bit of career self-destruction is instructive. White House spokespersons were willing to talk, but not on camera, not on the record, and not for direct attribution. So the news stories were analytical. What did we see on the nightly newscasts? Each network's White House correspondent stood on the lawn in front of the executive mansion telling us - without benefit of pictures or soundbites - what the thinking was inside the building visible over his shoulder. The lack of pictures and soundbites dictated that the stories be short. Had you set them in type and laid them into a newspaper column, they would have run only two or three inches. Compare that with the feet and yards, perhaps miles, of column space that print reporters produced on the same story, also working without those direct quotes. This was a dramatic demonstration that newspaper and magazine writers are less reliant on direct quotes to tell a story, so it's key that you make your points compellingly quoteworthy when you are dealing with the print media.

Also, it's important to ascertain the purpose of a print reporter's interview. Is she seeking background for a think piece or is the interview destined for inclusion in a news story? If it's the think piece, your direct quotes will likely count for less - they may never see the light of day, although the columnist may paraphrase your ideas. If the interview is for a news story, your quotes count for more; they are the only way for you to be directly represented in the story. While you're less likely to be directly quoted in the think piece, you can use a background interview to further your agenda even though your exact words won't appear. Note, though, that if you think you're giving a columnist information on a not-for-attribution basis, you need to think again. As I wrote earlier, these days it's hard for a reporter to maintain confidentiality. Therefore, I recommend only saying on a not-for-attribution basis what you would ordinarily say *for* attribution. Even if the reporter doesn't attribute, it usually isn't difficult to figure out the sources of many of these not-for-attribution assertions.

Let's refer again to the Trent Lott story. How tough was it to ascertain President Bush's attitude about the majority leader's ouster despite the president making exactly one public statement of rebuke and, in that statement, not calling for Lott to step down from the leadership? It wasn't difficult at all. Anyone who read a newspaper knew that President Bush wanted Lott out. Analysts kept writing of the White House's displeasure with Lott and the White House's desire that he step down. To read it literally, the building itself, rather than its principal occupant, had an opinion. The opinion expressed was, of course, the president's and the information came to the analysts in not-for-attribution discussions.

Earlier I recommended recording all your interviews. That goes for not-for-attribution interviews, too. Here is a case in point that involved me. When I was executive producer of "Good Morning America," *Time* magazine did a story about how our program had been beating "The Today Show" for months on end and about host David Hartman's seemingly unstoppable momentum. I was one of several show staffers interviewed for that story. The reporter told me I could go off the record any time I wanted and that if I had not-for-attribution material, my name would not appear as a source. Obviously, it was an invitation to dish dirt about the show and Hartman. Having no intention of placing my head in a noose, I declined to go off the record or to make not-for-attribution remarks. Also, I practiced what I preach and recorded the interview on audio tape.

When the story appeared it contained some negative comments, attributed to an unnamed "show source," about the interviewing prowess of the show's co-host, Joan Lunden. Television show staffs are prone to gossip, and, amid the finger-pointing, some malicious individual told Joan that I was the source of those comments. I was not the source and was able to put the matter to rest immediately because I had the tape of my interview. If I had not taped the interview, it would have been merely my word against gossip - and gossip is a very powerful force in the absence of facts.

The newspaper journalist who is writing a hard news piece as opposed to a backgrounder or opinion piece is less dependent on direct quotes than her broadcasting counterpart. Your exact words are icing on her cake. And while a news story without direct quotes isn't as interesting to read, we've all seen them. Help yourself and help the reporter by giving her good, usable quotes. Your opportunities for giving those quotes don't end when she leaves, either, and neither do her options. As a newspaper reporter, I frequently called sources after my primary interview to clarify points of fact or to pose previously unasked questions. You, too, can also follow up. As noted in Chapter 4, if you listen to your tape and discover a verbal typo, you should phone the reporter, tell her you misspoke, and give her the correct information. Also, if you left out one of your PMSs, call and tell her that there's another important point that her readers would likely want to know about.

If the reporter initiates the callback, then inserting your omitted PMS is less awkward, so think about inviting her to do just that. Before she leaves the interview venue, offer her the opportunity to call you to fact check her story. You don't want to ask her to let you read the story before it is printed; that's like asking for the right to censor it. But an offer from you to double-check the facts as she has written them is entirely in order. On some of the more thorough publications, like *The New Yorker*, a separate fact-checking department vets every assertion of fact. Many of these departments go into excruciating detail. However newspapers - with their tighter deadlines and scores of stories in each edition - do not fact check that way. So a thorough, ethical reporter may well take advantage of your offer to fact check her story, especially if there are technical, scientific, medical, or other arcane details in it. When she calls back to fact check, you can work in any PMSs you omitted in the interview.

Before sitting down to a print interview, it's a good idea to marshal on paper as many facts as you can, and to let the reporter have them to take away with her. Photographs and other visual aides help, too. Even if the newspaper doesn't run the photograph, a picture may enable the reporter to more accurately describe what you're talking about. If you are dealing with a new product, have a sample standing by and let the reporter use it. Sometimes this will yield a good third-party recommendation, as in: "This reporter tried the new MP3 player and found the audio reproduction to be the equal of the CD player in a fine, high-end stereo system." *Never* offer the reporter a free product; he might construe the offer as a bribe and report it as such. Reputable newspapers and magazines may buy or borrow a product for testing, but will not accept a freebee. Although there are unethical reporters who are "on the take," it is suicidal to assume you're dealing with one. In fact, even if a reporter solicits a gift, you should refuse. Any reporter who does that should be turned in to his employer immediately. And, of course, since you're following my advice to record your sessions with the reporter, you've got proof of his unethical venality.

HOW NOT TO DO A PRINT INTERVIEW

Discussing the importance of not copping an attitude in Chapter 3, I noted an interview Martha Stewart gave *The New Yorker* back in 2003. The interview was in connection with the insider trading accusations against her for her sale of ImClone stock in December, 2002. That interview bears some additional attention because it is a textbook case of how *not* to do a print interview.

First there is the timing. The controversial trade - in which Ms. Stewart sold all of her 40,000 shares of ImClone stock for $228,000 - took place on December 27, 2002. The sale came one day after ImClone's chief executive, Sam Waksal, learned the Food and Drug Administration was not going to approve a drug the company had developed. Waksal, who immediately began unloading his shares of ImClone, spoke with Martha Stewart, who was a longtime friend. After that conversation, Ms. Stewart sold her ImClone shares. For his part, Waksal agreed to plead guilty to insider trading, so much could be made - and was made - by the media of the Waksal-Stewart phone call that preceded Ms. Stewart's stock sale.

The Waksal-Stewart conversation and Ms. Stewart's sale of stock came immediately after Christmas, 2002, the conversation on December 26, the stock sale on December 27. The controversy erupted almost immediately. But Ms. Stewart did not speak to *The New Yorker*'s legal correspondent, Jeffrey Toobin, until sometime in mid to late January. Toobin's article appeared in the magazine's February 3 edition - more than a month after the controversial stock trade. In the weeks between the trade and the publication of the article, the media were free to speculate about the case with virtually no input whatsoever from Martha Stewart - and speculate they did. That speculation did great damage to Ms. Stewart's cause and to her finances. In *The New Yorker* article, Ms. Stewart indicated that the cost to her personally from lost business, depressed value of her company's shares, and legal fees totaled $400 million.

So her delay - not getting out in front of the story early on - was a big mistake. It looked as if Martha Stewart had been indifferent to public opinion and felt no need to address the charges in the media, whereas her accusers were not at all reluctant to go public. In fact, Ms. Stewart did have one previous brief brush with a reporter; she was questioned about the case by CBS News correspondent Jill Clayson during one of the domestic diva's regularly scheduled live appearances on the CBS "Early Show." This happened immediately after the charges surfaced, and Ms. Stewart responded to Ms. Clayson by saying that everything would turn out all right and she wasn't there to discuss the charges but to do a cooking segment. Chef's knife in hand and looking annoyed, Ms. Stewart resolutely continued chopping a cabbage with aggressive vigor. Among those who saw the episode there was an impression that she was ducking the issue, and

- perhaps - imagining that the cabbage was Ms. Clayson. The cooking segment became fodder for late night comedians and CBS discontinued Ms. Stewart's appearances on "The Early Show" after that.

A good rule for stories likely to become controversial is to get out in front of them, not to wait around until a reporter asks you to react. This is true even if you are able to say very little. A more media-savvy move for Ms. Stewart might have been to take advantage of the CBS appearance and indicate that she was donating the profits from the stock sale to charity. The cost of the donation would have been miniscule compared to the financial damage Ms. Stewart reported to Toobin. Also, if there were shades of gray in the case, regulators might have cut some slack to a public figure who had donated to charity any profits from her alleged wrongdoing. The media, certainly, would have been much harder-pressed to crusade against a caring and open Martha Stewart than against a seemingly evasive and indifferent Martha Stewart.

Ms. Stewart's second mistake in her *New Yorker* interview was going off the record. It is clear from even a casual reading of Toobin's article that she is the source of some of the unattributed assertions that buttress her side of the argument. In fact, Toobin writes at the beginning of his piece that Ms. Stewart agreed to talk with him about her feelings, but that she declined to discuss the facts of the case on the record - a clear indication that she discussed the facts of the case off the record. Had she not addressed the facts at all, it's likely Toobin would have noted that instead of writing that she declined to discuss them on the record.

Her third mistake was to have her PMSs right there in front of her where her interviewer could see them. Toobin reports that she had a pad in front of her with points she wanted to get into the interview. Having your notes in front of you invites the journalist to tell his readers just that - that you had your notes in front of you. Surely Ms. Stewart, an accomplished and extraordinarily bright woman, could have memorized her message points.

Ms. Stewart's fourth mistake was inviting Toobin to do the interview in her home, a restored early 19th Century farmhouse. That was probably a calculated risk, but it did not pay off because part of the piece was a house tour and animal census and neither furthered Ms. Stewart's cause. While Toobin didn't ridicule the attention to detail at Ms. Stewart's house, most of us would consider as borderline absurd the lengths to which she had gone to create her private world. Among those lengths were custom-tailored fabric frost covers cut to the individual shape of each outdoor shrub. Toobin mentions them without sarcasm; the readers certainly can supply that reaction without prompting by the writer. As to the animal census, Toobin describes a house which sounds like some sort of menagerie for domesticated animals. According to the article, there were two dogs, five cats and thirty singing canaries - but only because it was canary mating season. The house itself "reads" like some sort of stage set, with Ms. Stewart attended by a substantial staff of spin doctors and domestic help. This served to distance Ms. Stewart from the public she was trying to court.

The title of Toobin's piece was "Lunch at Martha's," although the interview began before lunch, ran through the meal, and extended beyond it. As indicated in Chapter 4, a meal is a meal and an interview is an interview, and it's a bad idea to mix the two. The normal pitfalls of a mealtime interview - interruptions by servers and the distraction of food - were exacerbated when Ms. Stewart spontaneously gave Toobin the recipe for one of the many Chinese dishes they were having and insisted he write it down. At that point, without Toobin's adding any nuance to his account, Ms. Stewart descends into self-parody.

Another hideous moment for Ms. Stewart's cause arose when she pointed out to Toobin that in ancient Chinese society the higher one's social class, the thinner one's chopsticks were. She then announced that she sought out and bought the thinnest chopsticks she could find. Then she added: "Maybe that's why people hate me." That was too good a quote for Toobin to skip.

That thin chopstick sensibility pervades the tone of Toobin's piece. Ms. Stewart's attitude was so manifestly self-absorbed and so indifferent to the public that she emerged looking worse than if she had not done the interview at all. She certainly failed in her attempt to rally public sympathy for her plight. She had not merely ignored the WSIC listener, she rather actively alienated him. Interestingly, Martha Stewart's next interview - a television session with Barbara Walters - was as good as her print interview was bad. But by the time she granted that interview, the damage was done; Walters interviewed Stewart on the eve of her brief stint in federal prison. It's entirely likely that Martha Stewart's greatest crime in the public's eye, was copping an attitude.

ONLINE AND E-MAIL INTERVIEWS

Online interviews fall into two categories: sessions conducted by journalists for online publications and interactive chats directly with the public.

The first are interviews for online publications such as the mass-appeal *Slate,* for more narrowly focused online journals of various industries and disciplines, or for online blogs. The second are scheduled sessions in online chat rooms - where the questioners are not journalists but journalism's end-users. This is the closest most spokespersons get to dealing one-on-one with the audience they normally reach through interviews with journalists.

In the online journal and blog interview, the reporter may conduct the Q&A session by conventional means - on the phone or in person - much the way a print journalist would. But some online journalists, and increasing numbers of print journalists are willing to submit questions to an interview subject via e-mail. The interview subject then e-mails back his answers and if the reporter has follow-ups, he e-mails these, too. The advantage to you, the spokesperson, is obvious. Composing your answers off-line and then e-mailing them to the reporter gives you total control, insuring that you can work in all your message points and that you can make your responses highly quoteworthy. Most journalists prefer the give-and-take of a live interview conducted either in person or over the phone, because their follow-ups are organic to your responses. Also, most reporters will stipulate in their stories that your answers were e-mailed responses to e-mailed questions. But so what? If your quotes are used and they are effective, your agenda has been served. Further, the reader generally doesn't care that the interview was an e-mail exchange. You can buy yourself far more thinking time with an e-mailed interview than with any other media encounter. Just be sure you take full advantage of the opportunity by carefully parsing your answers, printing them out, and reading them before launching them into the cyberspace by hitting that on-screen "send" button. Doing this will insure accuracy and quoteworthiness.

The online versions of conventional media - especially newspapers - are growing stronger and more important. An indication of this direction is the fact that fully 100 of the *New York Times'* newsroom employees do more work on the web edition than on the print version of the paper. An ever-increasing number of print reporters are now filing stories for both print and online editions of their outlets and many of them are also writing blogs - often containing more detailed information and more behind-the-story insights. At the same time as print newspaper circulation has been dropping, journals' Internet readership has been growing. Today, more people than ever are using the web as their primary source of news, and, according to a story in the April, 2007 edition of *The Columbia Journalism Review*, the trend is likely to continue, since newspapers are seeing a 20 to 30 percent annual increase in web-based revenue. The web is attractive to cash-squeezed print journalism because the production costs associated with the online editions are half those of the paper editions. ("No trucks, no trees," is how the Boston Globe's publisher described the cost benefit in the *Review*'s story.) As this trend grows, we are sure to see further dependence on e-mail question-and-answer exchanges.

CHAT ROOMS

Internet chats more often than not appeal to an audience that is already interested in your subject; one that is curious to know more. As in an e-mailed interview, you should craft your PMSs and grabbers in advance and have them available in your computer. That way you can simply cut and paste them into responses to chat room inquiries. Also, be sure to refer the chat participants to websites that support your point of view.

The chat room is the Internet's equivalent of a radio call-in show. But the big difference is that there's no interlocutor on the Internet, as there is on a radio show. In fact, the radio host is likely to act as an agent provocateur, stirring up his audience by sniping at you with hostile questions and a challenging attitude. Radio, the first electronic medium, offers additional challenges and opportunities as well. Radio requires you to master some specific tools and skills. More on that coming right up.

Whether you are interviewed for a cyber journal or *The Wall Street Journal*, the key rules are the same: prepare your points, inform yourself about whom you're really addressing, fashion quoteworthy statements, practice working your points into an interview, and don't cop an attitude, lie, or evade. Very few interviews will appear to be daunting experiences if you have your own agenda and are prepared to employ the skill set you've learned here to prosecute that agenda. Next up, we'll discuss some of the skills you'll need to master for radio interviews, and we'll look at the terrific opportunities afforded by interviews conducted over the phone.

CHAPTER 9

ON THE AIR; ON THE HORN: RADIO AND PHONE INTERVIEWS

When I joined ABC in 1968, the news division had a pro-
digious radio operation, staffed by highly professional and dedicated men and women. ABC News had divided its many radio
affiliates into four mini-networks and the operation churned out
four newscasts an hour, twenty-four hours a day, seven days a
week. ABC Radio News tailored its four newscasts to different
types of radio stations, ranging from the quick-paced, hip, and
contemporary to the more serious information outlets.

Later, when I was executive producer of "Good Morning
America," which was way back in the antecable days before
CNN was even a gleam in Ted Turner's eye, there were only
three national television networks doing news so I had in my
office the obligatory three silent TV sets monitoring ABC, CBS,
and NBC. But I also had installed an ABC News radio line
which I used to turn up to full volume six or eight times a day so
I could hear a good, professional radio summary of the latest top
news. Summary is the key word here. Those broadcasts were
highly compressed news, a succession of very short stories featuring briefer soundbites than even television newscasts. Hourly
radio newscasts remain to this day short form journalism, but
now a distressing number of stations do no newscasts at all. Information and talk stations are at the other end of the spectrum;
many feature long interviews and expansive, detailed stories that
can rival in content even a medium length newspaper article.
National Public Radio's "Morning Edition" and its evening drive
time "All Things Considered" are two shows that come to mind
when I look for all that's best in the radio medium. But even the
on-the-hour and on-the-half-hour newscasts on these shows are
short form journalism. Most larger cities have at least one all-
news radio station; these outlets churn out news twenty-four
hours a day, but their stock in trade is the short, headline-style
story, not the in-depth piece featuring substantial explanations,
comprehensive soundbites, and contemplative analysis. Also,

all-news stations repeat stories a lot because they know that there is a substantial audience "churn," with listeners tuning in for short busts of information and then quickly tuning out. That said, the all-news stations are voracious consumers of content and need a lot of material to stuff that 24/7 pipeline. If you are going to be part of the stuffing, your remarks need to be extremely concise and pithy.

RADIO INTERVIEWS

Many spokespersons fail to differentiate between the broadcast media. While radio shares some similarities with television, the differences are important.

RADIO IS NOT TELEVISION
WITH THE PICTURE TURNED OFF

Let's deal with the fundamentals that all radio interviews share: no pictures and no reread factor. Radio is unlike any other medium because it is the only one that offers its audience no visual clues or cues at all. In a radio interview you have your words and nothing else. The listener can't see your sarcastic smile, your raised eyebrow, your happy grin. You are a disembodied voice.

As with the television viewer, the radio listener has no way of going back in the story and checking out what a spokesperson said. What the listener hears initially is what she takes away. So it's up to you to enable comprehension the first time around by making your soundbites accessible and comprehensible. It is a rule of all media mastery that you speak clearly, simply, and in short but complete sentences. Nowhere is that rule as critical as it is in radio. And add another mandate: You need to speak slowly enough for listeners to hear and understand you.

ENERGY IS RADIO'S EQUIVALENT
OF TELEVISION'S PICTURES

Speaking slowly does not mean speaking listlessly. On radio, you should - no, you *must* - energize your voice and give it character and color. You have only that one tool, your voice, to capture the listener's attention. Make your voice commanding by using inflection and stresses, not by talking at machine-gun speed. You can sound energetic even when you are speaking slowly enough for the most preoccupied listener to absorb what you're saying. A lot of professional radio personalities achieve vocal energy by acting out as they speak or read. That is, they grimace and gesticulate with exaggerated movement. To brighten their speech, they do something old radio pros call "putting teeth in it." Putting teeth in a line means delivering it with a huge smile on your face. It looks ridiculous but sounds great. And, since it's not TV, no one sees the jack-o'-lantern grin. Try it. Record yourself on audio tape reading a line with a normal facial expression and then reread it with a big smile on your face. When you play back the tape, your ears will hear that smile.

Many stations, especially on the AM band, have initiated all-talk formats. There are sports talk radio stations, political talk radio stations, business talk radio stations, and general informational radio stations. The trade publications call the talk radio stations "yakkers." A substantial number of the yakkers, especially those featuring political talk, employ hosts who seem perpetually angry about something. As angry as the talk jockeys are, their audience members seem to be angrier; at least those who call in often manifest even more volcanic fury than the hosts. The only thing these listeners like better than a heated argument is a verbal assault by the gab jock on someone with whom they disagree. For our purposes, talk radio falls into two categories: the listener-interrupted monologue and the listener-participation interview. In the former, the host delivers a commentary on the day's events and may field questions and comments from listeners. These shows rarely have guests and do no interviews. On the listener-participation interview shows, the host grills the guest and then throws the questioning open to the audience. An upside of these shows is the length of time they accord a guest. Frequently there is only one booking in a half hour segment of the show so there's really a lot of time to expound your views. The downside is that these shows are looking for action, drama, and conflict; in other words, a loud, emotional argument. To these shows, there is nothing like angry, hysterically shouting opponents to attract and hold an audience.

Even if you aren't booked as a guest on a radio show, it is possible to book yourself if there's a call-in component. Simply by phoning in to the station, you can get yourself some air time. Talk jockeys will normally permit a caller to make a single statement or ask a single question so you can't go into one of these situations expecting to leave behind four or five PMS's. But there's no reason why you can't slip in one, or even two if you're graceful about it. Just remember, you must do all the branding yourself: "I work for Ynot Corporation and we're totally in support of...."

Call-in shows that place a premium on conflict place minimal value on full and complete discussion of issues. Radio shows that book guests - as opposed to the phone-in shows - will allow you to speak for a longer time, but be aware that before going on the show, you need to ascertain to whom and thorough whom you'll be speaking. Of all the media I deal with, that information is most critical with talk radio programs because it is so easy to get sandbagged by the host and audience of a show you don't know. So when a radio station calls to book you, it's critical to find out whether you're going to be praised, fawned over, skewered, belittled, ridiculed, or assaulted. That information is key to your preparation. If you can't listen to a radio broadcast before your interview, ask around and find someone who has listened to it so you can prepare for what's coming. And don't ignore the Internet; many radio stations not only broadcast over the air, but also make their programs available online and in podcasts, so you can check out what's in store for you by using your computer to visit a station's web site.

I don't mean to give the impressions that all these radio shows are audio replays of the Spanish Inquisition. Indeed, some are comparable to fan magazines, with host and listeners taking turns praising guests with whom they agree. But at the other end of the spectrum are some very tough hosts who enjoy the loyalty of loud and opinionated listeners.

Your principal defense against an anticipated onslaught of ridicule is your inalienable right to not do the show. No media outlet has subpoena power; none can compel you to submit to an interview. If you are certain that you are going to be subjected to unreasonable treatment, that you are not going to be permitted to make any points, that you are being booked only to be the target of scorn, decline the invitation. If they've already booked you and you learn belatedly that the experience likely will be akin to audio waterboarding, unbook yourself. Declining an invitation is easy; virtually all talk radio is live, so it's understandable if you have a conflicting appointment that prevents you from accepting an invitation to your own public beheading. In cases where you accept an invitation and then learn enough about the show to know you're going to be skewered, unbook yourself as early as possible so the show can find a replacement in plenty of time and not harbor too much resentment against you. There are any number of perfectly reasonable excuses for retracting an acceptance to appear: appointment conflicts, legal counsel recommendation, company or organization policy. While a television station might stage a dramatic confrontation between an opponent of yours and an empty chair meant to represent you, this gimmick doesn't work at all on radio. The worst that can happen is the talk jock will mention once or twice that you had accepted an invitation to appear and then changed your mind. After only a couple of repetitions this begins to sound petty and it's likely the talk jock will abandon the theme and move on to someone who is in the studio and available for his assault with a barrage of deadly questions.

Of course, if you are the sort of person who feels any publicity, no matter how adverse, is better than no publicity, go ahead and stick your neck out. You may win; you may not. In fact, by your own standards you may win even if a lot of listeners feel you've lost. When the syndicated Howard Stern radio show began airing in the Los Angeles market in the 1980s, I listened to the inaugural broadcast. Weight-loss guru Richard Simmons called in to congratulate Stern on his West Coast debut. Stern lashed into Simmons and kept up a stream of hateful invective for what seemed like a cruel eternity. I remember thinking, "Hang up, Richard. Cut it off." But Simmons stayed the course, although Stern had reduced him to tears. At the time I was supervising producer of ABC-TV's "Home Show" and Richard was a frequent guest on the show. When I next saw him, I told Simmons I had heard the broadcast and I felt Stern had treated him shabbily. "Oh," said Simmons, "he always does that when I'm on his show." Always? This had happened before and Simmons came back for more? To Richard Simmons, the humiliation was worth it because it gave him an opportunity to reach out to the over-weight people among Stern's listeners.

TALK RADiO PREPARATION

Once you make up your mind to accept an invitation to appear on a radio talk show, find out the circumstances of your appearance. Ask if you'll be the only guest and the length of your segment. Also, ask how long you'll be talking with the host before he'll take listener calls. Armed with that knowledge try to get all of your PMSs into the host's interview before he opens the phones to the public. If you can manage that, you will have set the agenda and the callers will be more likely to address your points with their questions and comments. Once the calls start coming in, remember to keep your points at the forefront. Often callers don't ask questions but use their time on the air to make statements. If a caller agrees with you, endorses what you said, or praises you, thank him and reiterate the point to reinforce it. This is not the time for saying, "Aw shucks, thanks a lot, caller." It's a time to put your message in audio boldface. If the caller opposes one of your points, I have a three-step variation on our four-step technique for answering a hostile journalist's question. Here are our original question bridging technique and the equivalent response to a caller statement:

**TOUGH QUESTION FROM
A REPORTER**
Short form answer.
Build a Bridge.
State your PMS.
Shut Up!

**TOUGH OR HOSTILE
PHONE-IN STATEMENT**
Disagree at Once.
State your PMS.
Shut Up!
There is no Step Four.

¶ **Disagree at Once.** There was no question; instead, the caller made a statement, so you don't have to come up with an answer. Your simple response, "I disagree with that," both challenges the caller's statement and builds the equivalent of a bridge. "You're dead wrong," is even stronger than "I disagree," and in the rough-and-tumble world of talk radio, you'll want to be extremely assertive.

¶ **State your PMS.** You'll want to do this forcefully and quickly. Don't repeat the caller's assertions; that just emphasizes *his* point of view by giving it more airtime. Get your Positive Message Statement into the listeners' ears as early in your response as possible. By doing this you are resetting the agenda from the caller's to your own. If the host is on the caller's side, he may try to shoehorn in a question sympathetic to the caller's point of view. If he does, then use that question to bridge to another of your Positive Message Statements.

¶ **Shut Up.** In an interview setting the final rule was to shut up - that is, to avoid bringing your answer back to his question as in, "So that's why this is not a disaster waiting to happen." In response to an assertion from a radio caller, you want to do the same thing; you want to end your statement on your own message point, not return to his. So deliver your PMS and shut up.

Let me demonstrate this technique with something truly controversial: Ynot Corporation's plan to build a nuclear-fueled electrical power plant in the New Jersey Meadowlands, just outside New York City. This project is going to be a tough sell so you have worked up four strong Positive Message Statements which you've kept short and simple:

1. The plant will be nonpolluting. Unlike fossil fuel plants, nuclear facilities emit neither particulates like soot and ash, nor greenhouse gases, like carbon dioxide. Ynot's Meadowlands plant will neither pollute nor contribute to global warming. (30 words, two sentences.)

2. The plant will reduce U.S. dependence on foreign sources of energy. At current import prices, an oil-fired plant generating the same amount of electricity will enrich foreign oil suppliers by more than $200 million every year. (26 words, two sentences.)

3. The plant will be safe to the point of being foolproof. The technology used in the Ynot Meadowlands plant has a proven, 45-year-long safety record in nuclear-powered U.S. Navy vessels. (22 words, one sentence.)

4. The plant will save consumers money. Customers will save money. Technology advancements mean Ynot Meadowlands will supply cheaper electricity to consumers over the plant's life than a similar capacity oil, coal or natural gas facility. (30 words, Two sentences.)

Despite your positive messages, this is going to be an emotional issue. People remember Chernobyl, the Soviet nuclear plant that melted down in 1986, releasing dangerous levels of radioactivity. In addition, they have a fear-provoking example closer to home: Three Mile Island, which the media and nuclear critics portrayed as an American Chernobyl, although there was no significant release of any radioactive material at that Pennsylvania plant. Because this is a hot-button issue, you have armed yourself with facts and figures: the difference between the poorly engineered and shoddily maintained Chernobyl plant and American designs, the fact that no one was harmed at Three Mile Island, the number of U.S. Navy ships powered by nuclear reactors, the fact that France safely generates most of its electricity using nuclear reactors, and the U.S. Department of Energy's record for guarding spent nuclear waste against terrorists and other potential thieves.

You're on a radio call-in show. The host has grilled you for a while, and the phones are flashing because you're dealing with such a controversial matter. The talk jock takes his first call. In a heated and emotional tone, the caller says: "I live near the Meadowlands and no one's gonna put a nuclear power plant in my backyard! If the government's too chicken-livered to stop 'em, I'll go to court with my neighbors and tie this up 'til the cows come home. And if the court gives you a go-ahead, we'll lie down on the highway and block the construction trucks. You build what you're proposing and you'll be exposing my kids to dangerous radioactivity. I don't see you living next door to a nuclear power plant with your kids."

Now you're going respond with the "Disagree at Once, State Your PMS, Shut Up" technique. The most logical message to work in here is your third one: The plant will be safe to the point of being foolproof.

There was no question, just a frightened and pugnacious statement. So here's a response that uses our three steps: "That's not the case at all. [Disagree at once - without repeating his point of view] Safety is our number one priority. That's why we designed this plant to be safe; safe to the point of being foolproof. Our Navy used this same technology aboard four hundred ships over forty years, without a single nuclear mishap. Ynot's plant will be just as safe for our workers and neighbors. [State Your PMS and shut up]" By using this technique, you have not gotten bogged down in a discussion of his children's safety - an emotional approach on his part which will have great sway with the public since it appeals to fear - and you've kept it short and simple. The "pull quote" part of your answer, Beginning with "Our Navy," is 30 words long, expressed in two sentences and is comprehensible at the sixth grade level. (Remember, in ordinary media encounters you aim no higher than tenth grade comprehension, the national average grade level. But with emotional issues like this one, you must gear comprehension levels down to sixth grade level because even the most sophisticated adult processes fear-inducing arguments like a frightened 11-year-old.)

RADIO SINS AND RADIO VIRTUES

Let's say you are approached to do a radio interview with a talent you are reasonably sure will not assault you with a constant barrage of deadly questions, one who will permit you to get in your points during a vigorous but fundamentally fair interrogation. This is an opportunity to get some message points out, but you want to be sure you emerge from the experience a radio saint, not a radio sinner. There are the five deadly radio sins and five corresponding virtues you need to know about. Not committing the sins and embracing the virtues, will make you into a competent radio communicator.

RADIO SINS AND VIRTUES	
Sin	*Virtue*
Loquacity	Brevity
Silence	Energy
Complexity	Simplicity
Brand Aversion	Branding

¶ **Loquacity Versus Brevity.** In Chapter 4, I wrote about the need to keep answers short and simple. Let's deal with the short part first. You already know that radio is a non-visual medium without a reread factor. A very long statement can sound like a speech or a sermon, rather than a conversation. It is much more interesting for a listener to eavesdrop on a conversation than it is to listen to a speech. In a tough interview, many of us have an impulse to filibuster, reasoning, "If I keep talking, he can't ask me more questions." Watching National Security Advisor Condoleeza Rice testify before the 9/11 Commission, I was struck by her logorrheic answers. I had the distinct feeling that Ms. Rice, knowing each commissioner had ten minutes to question her, thought she could keep tough queries at bay by giving two- and three-minute answers to every question. In fact, several commissioners called her on the tactic. On the radio, speaking at excessive length not only may fail to forestall other questions, but also it may spur the interviewer to ask tougher questions. And even if it doesn't, your long-winded answers are sure to frustrate listeners and cause their attention to wander. Once an answer has gone on too long, many radio interviewers will throw manners to the wind and interrupt you with the next question. So speak in short sentences and short paragraphs: one thought to a sentence, and one PMS to an answer. Brevity is not "Yes" and "No." I've already said that "Yes" and "No" are not answers but are rather the beginning of answers. Some time ago I heard an interview with a young rock musician on a local Los Angeles radio station. The DJ asked a question and the rocker answered, "Yes." There was the briefest of pauses, as the DJ waited for amplification. When none was forthcoming, the DJ asked a second question and got a second, "Yes." Again, nothing beyond the single syllable. So the DJ did what any radio broadcaster would do in such a situation: he cut the interview short.

¶ **Silence Versus Energy.** Just as nature abhors a vacuum, radio abhors silence. Think about this: if you were channel surfing on television, tuned to channel five, and there was nothing on-screen - no picture, no sound - you'd move on to another channel. If you were in a strange town you'd assume that in this market, channel five has no station assigned to it. Similarly, a listener hunting through the radio dial and hearing no talk, no music, nothing but the "sound of silence," assumes that there's no station and moves on. Radio interviewers know this and don't want to lose the station surfers, so if you are silent for too long after a question, it's likely your interviewer will begin talking to fill the void. When he's talking, he's using the medium's most precious commodity - airtime - and you are not. You can't deliver *your* message when *he's* talking.

` Even as you remember the danger of silence, keep in mind the first deadly sin, loquacity. You want to talk, but not forever. The virtue I've paired with silence is energy. I've already written a little bit about the need to make your voice interesting because in radio there are no supporting visuals. An energetic voice is an interesting voice. Your energy conveys enthusiasm for your Positive Message Statements. Again, don't confuse energy with speed. An energetic voice is not a fast-talking voice, rather it is a voice that employs coloration, emphasis, brightness - vocal qualities - not speed. If you go fast, you may qualify to join the Fast Talkers of America Club, but you'll leave the audience in your verbal dust. Listen to the really good radio communicators: they stress words a little unnaturally for everyday conversation, they change the pace of their delivery, and they vary their volume, raising it slightly to put in boldface words or phrases they want to emphasize. I was in the audio booth one day while the late Howard Cosell did his two minutes on "Good Morning America," and I watched the volume needles as they did a wild dance. Cosell would speak very quietly and then suddenly raise his voice to a near shout for emphasis. His pace, too, would vary from very slow to moderately fast - but never so fast you couldn't catch his words. Known for his television appearances, Cosell - like most sports booth announcers - was really an audio performer, and he made wonderful use of color and energy to make his voice interesting. He didn't have the resonant bass often associated with radio voices, but he used his reedy, nasal voice as well as anyone in the medium. So you don't have to sound like James Earl Jones to interest a radio listener. While it takes a lot of practice to get to a career announcer's stage of professionalism, you can do what they do on a more modest scale by varying your tone and your speed, by gesturing in an exaggerated way and by "coloring" your voice by "putting teeth" into your words from time to time.

¶ **Complexity Versus Simplicity.** With no reread factor as there is in print and no graphics assist as there is in television, radio listeners get one brief shot at comprehending what you're saying. In media training sessions I used to tell participants that rather than "dumb down" their answers, just pretend to be talking to their aunt across the table at Thanksgiving dinner and speak at the appropriate level for her to understand. In Chapter 3, I told Kerry Millerick's story about being chastised for writing copy with a 12-year-old audience in mind when, according to his producer, he should have been writing for five-year-olds. The danger of making things too simple is you'll insult your audience. If you speak to them as if they're five years old, you risk turning them off. Simplicity is not necessarily dumbing down what you say; it's just making sure that the audience has the opportunity to grasp your meaning. That means simplifying as much as you can without changing the meaning of what you're saying. Earlier I mentioned the arrangement we had at "Good Morning America" with the author Isaac Asimov, who agreed to fill in anytime a guest failed to show up. Asimov was a science fiction author of wide renown, but he was also a great popularizer of science fact, and many of his books shed light on scientific mysteries for the general public. To me he was always at the top of his game when he was able to make comprehensible to our audience a complex scientific theory or development. He kept it simple, explaining things in layman's terms and using examples whenever possible. But he never condescended to the audience. That's the secret of simplicity.

¶ **Brand Aversion Versus Branding.** Just before I began writing this chapter I listened to a radio interview with a British female pop singer. Like many listeners, I joined in progress. During the portion of the interview I heard - a good three or four minutes - neither she nor the interviewer ever identified her or her band, although both made reference to "the band." Nor did either of them name her album. Both missed multiple opportunities to tell listeners what they were discussing. At one point the interviewer said, "I understand the version of the CD that's been issued in this country has three additional tracks on it that weren't on the British original." Now how much effort would it have taken to insert the name of the CD in that statement?

"That's right," Ms. Unknown said, missing an opportunity to correct the interviewer's omission, "I'm very excited about it because when they cut one of those songs out of the U.K. version I sat down and cried. It was my favorite song of all the songs we recorded." It may have been her favorite, but she failed to name it. To add to a listener's frustration, after Ms. Unknown told that story, the DJ said, "Let's listen to it," and then played the still-unidentified song on the still-unidentified CD by the still-unnamed artist. "That's great," he said at the end, giving a strong third party endorsement to a product this listener could not identify. "Why thank you," she said. Now, if I had liked that song and went to the online iTunes store, what keywords would I have typed into the search box? "My CD?" "Missing song?" Even if I had gone to the Virgin Megastore, where clerks are knowledgeable, it would be a long shot that one of them would be able to identify "that new album by a British woman with a song on it that wasn't on the original U.K. release." But that was all the identification I could muster from the interview.

It is the job of the radio host to identify his interview subject for his listeners. A good radio interviewer does that with regularity - every third or fourth question. Watch Larry King's interview program on CNN and you'll see what I mean. King's half century of radio experience - and the fact that his show is also broadcast on radio - lead him to use his guest's name frequently and to always announce upon returning to the program from a commercial, "We're talking with Senator Goodhue of South Carolina."

A good radio interviewer will also help you brand. She'll not only give your name, but also will mention why you're on the show. Terry Gross on NPR's "Fresh Air" will say from time to time, "We're talking with George Merlis, author of *How to Master the Media*." And she'll ask questions like this: "George Merlis, in your book *How to Master the Media* you contend that it's up to the guest to mention his brand during an interview. Why is this necessary?" But not every interviewer is that professional or conscientious, so it's up to you to do that branding. For instance, to a host who doesn't use the book name, I might say, "Well, [insert name of errant interviewer], my book, *How to Master the Media* gives readers the tools to be the best guest on your show that they can possibly be so that they help you do your job of entertaining and informing your audience." Again, it's not, "Well, *my book* gives readers the tools...."

Not too long ago I was media training a recording artist who asked me, "How do I get my name in if the radio interviewer never uses it. Won't that sound egotistical?" I explained to him that it was, indeed, a lot easier to work in a band's name than a solo artist's name. It's also easier to work in a book title or a company's name than your personal moniker. For example, "Well, our band, Wolfbite sounds a little like...." comes to the tongue a lot easier than, "The Frank Ritchie sound is a little like...." There was a tendency some years ago for recording artists to speak of themselves in the third person. I vividly remember Diana Ross on "Good Morning America" beginning the answer to a David Hartman question along these lines, "Well, that wasn't the right career move for Diana Ross so....." And she kept talking about herself in the third person. In the control room we joked about the identity of the Diana Ross lookalike David was interviewing. Shortly after that, I noticed that a whole raft of show business figures were speaking about themselves in the third person. Thankfully, that bizarre trend ended in the entertainment world, but it is alive and well in politics. When he was running for president in 1996, Senator Bob Dole spoken often about "Bob Dole," as if he were discussing another person. Sen. Dole's practice - eschewing the pronoun "I" in favor of using his full name - invited ridicule and, among others, "Saturday Night Live" was only too happy to accept the invitation, casting one of its regulars as Bob Dole who used his name in virtually every sentence he uttered. The senator may have been an extreme case, but listen carefully and you'll find politicians referring to themselves as "we," as if they were a royal presence, as in, "We're marching in the Fourth of July parade here in Iowa because Iowans believe in retail politics, pressing the flesh, talking in person to a candidate."

Since you don't want to talk about yourself in the third person, it is difficult - but not impossible - to identify yourself if a radio interviewer fails to do it for you. The easiest way to do it is to quote someone else. "You know, it was a real honor when *Rolling Stone* wrote, 'Frank Ritchie is the new Elton John.'" Another way is to include yourself in a story: "I dropped my middle name, Philip, when I was 12 and became just Frank Richie." Obviously, you resort to these awkward strategies only if forced to by your interviewer's failure to identify you.

Telephone Interviews

Often a radio interview will be conducted over the phone. So, too, will many - if not most - print interviews. In a phone interview you are like the radio listener - you have no visual clues to your interviewer's attitude, expression, or demeanor. Still, phone interviews offer some unique advantages over in-person interviews. As with many things, those advantages come with a downside, too.

For the media, the advantages of phoners are obvious: a print or radio reporter sitting at his desk and working the phones can reach many contacts in the time it might take him to travel to one venue and interview a single source. Additionally, the phoner gives the reporter the flexibility to call you, interview you, call someone else, get a different point of view on the subject, and call you back to get your reaction - setting the stage for a good, rousing conflict of quotes in his story Even "beat" reporters use the phone extensively. A reporter assigned to Congress is more likely to phone various congressional sources for quotes and information than he is to wander the halls of the institution, knocking on doors to see sources in person.

I estimate that 80 to 90 percent of the interviews I conducted during my newspaper career were phoners. I wrote hundreds of stories without ever seeing the interview subjects with whom I was dealing. I had a fair number of regular sources and contacts whom I never met in person; they were solely telephone acquaintances.

A phone call from a reporter will not necessarily come to your office during normal business hours. A reporter might call you at home and at extremely odd hours. Most morning newspapers lock their first editions after 9 or 10 p.m. Reporters seeking information on stories may work the phones right up until that deadline. So if you're a source, don't be surprised to pick up a late evening phone call and find a journalist on the line. As a reporter for the *World-Telegram and The Sun,* I placed more than a few calls to news sources in their homes well after their bedtimes. Calling people at 11 p.m. or midnight a for comment on a story usually yielded far more unguarded statements than I got when I called during business hours. It also yielded more than a few exasperated cries of, "How dare you call me at this hour of the night?" followed by the slamming of a handset.

Even television, that most visual of media, will sometimes uses phone interviews when there are no other options. Usually this involves a breaking story and an interview subject who is at a location inaccessible to cameras. The day Islamic extremists assassinated Egyptian President Anwar Sadat, I made a decision to keep "Good Morning America" on the air beyond its normal two hours and we filled the earliest part of the third hour by interviewing prominent commentators and experts over the phone until we could get live guests into our New York and Washington studios. By remaining on the air using phoners, we were in position to be the first network program to report that Sadat was dead and not, as Egyptian spokespersons initially reported, merely wounded.

THE UP- AND DOWNSIDES OF PHONERS

The advantages of phone interviews for the reporter are obvious. And there are advantages for you as well, but there is also a downside to phoners. Let's deal with the negative first. Think about how we normally converse on the phone. Without eye contact, we tend to be more open, more confidential, and more revealing of our feelings than we are in face-to-face conversations. Unable to see the response of the other party, we imagine his acceptance of our argument and his agreement with our points - why else does he stay on the line? That assumed agreement leads to still more openness on our part. That openness is a pitfall in phone interviews with the media. We are talking to a reporter using the same instrument that leads us into natural, relaxed conversation with our best friend, but a reporter is never our best friend. The telephone has a way of lulling us into a state of self-revelation and in a phone interview that may lead us to stray from our agenda, casually stroll right up the gallows steps, and hang ourselves with our own words.

So it's incumbent on you to be on guard when doing media phoners. When you talk to a reporter on the phone, you are working, not chatting. And no matter how conversational the reporter gets, she is working, too. In fact, that casual, conversational attitude she strikes on the phone is most likely just a highly refined technique she uses to get sources to be more revelatory than they really want to be. That said, the very same aspect of phoners that allows you to forget you're talking to a reporter - the absence of any visual response - also allows you to use the phone to its greatest advantage.

A phone interview is like an open-book test. You can - no, you *should* - have your Positive Message Statements laid out on a table or desk in front of you. If you've noticed that there is a flaw in your interview technique, you can post notes to yourself such as "Slow Down!" or "Give Specifics!" or "Remember Why Should I Care!" Having these cues at hand will remind you of two things: First, you are not having a casual chat, but are working; and, second, that the goal of your work is getting your agenda through the reporter to her readers or listeners. You are not cheating on your college geology test if you read your own Positive Message Statements during a phoner. They are not crib notes; they are your points. The reporter may well be reading her questions, so why not read your answers? Further, I recommend putting each of your message points on a separate index card. When you work one into the interview, turn the card over - that way you are less likely to repeat any of your agenda points unnecessarily and you'll have a clear indication of your remaining points.

To guard against becoming too chatty during phone interviews, I encourage my clients to stand up and gesture broadly; you should do that, too. If you do stand and gesture, you're unlikely to fall into the trap of putting your feet up on the desk, letting down your guard, and saying something you will later regret. Also, expansive gestures help you make your voice more interesting for radio interviews conducted over the phone.

CALLS OUT OF THE BLUE

If a reporter phones you out of the blue and he wants to do an interview right then and there, say "No." These calls are the equivalent of a TV ambush interview. You need to buy yourself enough time to get organized. You also want to find out if the reporter is who he claims to be and if the story he's working on is actually the story he described to you or if that is a just a cover to engage you in a conversation about something else. In fact, the "reporter" on the phone may not be a reporter at all - something you'll learn by calling him back at his publication or radio station. That caller could be a competitor on a fishing expedition or someone with an ax to grind. I heard of one possibly apocryphal case where a private detective, identifying himself as a reporter, called someone in an attempt to lure him into making slanderous remarks against a particularly litigious client who was looking for grounds to file a lawsuit. You are perfectly within your rights to suggest a later time for the interview. Tell him, "I can't talk to you right now, I've got a meeting about to start. Let me call you back in two hours." If he says he's on deadline, be suspicious. Oftentimes he's not on deadline at all, but is saying he is because he fears you won't call back. Sometimes his deadline is self-imposed; he wants to complete his interview with you so he can call a second source and get reaction to your comments. Sometimes, he simply doesn't want to wait until he actually is on deadline to write his story. When I began working as a reporter for *The World-Telegram,* I sat next to a veteran newsman who was *always* on deadline. It was funny to hear him tell someone at 10 a.m. that he was on deadline and then hear him tell another source he was on deadline at 4 p.m. The real deadline for the section of the paper we worked on was 6 p.m. Nonetheless, his ploy of "I'm on deadline" almost always worked.

If the reporter phoning you is really on deadline, he may have waited until the last minute for a reason - specifically so you don't have time to prepare an adequate response. This was a trick Bob Woodward and Carl Bernstein of the *Washington Post* often used during their Watergate investigation, and they chronicled that practice in their book *All the President's Men.* As an example, they would call Attorney General John Mitchell just before deadline so that there was no time for his team to concoct a response or to do damage control. Now this isn't to say that reporters only call on deadline to entrap you. Sometimes, news breaks right up against a deadline. When it does and they're trying to get comment on the breaking developments, the deadline is very real and there is no trickery involved. You will know those instances by the circumstances of the story. If your plant sprang a leak of toxic chemicals half an hour before the local newspaper's deadline, the reporter is not playing games when he calls you and says he's on deadline. Still, never talk to a cold caller right away; call him back - even if your delay is only five or ten minutes. You need time to organize yourself and your ideas for each interview.

Those deadline calls will frequently come to your home, even if you have an unlisted number. Reporters are adept at ferreting out unlisted numbers, cell phone numbers, and even home e-mail accounts.

Once you've made satisfactory arrangements for the interview, array your PMSs in front of you, round up any additional notes you may need, and - as a guard against misstatements - invite in a witness to hear your side of the interview. Then set up your recorder. Most phones can be hooked into a simple, inexpensive device that permits recording of both sides of a conversation. (I bought one at Radio Shack for under $20.) Additionally, many home answering machines can record both sides of a phone call.

When you are set up, call the reporter, alert him that you are recording the interview, and tell him how much time you can devote to him ("I can give you ten minutes - I'm sure that will be adequate.") As always, if the interview is going very well, you can extend the ten minutes for as long as it suits you. If you're dissatisfied with the interview's progress, stick to the time limit you announced at the outset. You'll want to put a stopwatch to the conversation so you know exactly when you can bail out if it is going poorly. With each question the reporter asks, study your PMSs and see whether the question leads logically to one of them or whether there is a relatively easy bridge you can build between a short form answer and a PMS. Again, don't be shy about reading your PMSs. He can't see you and it's the best way of getting them into the interview. After you've gotten in all your points, turn your index cards back over and repeat any agenda points you want to emphasize - just remember to vary the phrasing slightly the second time.

My most successful interview was a phoner with *TV Guide*. I quite literally read my part from a script I had written. I did not just have a list of Positive Message Statements; I had quips, jokes, pithy comments - all of which I had written in advance. The circumstances were these: when I was executive producer of "Good Morning America," show business reporter Rona Barrett was lured away by the "Today Show," and as a replacement we hired and then quickly fired a woman I'll call Mary Sunshine. Mary had done the best audition I'd ever seen and followed it with thirteen weeks of disappointing performance. It was as if she had expended all her talent in the audition. Additionally, Mary got distracted by the perks of her job and spent too much of her time and energy on them and not enough on gathering gossipy show business news for the show. One glaring example: she spent two-thirds of her very generous wardrobe allowance on shoes, although on-air she always appeared seated behind a desk talking directly to camera. In 13 weeks, viewers never once saw her feet and those pricey shoes she'd bought!

When ABC fired Mary, she did not go quietly into the night but called *TV Guide* with her version of this abbreviated career. The magazine saw a good conflict and hence a good story - little David (Mary) versus big, bad Goliath (ABC). As the show's executive producer, I was Goliath's spokesperson - if not of Goliath himself. I knew *TV Guide* was going to go into this story with a pro-David attitude. How could they not? So I had my work cut out for me. Aware it was going to be an uphill battle, I sat down at my typewriter - which tells what ancient history this story is - and wrote out every point I thought Mary might make in her interview. I then wrote responses to every one of them, making those responses as quoteworthy as I could.

The *TV Guide* writer was in California, where Mary Sunshine lived, and I was in New York, so my interview was a phoner. I had my tape recorder hooked up and my index cards arrayed on my desk in front of me. As the interview progressed, I realized from the reporter's questions that I had anticipated all Mary's complaints. For each question that came out of those complaints I had not just an answer, but a concise, pithy quote. Now, when I was preparing for the interview, I had come up with one line that really pleased me and I thought, "This one ought to be the last line of the article." When the article appeared, it *was* the last line. After describing the shoe travesty, I said: "The problem with Mary Sunshine was she fell in love with her limousine and forgot where it was going." It not only ended the article, but epitomized its tone. On that rare occasion, Goliath won.

I tell you this story not to pat my own back for being clever, but to show just how effective you can be by having complete message points prepared in advance and by reading them during a phone interview. Remember, your preparation is only half the assignment. Your notes are there to be used. On a number of occasions in media training sessions, I've had clients go through the exercise of preparing messages for phone interviews only to leave them sitting on the desk in front of them, unread and unused. When I see them doing that I throw this question into the interview, "Aren't you going to use those great notes you've prepared?" That usually gets a laugh, but it also produces the desired reaction: they begin using their notes. For reasons unclear to me, some people are uncomfortable reading - or even referring to written material - during an interview. Get over it. Take advantage of the unique opportunity you have in a phoner; use your notes to get all your points across. All the preinterview preparation in the world is of no use if you don't use what you've prepared.

There's a very good reason that the first commandment of interviews is Thou Shalt be Prepared. Without that advance preparation, an interview is a game of chance. And media exposure is too valuable to leave to chance.

In the next chapter, I'll review another occasion where you can have your PMSs in front of you - news conferences - and I'll deal with the unique challenges of performing on-camera demonstrations.

CHAPTER 10

WHEN YOU'RE IN CHARGE: ON-CAMERA DEMONSTRATIONS AND NEWS CONFERENCES

There are two circumstances when your media encounter is specifically about your agenda and, usually, only about your agenda. These are news conferences and on-camera television demonstrations. In the latter, you are booked solely to explain and/or demonstrate your product (I include as products how-to books, such as cookbooks). Therefore, the entire segment likely will accommodate your agenda (i.e., your product) and you have far more control over the situation than you would in a conventional broadcast or print interview.

In the news conference, reporters and camera crews have come to the venue at your invitation to hear the news you will make. In other words, your agenda has drawn them, so you are in charge - at least at the beginning. Later in this chapter, I'll show you how to remain in charge throughout a news conference or regain control should things start to get out of hand. After reading this chapter, you'll have specific tools to help you maintain your cool and handle even the most challenging news conferences or on-camera demonstrations.

ON-CAMERA DEMONSTRATIONS

For our purposes, a demonstration can be something as simple as voicing-over some prepared videotape you've supplied to the program, or it may be holding up a prop and showing it to the camera. More involved demonstrations are actual how-to segments like food preparation, repair, design, or technical projects. The following are some tips for any physical demonstration before a TV camera:

MAKING ON-CAMERA DEMOS WORK
¶ Rehearse, rehearse, rehearse.
¶ Move slowly.
¶ Hold items steady.
¶ Hold items for a long time.
¶ Make sure your dominant palm
faces the close-up camera.
¶ Talk while you work, but talk about the work.
¶ Be prepared to accordion your demonstration.

¶ **Rehearse, rehearse, rehearse.** You'll recall that our fourth commandment of interviews was practice, practice, practice? Well, for demonstrations, rewrite that as rehearse, rehearse, rehearse. At home or in the office, practice doing the demonstration at different lengths: two minutes, three minutes, four minutes, and - may you be this lucky - five minutes. Prepare all your pieces, ingredients, and tools beforehand. Lay them out in a logical order so the camera follows them left to right (meaning they are right to left for you because you are facing the camera). Use a video camera and tape your rehearsal. First time through, have the camera on a wide shot to simulate the TV studio's master. But on your second run-through, focus on the close-ups, so you can see if they are working. If at all possible, feed the output of your video camera into a TV set so you can monitor your movements as you go. Don't be thrown by the image: TV is a *direct* image, while we are used to seeing ourselves in a mirror, which is actually a *reverse* image. When you move your right hand to the right the monitor makes it appear as if you are moving your left hand to the left. The television image is the accurate one because it is another person's view of us. But since most of us usually see ourselves only in a mirror, the TV monitor's image may be very disconcerting at first.

(Just for the fun of it, see out how much mirrors distort reality by going to www.vggallery.com/painting/p_0527.htm and looking at the self-portrait Vincent Van Gogh painted after he cut off his ear. The portrait makes it appear Van Gogh cut off his right ear. In fact, he cut off his left ear, but he painted his mirror image, hence the error.)

¶ **Move slowly.** Jan Rifkinson, the first director of "Good Morning America," used to tell guests who were doing demos, "Move as if you are under water," which is a sound piece of advice. Visualize how the resistance of water keeps you from making rapid movements when you're in a lake or pool. That's exactly how you should move when on camera, both in your rehearsals and when you're doing the show for real. Close-up cameras have difficulty following rapid movements; you can sometimes yank items right out of the camera's frame if you move them too fast. Even if the items stay in frame, rapid movement may seem like a blur to the viewer at home.

¶ **Hold items steady.** The close-up camera exaggerates any sort of motion, so if you hold something in a shaky or unsteady manner, it's hard for viewers to see it. This is especially critical if there is anything they have to read - such as a book jacket or CD cover. The easiest way to hold an item steady is to have your hands resting on the table or counter while you hold it; the solid base on which you're resting your hands will keep them from moving. If you must hold an item up, try holding it with both hands, elbows bent 90 degrees and locked tight against your ribs. This gives your forearms and hands support and rigidity.

¶ **Hold items for a long time.** If you think you've held something in place for enough time, you're probably wrong. Extend the hold by at least 50 percent more time. You do this to let the camera catch up with you. If you hold up a book, a CD, or a plate of freshly prepared asparagus and take it down quickly, the camera may not have enough time to find it, frame up on it, and get it into focus. In the studio, before you begin, ask if they'll place a monitor in your line of sight so you can sneak a peek and make sure that your item is on camera long enough for viewers to identify it. (A demo is the *only* TV appearance during which it's O.K. to look at the monitor.)

¶ **Make sure your dominant palm faces the close-up camera.** If you are standing at a demonstration counter with your elbows bent and your hands outstretched, palms perpendicular to the counter, the close-up camera should be on your left side if you are right-handed and on your right side if you are left-handed. In other words, the close-up camera should be shooting *into* the palm of your dominant hand. If you are wondering why, let's take the case of a right-handed guest doing a demonstration.

If the close-up camera is shooting from his right, the back of his dominant hand is going to cover the details of the work he is doing.

It is surprising how many television directors don't know this very basic rule for shooting close-ups of demos. You can't direct your own segment, so what can you do about it? I suggest that during the run-through you ask which is the close-up camera and, if it's on the wrong side, gently point out to the director or to the stage manager that you are right-handed (or left-handed) and your right (or left) hand will block the close-up camera. If there is no run-through, before you go on ask the stage manager which is the close-up camera. If it is on the wrong side, move even more slowly and periodically take your hand away from the work so the camera can get an unencumbered shot.

¶ **Talk while you work, but talk about the work.** As bad as directors who don't know where to place their close-up cameras are hosts who ask you off-point questions while you are doing a demonstration. Imagine you are about to show the host how to score a mango. As you begin, you mention that the mango is the most popular fruit in the world, even though it is far less popular in the United States. Picking up on the word fruit, she asks you whether the tomato is a fruit or a vegetable. If you answer the question while continuing to score the mango, the viewers lose out on having you narrate while you demonstrate - the most basic element of a demonstration. The solution: stop scoring that mango while you answer the question and then segue back to the demonstration and talk about what you are doing as you do it.

¶ **Be Prepared to Accordion Your Demonstration.** Just before you go on, you may be told you'll have four minutes. You go into your four-minute mode - but you're only two-thirds of the way in and the stage manager is frantically signaling the talent to wrap it up. This happens all the time on live shows, where segments after the first or second act are often squeezed because those earlier acts ran long. When the talent, responding to the stage manager, says to you, "Now, moving along, how do we get to the final product?" you need to accordion your demo. If you had rehearsed, rehearsed, and rehearsed some more and if, in these rehearsals, you ran through your demonstration at a variety of lengths, you can easily move to the shortest version for the remaining steps. You may feel cheated by this rush job, but you won't appear flustered on the air.

You can deliver some of the most effective messages in a demonstration. When you're doing something on camera, you command the viewer's attention. Just remember that in addition to the "show" there's the "tell." You want to work your PMSs into your discussion of what you're doing.

News Conferences

A news conference is an opportunity to reach many media outlets simultaneously. But it also presents a singular set of challenges to a spokesperson. More about those in a moment; first let's consider when and why you might want to call a news conference.

A variety of circumstances demand news conferences. Some government agencies hold press briefings daily or weekly to fill in the press corps on the activities of the agency. Companies typically hold news conferences to announce new products, reveal major economic plans, or respond to developments either good or bad that may impact their earnings. Nonprofits often call news conferences to announce new initiatives, new fundraising activity, or developments made possible by their efforts. In times of labor strife - or impending strife - it is not unusual for both labor and management to set out their positions before the public in a series of dueling news conferences. A news conference sends the signal that your story is more important than the ordinary grist for reportorial mills; that it demands the news media's in-person attention.

Sometimes, news conferences are conducted when there is no news; they are designed simply to keep speculation and bad information from creating an inaccurate public impression. During the 2002 sniper attacks in the Washington, DC, area there were daily news conferences, usually led by Charles Moose, the police chief of Montgomery Country, Maryland. At many of these sessions, Chief Moose had no real news to report, but he kept briefing the media on a regular basis to let the nervous public know police agencies were investigating the shootings and were following all leads. By conducting such news conferences, Chief Moose could also rebut speculation and dampen rumors. While reporters might grumble that there had been "no news," if

185

the press briefing prevented dissemination of speculation and rumor, it served the purposes both of the police and of journalism by keeping inaccurate information in check. On other occasions Chief Moose used news conferences to try to communicate with the snipers. In those instances, the conferences themselves became part of the story in addition to being the mechanism for covering the story.

**A NEWS CONFERENCE STARTS
WHEN THE MEDIA SHOWS UP**

Chief Moose got off to a rocky beginning with his news conferences. At the start of the first one, he told the assembled reporters, "You are going to follow these rules.... Don't make me look like an @#%**." Aside from appearing authoritarian to the media, which was bound to get their adversarial juices flowing, the chief probably appeared uncouth to those in the public who were viewing one of the many live feeds of the news conference. He recovered in later news conferences and handled them well.

WHAT TO BRING TO A NEWS CONFERENCE

Give the assembled press supporting documentation and visuals at the news conference. If you are announcing a new product or service, include thorough descriptions in the handout materials. Lay out in detail the most minute and technical data in these handouts. You should give the media photographs, diagrams, videotape, audio tape, CD-ROMs and/or DVDs to enhance your presentation. Insofar as videotape or video DVDs are concerned, you are usually better served by handing out a B-roll package - the elements a reporter can use to make a story - than by handing out an edited story. In most cases, samples of the product should be available for the reporters to play with; this often yields first-person accounts which, if they are favorable, amount to impartial third party endorsements.

If a news conference kicks off an event, you may want to supply both background video and a live video feed. One of the most successful projects I ever did involved just that - B-roll and a live video feed. Honda was about to ship to Japan the first batch of Accord coupes, made in the company's plant in Ohio. We staged the news conference on a pier in Portland, Oregon. We supplied the assembled media with B-roll of the manufacture of the autos, and we covered the news conference live with three strategically placed cameras and fed the event worldwide via satellite. The payoff came when the Accord coupes rolled out of the parking lot, up a ramp, and onto the ship that would take them across the Pacific, the very first Japanese cars made in America and exported to Japan. Hundreds of TV stations nationwide picked up and used some of that coverage, as did numerous broadcasters in Japan and two of the three broadcast network nightly newscasts in the U.S.

The lesson here is you'll really enhance your news conference if you give the attending television outlets additional video to take away with the printed material and still photographs. Newspapers love visuals in the form of stills, charts, and graphs, almost as much as television loves rolling video. Additionally, many newspapers now will use video of an event on their web site, another good outlet for B-roll packages. For radio, if you're dealing with any product or project that involves sound of any kind, make audio cassettes and/or CDs with those sounds and distribute them to the radio stations that attend the news conference. You may also want to include in the audio handout material soundbites from persons unavailable for the actual news conference.

News Conferences Are Not Interviews

As anyone who has watched a presidential news conferences on live television knows, a massed press can be a lot tougher than a single reporter. In a one-on-one interview a reporter usually builds a line of questioning, much as a writer would build a story. He follows up on answers and there is an organic growth to the exchange. Not so in a news conference. Many reporters will come to the event with their own agendas - some of those will mesh with yours, others may conflict. In a one-on-one, you know after a few questions where you stand, whether it will be easy or difficult to accommodate your agenda in the session. But because you are confronting multiple agendas in a news conference, you usually face both accommodating and obstructing questions. There is also an almost inevitable herd instinct at play in a news conference. Dodge a question in a one-on-one interview and the reporter may or may not press the point. Dodge a question in front of a dozen reporters and at least a few of them will be waving eagerly to get your attention so they can put your feet back to the fire.

And that's just the beginning of the differences between a press conference and a one-on-one interview. Even if you've gotten comfortable enough with your media mastery skills to consider an interview with a single reporter to be an opportunity, you may find a news conference, where you'll face a dozen reporters at once, daunting. After all, when you prepare for a one-on-one, you can bone up on the reporter's work, his leanings, and his publication. You can assess attitudes and style. But you can't do that for the dozen publications and broadcast outlets that will be sending representatives to your news conference. Before a one-on-one, your research can help you gauge the level of sophistication of the reporter's readers or listeners and you can tailor your answers to her audience. In a one-on-one, you likely will have a warmup period, which you can use to plant seeds for questions that will serve your agenda. None of that is available to you in a news conference. You may have reporters representing the most sophisticated publications and representatives of supermarket tabloids. Moreover, there is scant opportunity for warming up - you can't very well chat up five or ten reporters before the formal beginning of the session.

Your news conference attendees may represent a variety of media as well. There will be television cameras, still photographers, print reporters, and radio correspondents. You may be speaking into a veritable forest of microphones, and you may be facing not one or two but half a dozen bright television lights and the repeated blinding flashes of still cameras. Instead of the conversational tones you've come to expect from one-on-one interviewers, the reporters may shout their questions at you. Because they are in competition with each other to get their own questions asked and because they know that the time available to them is finite, their manners may go by the board.

A news conference poses a host of challenges for you: How do you answer a rude, shouted question? Do you adopt the cosmetic style and posture of a television interview? Do you keep your answers simple, even though some reporters represent sophisticated and specialized media outlets? How do you keep one reporter from dominating the session by asking a string of follow-up questions or making a speech? How do you end a news conference if the reporters' flow of questions shows no sign of abating? How do you deal with redundant questions?

Despite the challenges, a news conference is a unique opportunity to reach multiple media outlets - and their audiences - with great economy of time. And an array of simple techniques will help you maximize that opportunity.

You might be conflicted: should you speak to the lowest common denominator or should you tailor each answer to the particular audience served by each attending reporter? Attempting the latter puts an undue burden on you; you'll have to keep changing your tone and level of sophistication throughout the news conference, and you'll have to remember to whom you're speaking with each answer. Moreover, if you answer any question with the most sophisticated audience in mind, you run the risk of having the same question asked again by someone who represents a mass-market outlet and wants your answer in language his readers can comprehend. So for a news conference, go with the basics. Oftentimes the basic answer will suffice for all the media present. For example, I do a lot of work prepping scientists for news briefings. The range of reporters at the conference may run from *USA Today* to the journal, *Science.* Clearly, the *Science* readers are a lot more sophisticated about the science than the average *USA Today* reader. I tell my clients to use the *USA Today* answers and then, if the *Science* reporter needs additional information, he can usually glean it from the printed handout material that you distribute at the news conference. Address the oral part of the news conference to the mass audience. Sophisticated supporting documents should satisfy the specialists who need a more advanced level of detail. An added benefit is that various publications - even those catering to the mass audience - may post the more sophisticated material from your handouts on their web sites as a service for those who might want or need such data.

OPENING REMARKS: YOU'RE IN CONTROL

Your dread of a single reporter may multiply many times over when you are to face a horde of them in a news conference, but remember this: the reporters are attending in response to your agenda. When you or your publicity representatives announced the conference, you told the media that you're about to make news, and that news was of sufficient interest for them to attend. You have initial control over the agenda because you've told them, usually in very general terms, what the announcement is about. ("Sen. Goodhue will announce his plans concerning the presidential election," "The Ynot Corporation is going to announce the first major innovation in the Bumblepuppy product line in three years," "Stupendous Foundation is going to announce a major grant in the health care sector.") The first thing you do in a news conference is take the podium and make opening remarks that further define the agenda. Never begin a news conference without making an opening statement. If you don't take advantage of that opportunity, you are yielding control of the agenda right at the start.

Before the media assemble, place your opening statement and your Positive Message Statements - in bullet points on separate index cards - on the lectern, so you'll be ready to use them during the session.

Don't read the first or last sentences of your opening remarks; deliver them from memory. If you begin by engaging the room - and not staring down at your notes - and conclude your introductory remarks the same way, you will command the attention of your audience. Make your opening and closing sentences assertive and quoteworthy. Television is more likely to use remarks addressed to the audience than those read from the lectern. So start and finish your opening statement with strong stuff that you've rehearsed, memorized, and can deliver with vigorous authority. Here's an example: "Today, Ynot Corporation is announcing a major breakthrough in the production of environmentally friendly home fuel cells - a breakthrough that will allow every home in America to generate its own electricity at a fraction of the price we now pay for power." And, similarly, this last sentence: "And so the Ynot Fuel cell will help reduce our dependence on foreign energy sources and, at the same time, significantly reduce air pollution." If you can deliver lines like these without referring to your notes, the TV cameras at your news conference will love you for it.

DRESS THE LECTERN

Earlier I advised placing your PMSs on the lectern in front of you at a news conference. An occasional glance down will refresh your memory about which one you can deploy to answer a given question, and that gesture does not look unnatural. It will look peculiar, however, if you address your answers to the lectern and not to the reporters in the audience. Use the written PMSs only for reference; do not read them. It's a good idea to reduce your PMSs to bullet points so you won't appear to be reading a script. If each point is on a separate index card, you can flip that card after you deploy the message point. This keeps you from making points redundantly and encourages you to work in all your agenda messages. What to do with notes and index cards at the end of the session? Leave them there on the lectern. Detail an associate to clean up after you. Why plant them before you begin and why leave them there at the end? I'm sure you've seen speakers approach a lectern and, as I call it, get dressed. They walk up, fumble for their notes in a pocket - or, worse yet, in a briefcase. Then they organize the notes on the lectern, all the while looking down. Once organized, they begin reading the notes without engaging the room. Approaching a lectern this way certainly does not command attention or confidence; a speaker who is so dependent on his written materials loses some of his credibility. And that's why it's a good idea to dress the lectern in advance, stride up behind it, and begin with that memorized opening line. At the very end, after the Q&A, don't waste time and diminish your command of the moment by picking up all the detritus on the lectern; leave that chore to an associate who'll do the cleanup after you have left the stage. It's important, though, that *someone* round up that material; you don't want to leave notes where an inquiring reporter might snatch them up and use them to write a snide story about how you prepared for the news conference.

ADDITIONAL NEWS CONFERENCE TIPS

¶ **Don't rest your elbows on the lectern.** It looks sloppy and on television sends the wrong body language message. Also, don't grasp the lectern. If you do you're unlikely to use your hands to gesture. I've seen speakers hold on to the lectern as if it were a lifeboat lowered into the icy waters of the Atlantic when the *Titanic* sank. The lectern is there for your notes, not to hold up your frail being. If you want to command the news media's respect and attention, stand on your own two feet.

¶ **Dress the room correctly.** How many television stories have you seen that included tape from news conferences where the only supporting graphic was the name of the hotel posted on the lectern? You are not there to promote a hotel; you are there to promote a cause, a product, a position, or a policy, so bring signage to hang on the lectern and, if possible, more signage to hang behind you. It may be the corporate logo, it may be the name of the cause, product, position, or policy. Regardless, visual aids help. Politicians cover the walls behind them with "wallpaper" that features a repeat graphic, usually with a campaign or party symbol and a brief slogan. No matter how the speaker is photographed, the wallpaper appears in the background, clearly legible.

DON'T STOP THINKING ABOUT TOMMORROW
When you're dressing the room, be sure all words on the background wallpaper are spelled correctly. In May, 2007, Sen. Hillary Clinton addressed a gathering in Silicon Valley in front of wallpaper that read, "Better Jobs for To*mm*orrow." While it's a safe bet Sen. Clinton didn't oversee the hanging of the wallpaper, she was the one latenight comics cited when they showed the gaffe.

If you find an error in your wallpaper, have it corrected, have the wallpaper taken down or, if all else fails, call attention to it yourself so you are distanced from whoever make the mistake.

¶ **Rehearse with media stand-ins.** It's a good idea to run through the prepared portion of your news conference in the actual venue, using stand-ins for the media. This is particularly useful in helping you place and play to still and TV cameras; you want to be certain the cameras will have a good, clear shot of you at the lectern. I attended a news conference in Las Vegas where the American flag was downstage of the lectern, partially blocking the TV cameras' shot from the elevated camera platform. If the news conference organizers had taken the trouble to stand on the camera platform in advance, they would have seen that the flag blocked the cameras and they would have moved it.

¶ **Initiate the question period.** At the end of your prepared statement, call for questions. You will always want to set a time limit on the Q&A session, as in: "I'll now take questions for ten minutes." This puts everyone on notice that you are beginning a limited-duration Q&A session and not an open forum for reporters to give their opinions. Any reporter who starts making a speech after you've given a finite length to the Q&A session is likely to be admonished into silence by his colleagues. In the event you do get a speechifier and his colleagues don't shut him up, you have control of the lectern and the microphone, so pick out a question in his rambling discourse and answer it. "I can see you're concerned about how we will distribute these fuel cells, and let me answer that." In other words, if no question is forthcoming, infer one.

¶ **Prime the pump, if you need to.** On rare occasions, the reporters may be slow to raise their hands and ask the first question. If this happens, prime the pump by asking yourself a question. Phrase it this way, "I'm frequently asked about how we can deliver these fuel cells on the schedule we've announced." Then go on to answer it. Always ask yourself a question that enables one of your PMSs. It can even be one of the questions from your prepared list of hostile questions - one that you can answer with a deftly built bridge to a PMS. It's likely you're going to phrase the question in a far less hostile manner than a challenging reporter will and, by asking yourself the question, you've preempted the reporters from asking it. If a reporter does ask a variation of your tough first question, you can say, "I addressed that in answer to the first question." (This same technique is effective if a number of reporters feel compelled to ask you the same question. If you've already answered it, tell them that and move on; you need not answer the same question repeatedly.)

¶ **Start with a "friend."** Obviously there's no need to prime the pump if the reporters jump at the opportunity to ask questions. In that case, it's a good policy to take your first question from a reporter who has treated you fairly in the past, because chances are he will do it again. Do not recognize for the first question someone who you know to be a skeptical or tough questioner. Why start your Q&A on a negative note? Often the first question or two set the tone for the entire news conference. Now, I know I wrote in an earlier chapter, "Don't assume that you have friends in the media." Calling on someone who has been sympathetic in the past does not guarantee a gentle question, but the odds are better for you. A reporter who was sympathetic in the past *may* change her spots in a news conference, but you can almost bet that someone who has been antagonistic in the past will be antagonistic at your news conference as well.

¶ **Work the room.** When you are delivering your opening and closing statements and when you're answering questions, speak to the whole room. For questions, start your response looking at the reporter who asked you the question, express a thought, then move on to the reporters on your left, express a thought, turn your attention to the reporters on your right, and so on. Don't do a radar sweep of the room; you're not looking for incoming aircraft and you won't engage anyone that way. Also, don't work a fixed spot in the room. As a reporter, I've been to a number of news conferences where the spokesperson addressed all his statements to a static spot at the back of the room. I once asked a back-of-the-room concentrator why he was doing that and he told me, "Well, I was told to always address my remarks to an imaginary clock on the back wall." Talk to an imaginary clock when you have warm human bodies to address? Nonsense! Talk to the people in the room.

If the question was a friendly one, work your way back and conclude your answer looking directly at the questioner. That way, if he's got a follow-up, you're in position to recognize him. If the question was a tough one, don't go back to him at the end of your answer. That way you can move on to someone else for the next question even if the tough questioner has a follow-up.

¶ **Keep an eye on the time.** If you've told the assembled media that you'll take questions for fifteen minutes, and if the conference has been tough, after thirteen minutes have elapsed announce that time's almost up and you can take "one or two" additional questions. If things are going swimmingly, you can let the clock run a little longer before announcing you have time for one or two last queries. Use the *one or two* question phrase because it enables you to stop after one question. And that's what you should do if the first question after that announcement is an easy one that accommodates one of your message points. If, however, the first question is a stinker, take a second one in an effort to go out on a positive exchange. If the second one is a stinker, too, just end it; things are unlikely to get any better.

¶ **End with a summary statement.** Thank the reporters for attending and deliver a summary of your most important points. Usually your closer should be a brief condensation of your opening remarks.

The news conference is an invaluable tool in crisis communications. Many organizations prepare action plans for crises - readying an institutional response to various worst-case scenarios. No crisis plan is complete without a communication component. Whether the crisis you may face is an industrial accident with severe community-wide ramifications, an incident of workplace violence, a disease outbreak, an act of nature, or an act of terrorism, an essential part of your crisis response plan must be media communications. The next chapter deals with crisis communications, and I preface it with the hope that you never have to call on these tips and tools.

Chapter 11

CRISIS COMMUNICATIONS: ARE YOU PREPARED FOR THE WORST-CASE SCENARIO?

On September 10, 2001, Rudolph Giuliani was the weakened lame duck mayor of New York City. He was widely despised for his brusque, authoritarian manner which had grown more pronounced during his second term. His personal life was such a train wreck it had become fodder for latenight comedians. One day later, September 11, 2001, Rudolph Giuliani became the *de facto* spokesman of the United States; he was the face of authority and reassurance in the immediate aftermath of the terrorist attacks against the World Trade Center and the Pentagon.

The mayor went from lame duck to hero overnight thanks in large part to his skill in communicating about the unprecedented crisis. He rose to the occasion, convincingly conveying the breadth, scope, and severity of the attacks that took the lives of three thousand innocent people that awful day. He appeared to be a steady anchor and a compassionate captain in a confusing tempest. Giuliani had an advantage over President Bush, the officeholder one would have expected to be that anchor, in no small part because of his proximity to the largest disaster - the World Trade Center was walking distance from New York's City Hall. The president, on the other hand, wasn't even in Washington that day; prior scheduling had him at a photo-op in a second grade classroom in Sarasota, Florida, promoting his education plan. Uncertainty about other attacks led the president on a zigzag course around the country and it wasn't until early evening that he returned to the White House. So for the nearly twelve hours between the time the first plane hit and the time the president addressed the nation on live TV from the Oval Office, the New York mayor had the crisis communications stage largely to himself.

It is hard to believe that there was no national crisis plan for something like 9/11, but if there was, the media communications portion was missing or ignored. In New York, on the other hand, Mayor Giuliani may have been working from instinct, rather than in accordance with a plan, but his actions are instructive to us in assembling a crisis communication strategy.

Four qualities in Giuliani's response stand out and they are essential for establishing and maintaining communications control in a crisis. They should be the basis of every crisis communications plan.

> **Mayor Giuliani's 9/11**
> **Crisis Communications Strengths**
> **Early response.**
> **Frequent and uncomplicated media accessibility.**
> **Consistent candor.**
> **Empathy.**

While it may appear difficult to plan empathy, which is the emotional component of a spokesperson's response, it is not hard to envision how the public might respond to a crisis. For our purposes, empathy in crises like a terrorist attack, a major natural disaster, a Virginia Tech type shooting, or any other dire, life-threatening event, can be defined as seeing the event the same way the public does and addressing the public's predictable concerns. In crises, the media, which normally see themselves as writing the first draft of history, often add to their mandate the job of sharing national concern and bringing the public together. In fulfillment of both those roles the media are eager for high-ranking, empathetic crisis spokespersons. In the case of 9/11, it was Mayor Giuliani, who did everything right.

President Bush had another opportunity to take communications control of a crisis in 2005 when Hurricane Katrina struck the Gulf Coast and destroyed huge sections of New Orleans. But he blew the opportunity with a slow response and often less-than-empathetic statements. Bush had been on a five-week vacation at his ranch in Texas when the storm roared into the Gulf Coast. He was just a short plane ride from the devastated area, yet it took him three full days before he flew over the affected areas and two more days before he set foot in the region. Worse, yet, during those days, the president left his ranch for previously planned photo-op side trips to Arizona and California to promote his plan for the Medicare drug benefit. His staff, concerned that Bush appeared indifferent to the suffering of tens of thousands in New Orleans, put together a DVD with all the news coverage and urged him to watch it so he would gain insight into the depth and breadth of the problem. But the president didn't watch the DVD until he was flying to New Orleans on September 2, five days after the storm struck. In addition to the delayed response, once Bush was on-scene in the devastated area, there were a number of serious communications gaffes. It was reported that Coast Guard rescue helicopters were diverted from their mission to serve as a backdrop for a presidential photo-op. Another report said the presidential visit shut down the New Orleans airport, delaying delivery of three tons of needed food. Then, in fairly rapid succession over the course of just a few days, the president made these three statements:

**SOUNDING LESS-THAN-EMPATHETIC
IN KATRINA'S AFTERMATH**

"**I am satisfied with the response. I am not satisfied with all the results.**"

"**Heck of a job, Brownie,**" (directed to Michael Brown, the FEMA director whose agency was responding so poorly that nations around the world, including even U.S. archenemy *Cuba,* were offering assistance)

And, on learning that Sen. Trent Lott's house had been destroyed: "**Out of the rubble of Trent Lott's house... there's going to be a fantastic house. And I'm looking forward to sitting on the porch.**"

Time magazine characterized that last remark as "astonishingly tone-deaf to the homeless black citizens still trapped in the postapocalyptic water world of New Orleans."

Additionally, a day before his in-person visit, the president said, "I don't think anybody anticipated the breach of the levees." Unhappily for him, video later made available to the media showed a teleconference he attended the day before the storm hit in which a hurricane expert and FEMA Director Brown specifically warned the levees might not hold if Katrina scored a direct hit on New Orleans.

In the Katrina tragedy, the president ignored the Giuliani lessons of 9/11- early response, frequent and uncomplicated media accessibility, consistent candor, and empathy. It is critically important that in establishing your crisis communications plan you and your colleagues pay heed to those lessons.

IGNORING HIS OWN EXAMPLE

In August, 2007, responding to critics who complained he had not done enough to protect recovery and cleanup workers from the toxins at Ground Zero, Giuliani said: "I was at ground zero as often, if not more, than most of the workers. I was exposed to exactly the same things they were exposed to. So in that sense, I'm one of them." Ground Zero workers, who had spent multiple twelve-hour days digging through the toxic rubble, were outraged. The next day Giuliani tried to recover, claiming that "what I was trying to say... is that I empathize with them because I feel like I have that same risk." But, like many another politician, Giuliani was spinning something he said *on camera*, and it is clear from looking at the video of his remarks, which was posted on YouTube, his original statement was offhanded and less-than-empathetic.

YOUR CRISIS MANAGEMENT PLAN COMES FIRST

Before you craft a crisis *communications* plan, you have to have a crisis *management* plan. If you don't have such a plan and you are ad-libbing your crisis response, then all the speed, accessibility and empathy in the world aren't going to help you. You will quickly be viewed as stage-managing the event, doing a smoke-and-mirrors presentation to mask an inadequate response to an emergency. This is a lose-lose situation. In crises, there is no "which comes first, the chicken or the egg" question. You must have the management plan before you have the communications plan; otherwise you've nothing to communicate.

Preparing a crisis management plan is outside the purview of this book, but I will say that the time to plan for a crisis is in advance and that every conceivable department or division that will respond in the crisis must be involved in the planning. A key to your crisis management plan's success will be communication, because most crises, require some public response and unless there are adequate communications, the public won't know what to do. A crisis management plan without a communications component is just as futile as a crisis communications scheme without a crisis management plan.

INFORMATION THE PUBLIC NEEDS IN A CRISIS

Obviously, crises vary in degree, intensity, and effect on the public. A company's bankruptcy is a tragedy, one that deeply affects employees, customers, and stockholders. It might even have a ripple economic effect on a community or a region. The effects of such a crisis, while severe to those involved, are limited insofar as the affected population. The deadly swarm of tornadoes that leveled the town of Greensburg, Kansas, in the spring of 2007 was a contained crisis. The entire country felt deep sympathy for the townspeople, but the threat and effects were regional. The 9/11 terrorist attacks and the subsequent anthrax mailings had far wider ripples. In the first, the American mainland suffered 3,000 killed in its first significant foreign attack since the War of 1812, and the threat of further terrorist strikes frightened millions. After anthrax-tainted letters began showing up the previously benign mail slot in every American home suddenly became the potential portal for a deadly disease.

Whatever the crisis, the pubic wants answers to four basic questions which your communications plan must address:

> **WHAT THE PUBLIC WANTS TO KNOW IN A CRISIS SITUATION**
> How dangerous is this situation to me and to my family's physical and economic health?
>
> If there is direct danger, what individual and family actions should we take to mitigate risks?
>
> What steps are you, the responders, taking to mitigate the situation and to insure it does not happen again?
>
> If there is no direct danger to me or to my family, how can we be of service?

INFORMATION A SPOKESPERSON NEEDS TO COMMUNICATE

In addition to answering the public's questions, spokespersons should be ready to explain how the responders are going to do these four things:

> **WHAT CRISIS SPOKESPERSONS MUST EXPLAIN**
> How the response will mitigate the effects of the crisis.
>
> How the response will efficiently execute mitigation and recovery plans.
>
> How the response will allocate mitigation and recovery resources equitably and fairly.
>
> How the response will avoid squandering resources, including recovery personnel, material, and funds.

WHO SPEAKS IN THE CRISIS; HOW THEY SHOULD SPEAK

¶ **Designate spokespersons in advance.** When a crisis breaks, you frequently see multiple personalities jostling for the media spotlight, trying to manage the crisis communications. This could not be more counterproductive because it sends a message that nobody is in charge. Who can forget Secretary of State Alexander Haig's media response after would-be assassin John Hinckley, jr. wounded President Reagan? Haig announced to the White House reporters, "As of now, I'm in control here in the White House." In fact, he was not; the vice president, George H. W. Bush, was in charge, even though at that moment he was out of town. The Constitution provides a chain of succession and the vice president, speaker of the house of representatives and president *pro tem* of the senate are all in that chain. It remained for White House spokespersons and others who apparently were more familiar with the laws of presidential succession than Haig, to straighten out the communications mess.

A good crisis communications plan designates spokespersons in advance, and the fewer they are in number and the higher ranking they are in office, the better the plan. The more authoritative the spokespersons, the better. Both as a journalist and a member of the public, I don't want anyone telling me about an impending pandemic unless he has an M.D. after his name and is a very high official of an agency or organization that tracks and combats infectious diseases, such as the Centers for Disease Control. Hearing this information from a political appointee just doesn't reassure the public. And I certainly don't want to hear from a high-ranking physician who says, "A," and then hear from the political appointee saying, "B." All spokespersons need to be on the same page. If your agency or organization will need outside experts to vet your messages, recruit them in advance, brief them on your crisis management and communication plans, and enlist their cooperation and aid. If you fail to have experts at your disposal, the media will find other, often less-qualified, figures to interview.

In the absence of official crisis communicators, the media will call everybody and anybody in an organization when a crisis breaks. It's imperative that everyone in the organization knows who the proper spokespersons are and refers reporters to those spokespersons. If people don't know who to refer the media to, you'll face a flood tide of speculative answers from people within your own organization who have only a partial picture of the crisis.

¶ **Get out in front of the crisis.** Late messages are as bad as mixed messages. Remember President Bush's response to hurricane Katrina? Not only was the impact of his message severely weakened, but also his late response damaged the perception of his leadership in that crisis. If you or your spokesperson doesn't get out and address the crisis quickly, other "experts," many of them self-appointed and ill-informed, will assume the mantle of authority. After the 9/11 attacks, Americans wondered if they should buy gas masks as a precaution against possible chemical attacks by terrorists. It took the federal government three weeks to come up with the recommendation *not* to buy them. During these weeks, self-appointed terrorism experts filled the interview chairs on the 24-hour news channels, warning of the dangers of chemical weapons. In the aftermath of this onslaught of fear-based ruminating, the public depleted Army/Navy stores and online military surplus companies of every gas mask on their shelves. If you don't respond in a timely manner, someone else will, and it may prove hard to wrest back control of crisis communications once the horse is out of the barn. Remember this: into any information vacuum, the media will suck up and then disseminate rumor and speculation from self-appointed, publicity-hungry "experts" who readily, even eagerly, make themselves available.

¶ **Empathy, not paternalism.** Another cardinal sin of crisis communications harkens back to our Commandment 5: "Thou shalt not lie, evade, speculate, nor *cop an attitude*." Copping a paternalistic attitude is the flip side of empathy in crisis communication. A perfect example of this is Alexander Haig asserting his authority over the country while President Reagan was having a bullet removed from his chest. If you can't communicate without talking down to people, don't talk to them at all. If you are paternalistic, everything you say will be disbelieved or resented. Another form of paternalism is withholding bad news from the public for fear it will panic or react badly. Eventually the information is going to come out and once it does, your credibility will be in shambles. The public can handle bad news if you present it in a mature, factual, respectful way. A series of 55 focus groups conducted across the country by the Centers for Disease Control and five universities found that uncertainty is more difficult to deal with than bad news and that *any* information is empowering in a crisis.

¶ **Don't speculate.** Again, we're revisiting Commandment 5. Speculation develops a life of its own; a very long life, in fact. Even if your speculation is partially right, it's dangerous because the wrong material poisons the correct information.

¶ **Put out the fires of rumor.** Wild rumors accompany every crisis. If you do not quickly bat down rumors with facts, they grow like viruses and once a rumor virus gains hold, it infects all discourse about the crisis. So it's imperative to move quickly to squelch rumors. Many Americans believed rumors of mass rapes of women and girls in the Superdome in the aftermath of Katrina. It didn't happen, but authorities did not refute the rumors in a timely manner and as a result many still repeat and believe the rape stories.

¶ **Show your credentials.** A small group of protesters stirred up fear in the Florida communities near the Kennedy Space Center during the run-up to the launch of a spacecraft because it carried some 70 pounds of plutonium to power its instruments. The government spokespersons working to reassure the public about these fears gained greater credibility from their academic credentials than from their bureaucratic titles. One woman worked into all her interviews the fact that she was an MIT-educated engineer who had written her master's thesis on nuclear safety. That was a lot more reassuring to the media and to the public than her official government title.

¶ **Don't answer what you can't answer. Do answer what you can answer.** "I don't know. We're working on it," is a perfectly valid answer, especially if followed by a description of what steps are being taken to work on it. On the other hand, don't withhold information, unless it is critically important to do so. You can't manage a crisis by withholding information. As Shakespeare wrote in *The Merchant of Venice*, "Truth will out." When it does, your credibility plummets and you find yourself managing both a crisis and a credibility gap. But what about information you really can't share? Respectfully tell the public that you are withholding some information and why you are withholding it. If you have no results to report, talk about the process that will lead to results. The public wants to know *something* is being done, even if it hasn't yet borne fruit.

KEEP YOUR SPOKESPERSONS IN THE LOOP

Part of your crisis communications plan must include mechanisms for keeping spokespersons in the information flow. They cannot address public concerns if they don't know what's going on themselves. You must never withhold information from your spokespersons because you want it withheld from the public. If that information gets out and the spokesperson did not have it, did not know about it, he no longer has any credibility with the media. "I can't discuss that; it's an ongoing process, and until we get results we don't want to speculate," is a better answer than, "I *didn't* know that."

A crisis communications plan must designate a team to decide what information to release and what to withhold. You can't begin scrambling to put together that team once a crisis breaks; everyone will be too busy. But if the team members understand in advance that their management duties include serving on the communications team, they'll be available. Also well in advance, the team must learn the demands and needs of both the public and the media, so that they don't revert to the all too familiar response of clamming up in the face of adversity. Often, crisis management teams find it easier to withhold information than to do the hard work of considering what to release and when to release it. The instinct of any organization is to protect itself and often that involves withholding information. This policy is self-defeating and it's important the crisis communications team, from top to bottom, understand that.

At this point you may feel as if you're ready to confront any media opportunity with confidence. But not so fast! Let's take the last chapter to review the basics and determine if you are really ready for *your* fifteen minutes of fame.

Chapter 12

GETTING READY FOR
YOUR FIFTEEN MINUTES

During the first year of "Good Morning America," the show's talent coordinators managed to book an interview with James Cagney, the actor. Cagney, one of Hollywood's original tough guy gangster stars, was then in poor health and lived a reclusive life with his wife on a farm about two hours north of New York City. He had not given an interview in a dozen years or more, so booking him was a real coup. A group of us - David Hartman, two camera crews, director Jan Rifkinson and one or two others - drove to his farm one afternoon and David sat down with the screen legend for about two hours of conversation.

At one point, Hartman asked Cagney the secret of his extraordinarily natural acting style. In his clipped New York Irish accent, Cagney said, "Nothin' to it. Ya walk in, look the other fella in the eye, and tell the truth." With those few words Cagney distilled not only acting but also media interviews. I would argue with him on only the first part of that quote: "Nothin' to it." There is quite a bit to it, at least there is in media encounters, and I suspect the same is true in acting. But if you, as a spokesperson, are as prepared as any good actor would be, then it is a lot easier to "look the other fella in the eye and tell the truth."

If you got to this page by reading the previous eleven chapters - and not by flipping to the end to see how it all turns out - then you have a good, solid sense of what you need to do before, during, and after an interview. Let's review. First, obey the five commandments of media communications and you will be able to look that other fella in the eye with confidence:

Commandment 1. Thou shalt be prepared. Knowing what you want to say in advance of an interview is the key to preparation. If you do not establish an agenda for each interview, you will be at the mercy of the reporter's agenda. Even when the reporter's agenda matches your own, you are cheating yourself out of an opportunity to be most effective if you don't prepare a set of messages in advance of the interview. And remember Merlis' Law of Interviews: *Anybody unprepared for tough questions will be asked them.* So if you prepare for the worst it's unlikely a reporter will blindside you in the interview. Also, as close to interview time as possible, check the latest news about you, your company, your project, and your industry. You don't want the reporter surprising you with the bombshell of a new development during your interview.

Commandment 2: Thou shalt know to whom thou art speaking. Remember, you are not talking *to* the reporter. You are talking *through* her to her readers, viewers, or listeners. No matter how conversational a reporter is with you, she is working. You should be working, too. Your job is to reach her audience with your Positive Message Statements.

Commandment 3: Thou shalt be quoteworthy. To reach that audience you have to communicate in ways that are so compelling the reporter says to herself, "I gotta use that." To communicate your messages effectively, you must express them comprehensively, with economy, and in memorable language. Most good interview subjects are thought-provoking and speak with a deft ease that appears innate but more often than not is a result of extensive preparation and practice. Use grabbers, word pictures and other colorful word devices. They command attention. And speak in soundbites. A good soundbite is a sentence or two or three that captures your audience's attention and delivers a message in a way that's sufficiently dramatic or witty to remain in the listener's or reader's memory. The ideal soundbite is no more than thirty words long, takes no more than ten seconds to speak, and is no more than three sentences long. (The operative words are *no more than*. An ideal soundbite can be, and frequently is, shorter that 30/10/3 maximum.) Incorporate the sense of an interviewer's question in your answer so your quote or soundbite can stand on its own and doesn't need an introduction from the reporter.

Commandment 4: Thou shalt practice, practice, practice. It is a not enough to prepare, you must also practice. Read your PMSs out loud to see if they work. Sometimes you won't be able to get your mouth around the phrases you've written; you don't want to learn that in the middle of a broadcast interview with a microphone recording your every word. The more you practice, the more comfortable you will be with your messages, and the more natural and conversational you'll make them in an interview. Have someone throw questions at you; it's better to hear them coming from another voice than to ask them of yourself. Record and review your practice sessions.

Commandment 5: Thou shalt not lie, evade, nor cop an attitude. Abraham Lincoln was right when he said, "It is true that you may fool all the people some of the time; you can even fool some of the people all of the time; but you cannot fool all of the people all of the time." Untruths and half-truths usually pop up just like the insufficiently weighted victim a mob hit man drops in a lake. Insofar as attitude, if you alienate readers, viewers, or listeners, they are going to be negatively disposed to your PMSs.

WHAT TO DO BEFORE, DURING, AND AFTER A MEDIA ENCOUNTER

To obey these five commandments, you will need to take some concrete steps before, during, and after any media encounter. Your failure to take all these steps doesn't guarantee doom, but taking them is a virtual guarantee of success. If you think of an interview as a performance, these steps equate to creating your material, rehearsing it, performing it, and then following up to insure you and the audience are happy with the performance.

BEFORE THE ENCOUNTER

¶ **Determine your agenda.** Create an agenda for the interview and craft your Positive Message Statements. When you write them out, keep in mind that your audience is not the reporter, but her readers, viewers, or listeners. Make your PMSs come alive with grabbers; they enhance your agenda and entice reporters and the public. Remember, when you are writing your messages and your grabbers, your end-users are always asking themselves, "Why should I care?" Always incorporate that sensibility into your PMSs.

¶ **Make a list of your nightmare questions.** Figure out the worst questions any reporter can ask you and, wherever possible, tie one of your PMSs to each of those questions. Study these question-and-answer links: they will be your mental road map from a tough question to an answer that serves your agenda.

¶ **Check out the media outlet.** Make an effort to ascertain the reporter's likely agenda. Learn what her publication or broadcast is like. Does it have a particular style or point of view? How might that point of view influence their coverage of your organization? How detailed does the media outlet get? Does it address a sophisticated or a general audience? What is the individual reporter's style in an interview? There are five questions to ask the reporter who will be interviewing you:
1. What is the direction or thrust of the story?
2. Who else are you interviewing?
3. How much of my time will you need?
4. How long will your article (or broadcast story) run?
5. Do you need or want any documentation, photos graphics, or videotape?

¶ **Rehearse.** Before any interview, you'll want to practice, practice, practice. Rehearse your responses to challenging questions. Have a colleague or friend aggressively throw questions at you so you will get used to answering with your PMSs. Tape these practice sessions and study your performance.

¶ **Be informed.** As close to the time of the interview as possible, check the latest news: watch an all-news cable channel, listen to a radio newscast, or, better yet, check out the news websites we've already listed: Google news (news.google.com) or *The New York Times* (nytimes.com) or the Associated Press at http://customwire.ap.org/specials/bluepage.html. (This site takes some work: click on any state and then on any publication or broadcast outlet in that state for access to the wire service's latest news.)

¶ **Arrive early and warm up.** If the interview is someplace other than your office or home, arrive at the venue early and establish yourself with the reporter during a preinterview warmup so she thinks of you as a human being. Use the warm-up to plant the seeds of your PMSs with her; perhaps they'll grow into questions that lead the interview to your agenda points.

During The Interview

¶ **Tape the interview.** You want a record of what you said and how you said it. If it's a television interview, make every effort to videotape it; otherwise audio taping is fine. Also, bring a witness; someone from your organization who knows the subject area of the interview. He'll be available to correct you if you inadvertently misspeak during the Q&A.

¶ **Use Counterintuitive Communications.** There are four fundamental rules you should adhere to during the interview; they are essential if you are going to succeed in addressing the reporter's audience - which is your goal. The four rules are likely to be counterintuitive to your normal conversational style:

1. **KPUF - Key Point Up Front.** Lead with your strongest stuff. This is the way the media speaks to us and it is the way we should speak to the media

2. **KISS - Keep it Short and Simple.** Remember our 30/10/3 rule - soundbites should be no more than thirty words, take no more than ten seconds to speak, and should be no more than three sentences. As to how simple - if you're dealing with a general audience, use the national average grade level: tenth grade. But for highly emotional and controversial subjects, communicate at sixth grade level.

3. **KOTJ - Knock off The Jargon.** Activate your jargon filter. Avoid acronyms and other verbal short-cuts. You and your colleagues will understand what you're saying but the rest of us will be left scratching our heads as we attempt to translate your remarks into English.

4. **Brand.** If it's got a name, use it. It's not "we" or "us," it's the name of your organization. If you're talking about a book, a product, or a policy, use its title or name.

¶ **Stay cool.** Remain calm during your interview; your attitude counts even in print interviews where the reader won't see your face the way a television viewer will. When writing her story, a print reporter can characterize you as appearing nervous or furtive. If you're asking, "How do I stay calm when I'm confronted with a reporter?" the answer is if you are prepared with your own agenda of PMSs, you will be calm and resolute.

¶ **Everything is on the record.** Don't go off the record, supply any information on a not-for-attribution basis, or ever use the phrase, "No comment." If you can't answer a question, explain why you can't and then offer help to the reporter in finding someone who can answer it.

¶ **Stick to your agenda.** During the Q&A, concentrate on your agenda. Since most people are taught to be polite, it is easy to get sidetracked onto the reporter's agenda by dutifully answering her questions. This is fine if her agenda meshes with yours, but that won't always be the case, so keep your PMSs at the forefront of your thoughts and work your answers around to them. Use our four steps to get back on track from her off-the-point or tough questions:

> **1. Short form answer.** You must acknowledge her question or she will ask it again.
> **2. Build a bridge.** Just a few words can get you beyond your short form answer and leave you on the threshold of your agenda. Use simple words or phrases for your bridges like: "on the other hand," "in fact," "however," "but," or "and."
> **3. State your PMS.** Cross that bridge and move on to one of your points. State it at greater length than your short form answer and anchor it with a grabber.
> **4. Shut up.** You don't want to add the anti-climactic, "And that's why…." and restate her off-point or hostile question.

¶ **Flag it.** If you are using the four-step process and you find yourself going on at great length in step one, here's a way to recover: flag your agenda point. Simply say, "The most important thing to remember is...." or "what I really want to say is...." and move on to your PMS. This alerts both reporter and the public that you're really getting to the meat of your answer. Flagging also works well if you find yourself violating the KISS rule - keep it short and simple. If you're going on and on and on, just focus attention on what you *really* want to say by flagging what's most important when you finally get around to saying it.

¶ **Be specific.** The media - and their audiences - love specifics. It is easy to infer the general from the specific, while it is impossible to infer the specific from the general.

¶ **Enumerate.** If there are three pieces of evidence that support your contention, announce that there are three of them and then tick them off one-by-one. Audiences respond to enumeration. It is more effective to say "there are three benefits," and then list them, than to speak about the same three benefits randomly.

¶ **Know when your interview ends.** An interview is over after the reporter or you leave the premises, not after the notebook, tape recorder, or camera is put away. As long as you are in the presence of a reporter, she is observing and mentally recording. The whole world may read or hear anything you say in proximity to a reporter or a microphone. In fact, anything you say in proximity to a reporter - even in a nonworking venue - may be grist for her mill. In 2001, at a party hosted by Conrad Black, one of Britain's major newspaper publishers, France's ambassador to the United Kingdom undiplomatically told the guests he thought Israel was, "A *&$@# little country." Naturally, the story broke in the British papers, which exhibited far less reticence about using his actual word than I did. Instead of apologizing, the diplomat said, "I thought this was a social occasion." Since the publisher had invited several reporters to the party - including his own wife, who is one of the country's leading political columnists - the ambassador's belief that he could say something so provocative without being quoted was stunningly naïve. Understand that there are no private moments with journalists. The ambassador, Daniel Bernard, had lots of time to ponder that lesson in his subsequent job in Algeria, a far less prestigious posting than London.

¶ **Watch your words and the reporter's words.** If there are loaded or negative words in a question, be careful not to repeat them when you are including the sense of the reporter's question in your answer. The "Isn't this a disaster waiting to happen" question is designed to elicit from you the words, "This isn't a disaster waiting to happen." Don't utter them!

AFTER THE INTERVIEW

¶ **Be cooperative.** Offer the reporter the opportunity to fact check her article or her broadcast script with you; you are not asking for approval rights over what she writes, just offering to confirm the facts.

¶ **Review Your Tape.** Screen or listen to your tape of the interview immediately after she leaves. If you discover you misspoke, then call her up and tell her you made a mistake and correct it. If you've omitted a key message point, call her up and tell her that her readers or listeners might want to know about one more point. Reporters won't hesitate to phone you if they come up with more questions while writing their story; you should feel free to call them and volunteer information you may not have gotten into the interview.

If you're dissatisfied with your performance, analyze what you did wrong. Every time you watch or listen to that tape, you're learning how to do it right the next time.

¶ **Complain if you've been treated unfairly.** If you feel a reporter has misrepresented you, complain. Reporters with a pattern of misrepresentation need to be held accountable. On the other hand, if the story was tough but fair, don't go wasting your time complaining, it could backfire.

DO YOU NEED
PROFESSIONAL MEDIA TRAINING?

There are a lot of companies and individuals offering media training, and you may want to avail yourself of those services. One way to tell if you need training is to write up a series of Positive Message Statements and a series of challenging questions and then have a friend or colleague interview you. (You'll want to have him read "The Interviewer's top Seven Dirty Tricks" in Chapter 4 before grilling you.) Videotape the session and study the tape to see how successful you were at working your PMSs into the interview. The cosmetics of your response are less important than your ability to work PMSs into the interview. Give yourself a point for every PMS you work into the interview. Deduct one for every PMS on your list that you failed to work into the interview. Did you score zero or less? You probably need training. If you got all your points in, you may be a natural and not need training. If you scored somewhere in the middle, assess your performance, and decide if a professional trainer can improve it.

The bottom line is only you can answer the question of whether or not you need training. If the answer is "yes," you may find it tempting to have your in-house public relations person train you. My experience has been that most in-house public relations people really don't want to do it. And with good reason; more often than not, a staffer should not do this sort of training. First, they may not be qualified. Second, if they work for you they may be extremely shy about giving you the proper grilling with tough, squirm-in-your-seat questions. And they may go easy on you when critiquing your performance. In-house personnel may also know too much, so when you respond in your organization's shorthand code, they will understand and let you get away with it, whereas an outside trainer will point out that you are failing to communicate beyond your own community.

The best advice is to look outside your organization and find a qualified and trustworthy group or individual. The qualified credential is self-evident, but the trustworthy is equally important because you may be revealing to this outsider intimate and potentially damaging information about you, your business, or your organization. Even if you think that there may not be proprietary information disclosed in training, I can tell you from experience that clients often reveal details they never intended to share during these sessions. So you need to engage the services of a media trainer whose first loyalty is to you as a client, not to the calling of journalism. I was recently summoned to do a media training session clear across the country because the client didn't trust the person they had been using in the past to not share with his friends in the media some sensational new information the organization was going to announce. I feel that if a trainer is untrustworthy some of the time, he is untrustworthy all of the time.

QUESTIONS TO ASK
A PROSPECTIVE MEDIA TRAINER
1. What are you training me for?
2. What materials do you leave behind?
3. Do you have a confidentiality agreement?
4. What is your background?

¶ **What are you training me for?** If the first word out of the trainer's mouth is "television," I would find someone else, unless you are going to appear *only* on television. Most people need training for *media* interviews, encounters, and presentations, not just for television. A media trainer who answers "television" is likely to stress the unique cosmetic considerations of the one-eyed beast over the *substance* you need to develop for all media interviews. Any coach you engage should customize the curriculum to meet your needs. For example, if it is highly unlikely you'll ever suffer an ambush by a TV crew, why waste a valuable chunk of training time with an ambush exercise?

¶ **What sort of materials do you leave behind?** Believe it or not, some media trainers don't give you worksheets, a workbook, or other written materials. Others collect the videotape of the interviews when the session ends, which means you can't review your performance at home to learn from your mistakes. More than one client has asked me, "Do you leave behind any materials?" When I asked why they were inquiring, they told me of trainers who took away all training materials, claiming they contained the trainer's proprietary information. I suppose this action stems from the misguided fear that the internal public relations staff of a company will use the materials to do their own training in the future. But you can't learn from your training exercises unless you have the tape or DVD of those exercises in addition to the other materials used in the training. Home review of all the training materials is an important component of preparation for future, real-life interviews. Moreover, those worksheets and videotapes are likely to contain your most feared questions and potentially embarrassing slips of the tongue made during practice interviews. You want that material securely in your own hands, not in the hands of an outsider, even if the outsider has signed a confidentiality agreement. Which brings us to our next question:

¶ **Do you have a confidentiality agreement to insure my organization's secrets will be protected?** This question should be unnecessary. Any trustworthy trainer should offer you a confidentiality agreement in his initial conversation with you; you should not have to ask about one. Confidentiality should be as high a priority for him as it is for you. Even if your organization has its own confidentiality agreement, I would ask that question in the event the trainer does not offer the information voluntarily. I would avoid any media coach who lacks his own confidentiality agreement; or one who tells you that his clients customarily supply an agreement. A trainer without his own confidentiality agreement is insensitive to the need to protect his clients. If you do require your media coach to sign a confidentiality agreement, be certain his camera operator, if he uses one, also signs.

¶ **What is your background?** There is no hard-and- fast rule that someone must have media experience to be a media trainer, but it certainly helps a trainer get inside the head of a reporter if he has been a reporter. A lot of media trainers today are former actors or public relations and marketing personnel with no direct, hands-on media experience. Some others are media "veterans" whose experience was at the lowest, nonreporting, noninterviewing, nonwriting levels. That said, some of them are very good. But how confident would you be if the pilot of your transatlantic airliner came on the intercom and said, "This is Captain Jones and my background is in aviation. I used to work the check-in counter and then I was a baggage-handler before becoming a pilot. Oh, and this is my first flight, so sit back, relax, and enjoy the ride."

Ask yourself, "Do I really want someone with no reporting experience playing reporter in my media training? Do I want someone who specializes in marketing to prepare me for '60 Minutes' type questions?" Some very large training organizations have stables of freelancers who do the training for them. Years ago, I worked with one such organization; it had a stable filled with thoroughbreds. Former top network producers and reporters were among the cadre. That team, had they the financial wherewithal, could have run a newsgathering and producing operation that would have rivaled any of the broadcast networks' news operations. Most of these veteran journalists had come to television out of newspapers or newsmagazines, so they had great print backgrounds as well. Unfortunately, that large and highly-qualified group no longer exists today, another firm bought the company and reorganized it, replacing the journalists with actors and publicists.

For your media training, you want someone who in practice interviews will treat you as a reporter will treat you. Additionally, the ideal trainer will have multimedia experience. A print interviewer's techniques usually are quite different, and in some cases far more seductive, than a broadcast reporter's techniques. If you are going to be doing interviews with various media, you want training from an expert who will do multiple types of interviews with you.

Some large public relations firms conduct media training by publicists and bring in a "visiting journalist" to do the interviews. This can prove to be a satisfactory arrangement, although some clients who have had that sort of training in the past tell me it was very discomforting having an active, working journalist hear their firm's confidential information.

INDIVIDUAL OR GROUP TRAINING

Normally, I prefer groups. For the client they are highly cost-effective. And even if money is no object, participants in group sessions learn a lot by watching each other - picking up pointers from colleagues' hits and misses. Also, a group is likely to come up with more good Positive Message Statements, more grabbers, and more tough questions than an individual. One-on-one training can take considerably less time, however - principally because the solo player is the only one interviewed and critiqued. Solo training is specifically appropriate when the session deals with a unique crisis that only one spokesperson will address or when prepping a spokesperson for a hostile or challenging investigative broadcast interview.

It's best to conduct the training away from your personal office, far from the temptation of e-mail, phone, fax, and importuning subordinates and colleagues. A conference room - preferably on a different floor than your office - can work well. A hotel meeting room a couple of miles away from your headquarters is even better because there's no way a subordinate or colleague can stroll in to interrupt with some bit of "can't wait" information. A number of my clients have their own small insert TV studios for public relations videos. These are ideal, if sealed off from the normal business of the day.

During the training - as during all media interviews - turn off cell phones and Blackberries. I had one client who couldn't turn off his cell phone during training because he was expecting to get word on a big deal at any moment. He spent the better part of the day taking and placing calls and, indeed, concluded the big deal. Unfortunately, he wasn't equipped to announce it to the media. However, he'd brought two colleagues with him and they turned off their phones, stayed with the program, and were prepared.

Media training does not end with the close of a session - like any education it prepares you for further independent study. Sometimes, before a big event or a specific interview, you'll want a refresher with your trainer. Without a refresher session, it is up to you to keep your PMSs fresh, to come up with new and better grabbers for them, and to do on-camera practice interviews with family or colleagues before embarking on a real interview.

Media mastery takes time and work. Few of us are natural spokespersons. But if you're going to do media interviews, the effort will result in unique opportunities. The more you work at it, the better you'll be at it. Not devoting the time and doing the work means you'll be the media's puppet or even - in extreme cases - their victim. Your investment of time and effort will pay dividends and empower you to speak through the media to the audience you really want to reach.

ABOUT THE AUTHOR

For more than two decades, George Merlis has used his experience as a print journalist and television news producer as the basis for media training hundreds of clients. As a TV producer, Merlis has overseen more than 10,000 broadcast interviews, the vast majority of them live. As a print journalist and investigative television news producer, he has conducted hundreds more interviews himself.

Merlis was executive producer of two of the three network morning shows, "Good Morning America" and "The CBS Morning News." He was also executive producer of the nationally syndicated "Entertainment Tonight" and USA Network's early venture into talk TV, "The Dick Cavett Show." Merlis has worked closely with talents as diverse in style as Ted Koppel, Diane Sawyer, David Hartman, Sam Donaldson, Geraldo Rivera, Gary Collins, Harry Reasoner, Bill Kurtis, Frank Reynolds, Bill Moyers, Peter Jennings, Barbara Walters, and Willard Scott.

His media training firm, Experience Media Consulting (www.MasterTheMedia.com) has trained a large gamut of spokespersons ranging from rock stars to rocket scientists and every category in between.

Earlier in his media career, as a print reporter and editor at the *New York World-Telegram and The Sun*, the *New York World Journal Tribune,* and the New York *Daily News*, Merlis covered a variety of subjects and wrote hundreds of news stories. In August, 1961, he was in Berlin to cover the building the infamous wall dividing the city. Twenty-eight years later, as a TV producer for ABC, he came full cycle on the story when he went back to Berlin to cover the destruction of the wall and the collapse of East Germany.

Merlis began working in television in 1967 when he joined ABC News. He served on the large network team that covered the Apollo 11 mission to the moon. He was also an investigative producer on ABC's "The Reasoner Report," where he reported, wrote, directed, and produced major stories about the food, chemical, petroleum, pharmaceutical, and automotive industries. He was also "The Reasoner Report's" environmental specialist.

Merlis won a 1999 National Emmy Award as executive producer, writer and director of the syndicated television program "Better Homes & Gardens." He also executive produced five long-running series for the Home and Garden Television network. Merlis produced a number of shows for Discovery Communications' networks, including the flagship Discovery Channel, the Science Channel, and the Travel Channel. For PBS, Merlis directed the lively panel show "Closer to Truth."

He wrote a novel, *VP*, and the nonfiction book *How to Make the Most of Every Media Appearance.* He co-wrote *Al Ubell's Energy Saving Guide for Homeowners* and *Save Energy, Save Money.*

MEDIA-MASTERY
WORKSHEETS
WORKSHEET 1 - PMSs

List five Positive Message Statements you want to work into your next interview.

1._____

_____

2._____

_____

3._____

_____

4._____

_____

5._____

_____

WORKSHEET 2 - WSIC

Fine-tune your PMSs to answer the public's "Why Should I Care" question. Characterize why they should care about at least one of your PMSs and ideally about all five.

1._____

_____

2._____

_____

3._____

_____

4._____

_____

5._____

_____

WORKSHEET 3 - GRABBERS

Create a grabber for each of your five PMSs. A grabber is a word picture or other verbal device that makes your message point come alive, turns it into a soundbite or a pull quote.

1._____

_____

2._____

_____

3._____

_____

4._____

_____

5._____

_____

WORKSHEET 4 TOUGH QUESTIONS

List your nightmare questions - those you find extremely tough to answer. After each question, write the PMS and grabber you want to navigate to in your answer.

Question:_____

_____

PMS to use in answer: _____

_____

_____

Question:_____

_____

PMS to use in answer:_____

_____

_____

Question:_____

_____

PMS to use in answer:_____

_____

Question:_____

_____

PMS to use in answer:_____

_____

_____

_____

Question:_____

_____

PMS to use in answer:_____

_____

_____

THE FOUR STEPS TO YOUR AGENDA
1. Acknowledge the tough question with a short form answer.
2. Build a bridge ("but," "however," "on the other hand.")
3. Deploy a PMS illustrated with a grabber
4. Shut up! Don't refer back to the original question.

Notes

_____

_____

_____

_____

_____

_____

_____

_____

_____

_____

_____

_____

INDEX